Hugh Downs

ON
CAMERA

ON CAMERA

My
10,000 Hours on Television

HUGH DOWNS

G. P. Putnam's Sons   New York

G. P. Putnam's Sons
Publishers Since 1838
200 Madison Avenue
New York, NY 10016

Library of Congress Cataloging-in-Publication Data

Downs, Hugh.
On camera.

1. Downs, Hugh.   2. Television personalities—United
States—Biography.   I. Title.
PN1992.4.D6A29   1986   791.45′092′4   [B]   86-8097
ISBN 0-399-13203-1

Printed in the United States of America
1   2   3   4   5   6   7   8   9   10

Acknowledgments

I would like to thank the following people for their inspiration and editorial counsel in making this book a reality: Steve Fenichell, Marlene McGinnis, my editor Martin L. Gross, and my indispensable assistant, Jean Ferrari.

For Ruth

Contents

Comeback 13

Radio 21

Early TV 47

The Tonight Show 65

The Today Show 103

Concentration 147

The Hiatus 165

20/20 181

Adventure 209

Final Cut 243

Hugh Downs, in his more than thirty-five years as a television personality, has appeared on national commercial television at least 9915½ hours as of 31st July, 1985.

Therefore, as editor of *The Guinness Book of Records*, I do hereby certify that as of that date, Mr. Downs holds the Guinness Record for on-air national commercial television time.

Norris McWhirter,
Editor, *Guinness Book of Records*

1

COMEBACK

Early retirement from network broadcasting is not necessarily the formula for a perfect life. I found that out almost by accident when I left my retreat in the Arizona desert and its radiant sunsets to come back to the streets of New York and the frenetic world of mainstream television.

Seven years before, at the age of fifty, I had chosen freedom over what is loosely called stardom. During two demanding decades I had hosted *The Today Show* on NBC and served as sidekick-announcer to Jack Paar, the high-strung star of the old *Tonight Show*. After nine years of rising well before dawn five days a week to host *Today*, at what many considered the height of my career, I had escaped. I left an exciting but stressful life behind for the solitude of the Sonora Desert, blissfully surrounded by endless sky in Carefree, Arizona.

Now I had come back to New York for just a week to fill in for David Hartman as host of *Good Morning America*, ABC's top-rated answer to *Today*. I had flown in a few days early to watch Hartman work from the sidelines, worried that I might have gotten rusty during my seven-year hiatus from the routine of dawn television.

I found a very different world from the one I had left. The technology was far more sophisticated, and demanded many more people, than when I had hosted *Today* throughout the 1960s.

But coming back into the camera's cool eye was far from

bitter medicine. Frankly, some of my long-cherished illusions about the desert life had proven to be something of a mirage. I had imagined spending my evenings on a terrace overlooking the valley's sweep toward Phoenix, watching the sun set over the red rocks of Arizona. The broadcast industry would beat a steady path to my door, bearing caravans of enticing offers. I, of course, would pick and choose at my leisure.

As it turned out, I really couldn't complain. My home in Carefree was hardly besieged, but television did hold out a number of worthwhile, if not exactly earth-shattering, projects. I narrated a series of environmental and historical specials for NBC, one of which won an Emmy. I hosted a series for PBS on aging in America called *Over Easy*. And I managed to find time between broadcast assignments to work on several books, do some teaching, become a Visiting Fellow at the Center for the Study of Democratic Institutions in Santa Barbara, and eventually succeed Wernher von Braun as chairman of the National Space Institute. The press might have called it retirement, but I didn't see it that way.

But if there was one electronic dream which would tempt me to abandon my quiet new life, it was the anchor job on a major "magazine of the air." Not another *Today* show, but a prime-time multisubject news hour. Something, frankly, like *60 Minutes*. It had even crossed my mind to fund a pilot for such a program myself, but that was not the way to sell a show to a network news department. Entertainment divisions frequently acquire new series from independent producers, but news shows are developed from the inside.

That Tuesday night in New York, after surviving two high-pressure mornings on the set of *Good Morning America*, my wife, Ruth, and I were relaxing in our hotel suite.

We turned on the TV. I was eager to learn how ABC would handle the premiere of *20/20*, their new, highly touted prime-time show. It had been just ten years since CBS had launched the most popular on-air magazine of them all, *60 Minutes*. Contrary to popular folklore, *60 Minutes* was no immediate success. In fact it had gone through six difficult seasons before gaining its present devoted nationwide following. Only after moving to Sunday evening, where there was little to threaten it, did *60 Minutes* secure its extraordinary niche.

This opening *20/20* had to be something different—perhaps even more challenging than *60 Minutes*—if it was going to make it. It was starting out in prime time, launched in precisely the same time slot in which CBS had unsuccessfully introduced *60 Minutes* a decade before. Though the critics would inevitably compare the two shows, *20/20*'s real competition would be high-rated escapist entertainment, the overly false world of weekday nights on the tube.

As the opening credits came on, a montage of flashy graphics depicted a set of old-fashioned wire-rimmed spectacles floating on a field of optometrist's eye-charts. The implication was clear. ABC intended to provide a sharper view of the real world. One with *20/20*, or perfect vision. This was not a new concept. The original *Today Show*, billed as the first magazine of the air, had called itself a "window on the world."

I waited with anticipation as the camera came up on two young men, one fair, one dark. I was surprised. I had never seen either of them on television before, network or local. Perhaps something unique was in the offing. But their opening patter had a peculiar, unprofessional touch.

> *HAYES:* I'm Hayes.
> *HUGHES:* And I'm Hughes!
> *HAYES:* Robert Hughes is not exactly a household name. Where do you come from?
> *HUGHES:* Born in Sydney about forty years ago, started off as a journalist, art critic, political cartoonist, general all-purpose literary grease monkey. Studied art in Italy for a few years and then moved to England to work for the BBC there, and then I was hired out of there by *Time* magazine about eight years ago and so came here.
> *HAYES:* Slipped into the country surreptitiously?

HUGHES: Uh, yep. Under a forged . . . palette.

Hughes then questioned his partner:

> *HUGHES:* And how about you, Hayes? Where'd you get that fancy foreign accent?
> *HAYES:* From North Carolina, Hughes. We all talk that way down there. I started there many years ago, came to New York about twenty-five years ago, been a magazine editor, a lot of that time at *Esquire.*
> *HUGHES:* Well, different work now. Let's get to it!

So here were Robert Hughes, art critic for *Time,* and Harold Hayes, a former editor of *Esquire,* appearing on a prime-time news magazine as anchormen. I was baffled by their rapid-fire, rarefied introduction. How had these two ever gotten on the air, on a network, in such a highly visible position? From the way they came across, I had a feeling they were wondering the very same thing.

The critics were not kind. One dubbed the two hosts "Tweedle Dee and Tweedle Dummy." Another called the unfortunate pair a "tag-team cute act." *Newsweek* said, "20/20 can't decide whether to emulate *60 Minutes* or imitate *The National Enquirer.*"

I have often disagreed with television critics. They tend to lavish their bitterest ink on mediocre fare, so when a true disaster turns up, they have nowhere to go. The opening program of *20/20* was a genuine broadcast disaster. The hallmark of the show was an embarrassing segment featuring a clay effigy of Jimmy Carter mouthing Ray Charles' rendition of "Georgia on My Mind." As if that wasn't enough, the grotesque clay caricature was backed up by a chorus line of peanut people wearing top hats and tails.

From the beginning, electronic media have been too much in awe of print people. ABC's blunder with this first *20/20* repeated a nearly identical error made by NBC twenty years before.

To replace the first *Tonight Show,* starring Steve Allen, NBC had mounted a dismal effort called *America After Dark.* It featured prominent newspaper writers and columnists Liz Smith and Earl Wilson. Some newspaper journalists, like Irv Kupcinet, host of Chicago's *Kup Show*, are capable of handling a television broadcast. But many are not. While no one would assume that just any broadcaster could write a newspaper column, it was taken for granted that any print journalist could run a broadcast.

My professional vanity was tweaked by this arrogance. And vindicated by the results. But, as frequently happens in television, the dark cloud had a chrome underside. The morning after the *20/20* debacle, I was sitting at my desk in David Hartman's office, having just wrapped up my third *Good Morning America* segment, when the phone rang. The call was from Roone Arledge, president of ABC News. I didn't know Arledge, but I knew who he was. He wanted an urgent meeting with me at an ABC suite at the Dorset Hotel at noon.

When I first heard about *20/20,* out in Arizona, I said wistfully to my wife that this was the sort of program I would have loved for myself. But even after that disastrous premiere, I had no reason to believe ABC might make a right-angle turn and ask for me. After all, I had been out of the network news game for the past seven years.

I couldn't think of any other reason why Arledge had called. I was vaguely aware that *20/20* was the first major news offering by ABC since this chief of ABC Sports had risen to also become president of the New Division. How had I been doing on the Hartman show? I asked myself. My only memorable mistake had been when I said "NBC" instead of "ABC." (Barbara Walters consoled me. She said she had done the same thing her first day at the new network.)

I assumed Arledge must have been watching *Good Morning America* all three mornings. It was an ABC show, and in his division. The fact that he wanted to meet with me in a hotel, outside ABC offices, suggested he wanted our conversation to be confidential. There was only one thing I could be sure of— Roone Arledge was not calling me in to host *Monday Night Football.*

When I walked into the Dorset suite at noon, Arledge and Bob Shanks, the producer of *20/20*, both stood up to greet me. I had known Bob a long time. He had been in charge of booking talent on Jack Paar's *Tonight Show*. Arledge, who had made his name in sports programming, looked something like an athlete himself. Broad-shouldered, fair-haired, and square-jawed, he also looked like he meant business. He dispensed with the usual formalities.

"Hugh, have you seen *20/20*?"

"Yes," I said. I thought it best to add nothing else.

He came straight to the point.

"We want to make some changes in *20/20*. The dual-host idea just isn't working. We need someone who has more experience with this sort of work. Are you interested?"

So Hayes and Hughes were out. And I was in—if I wanted in. I felt a bit like a beached admiral being called back to sea. I didn't know Arledge, but from his reputation I knew that once he made up his mind he was not likely to change it. From the frankly acquisitive way he was looking at me, I had a strong feeling his mind had already been made up.

Of course I was interested. At that stage of my career, nothing was more enticing than hosting a prime-time news show on a major network. But if forty years in broadcasting had taught me anything, it was to approach any new project cautiously.

I had no desire to preside over the demise of a show they were planning to fold. That was my primary concern. To be hung with a serious failure would not be a graceful way of capping my long career. I wanted solid assurances that the network was willing to continue its full-scale support of the show for a reasonable time period. Arledge assured me that ABC News was behind the show all the way.

The second condition was that I be permitted to uphold my obligation to *Over Easy*, the PBS show I was hosting out of San Francisco that dealt candidly with the subject of aging. I wasn't about to back out of my commitment to PBS simply because something else had come up. This was agreed to. I could fly to San Francisco after *20/20* and spend three days there taping *Over Easy*, returning to New York for the rest of the week.

My third stipulation was that the full resources of the news department be made available to us. I had a horror of being an isolated unit, competing with ABC News. I wanted to know if certain key network correspondents like Barbara Walters and Sam Donaldson would be available to us. Although it was too short, the only worthwhile segment on the first show had been Donaldson's interview with Teddy Kennedy at the site of his brother Bobby's grave.

I sought assurance that I would be sole anchor, on the grounds that multiple anchors in the same studio never really work. The only successful dual anchors in news were Huntley and Brinkley, and they had been safely separated—one in New York and the other in Washington.

Last, I wanted a position with the company. This was my most controversial request. It was not a demand, but I wanted to sit in on high-level meetings involving the management and the production of the show. I wanted to remain a contract artist but still keep a hand in policy setting. At that stage of my career I was hoping to step into a behind-the-scenes role as well as an on-camera spot. I had enjoyed some of that power for years as anchor on *The Today Show*.

But Arledge balked. He said ABC just wasn't prepared to do that. Since all my other requests had been informally met, I accepted the offer in principle. My agents at William Morris began discussions with ABC negotiators to draw up a contract.

The next day I went down to Philadelphia to do an independent documentary project. By Friday I hadn't heard a thing from ABC, and I was beginning to wonder whether the offer had fallen through. I had some location work along the waterfront, and Ruth was out of the hotel. Our eight-year-old grandson was alone in the suite when the telephone rang. I got back to the hotel to find him gone, and a message in his handwriting:

"Run called."

That was it. The green light. After seven years out in the desert, I was back in the center. At a major network. On camera.

2
RADIO

My broadcasting career began on a hot summer day in Lima, Ohio, in July of 1939. I had just completed my freshman year at nearby Bluffton College, and my one-year scholarship had run out. The end of the Depression was nowhere in sight. My father thought I should leave school and get a job, and I agreed: I was eighteen and perfectly healthy. But work wasn't easy to find in and around Lima, an industrial town of 40,000 in northwest Ohio that, like many others, had been hard hit by the national slowdown. However, my family had suffered financial reverses and I had to start helping out.

I was on my way home with a gallon of milk from a discount milk depot when I stopped by the little 100-watt station that sat on top of a bank building facing Lima's main square. My scholarship had been the reward for winning a public-speaking contest called "The Prince of Peace." I had been singing in the college choir, and had an untutored but not unpleasant voice. So I decided on a whim to duck into the local radio station to see if they might need an utterly green announcer.

When I was growing up in Lima, the station had been called WBLY, after its founder, a man named Bly. It had a notoriously wobbly turntable, so people took to calling it WOBBLY. WBLY had recently been purchased by the Fort Industry Company, based in Toledo, and given new call letters: WLOK. Summoning up all available courage, I strode right up to the reception desk and set my one-gallon milk container on it. I told the girl behind the desk I wanted to be a radio announcer.

To her credit, the receptionist did not burst out laughing. In fact, she didn't bat an eyelash. She also did not seem to notice, or care, that I was toting a one-gallon milk can as if it were a prop for my interview.

"We hold auditions on Tuesdays," she said matter-of-factly, as if I were a serious candidate. I had no idea what the word audition meant. I was about to walk out in confusion when the program director happened by. I explained to him that I was interested in becoming a radio announcer.

"I'm not doing anything at the moment," he said. "If you want to read me something right now, I'd be happy to listen."

He led me into a small studio off the reception room, seated me in front of a goose-neck ribbon-velocity mike, and handed me a piece of copy. It was an advertisement for a sale at a local paint store.

"When that red light goes on over that door," he said, "just start reading." He went out, closing the door behind him, leaving me alone with nothing but whatever native ability I had to read and speak English clearly. I sat for what seemed an uncomfortably long time waiting for that red light to go on. It finally did, and I started reading.

When I was through, he opened the studio door.

"That was bad," he said cheerfully. "Really quite bad. But," he said, "you never know. Great oaks from little acorns grow."

I had no idea how lucky I was. They happened to need someone right away. He offered me a job as a staff announcer, at the full-time rate of $12.50 a week. "You can learn on the job," he finished, and walked out. That was it. I was hired.

When I dashed home bearing this wonderful news, my father was not nearly as impressed as I was.

"Keep looking for a job for a week," he said. "If you don't find a job, go with the radio station."

Even after I'd put decades in broadcasting behind me, my father refused to believe I had found a real job.

Though Dad was not enthusiastic, he was always helpful. "If broadcasting makes you nervous," he said of my mike fright,

"Just stop and think that people have dials on their radios. If they don't like what you're saying, they can tune to some other station."

This idea, for some reason, was strangely comforting to me, for the thought of broadcasting made me nervous to the point of terror.

I was born in Akron, Ohio, in 1921, in an apartment house that's now a parking lot. I remember my father carrying me out onto the back porch so I could see a dirigible in the southern sky. Akron was the home of dirigibles, and my father worked for Firestone. But when I was two, we moved to Lima, where Dad took a job as a machinist with the Lima Locomotive Works, one of the industrial mainstays of the town.

In the plant where he worked, they handled locomotive drive wheels, a stack of which weighs several tons. One day a support chain broke and a wheel nearly fell on him. With a wife and children to support, taking risks of that kind just didn't seem healthy. So he managed to get himself transferred into a pit where they would lower locomotive boilers and cabs suspended on chains onto the chassis, supported by eight-by-eight oak uprights. One day a 200-ton freight locomotive came down slightly crooked. The oak uprights bearing the immense weight started to splinter. Dad hopped out of the pit, walked straight to the front office, and quit. This was at a time when jobs weren't easy to find, but soon he landed a job with the Willard Storage Battery Company, and gradually worked himself up to an eight-county distributorship. He drove a truck to service that extensive territory.

We lived in half of a double house in Lima. A young, half-Cherokee girl, probably about thirteen or fourteen, lived with her family in the other half. She used to play MacDowell's "To a Wild Rose" on the piano, and I was in love with her by the time I was nine. That affair was tragically broken up when I was ten, when we moved to a small farm outside of town so my father could do some farming in his spare time.

In 1934 Dad quit his job at Willard to set up his own company distributing Penn Power Bar Batteries. The business failed after four years, not because my father failed, but because the battery itself gave out. Penn Power Bar had taken a few manufacturing shortcuts that boosted the available voltage but caused the battery to go dead because the plates buckled.

The batteries were sold with guarantees on which the company failed to back the distributors, and the business finally collapsed in 1938, just when I was starting at Bluffton. Dad's partner declared separate bankruptcy, but my father went to work for Westinghouse and started to pay all the debts back. It took years to clear what he owed.

That was how I happened to stop by that radio station in the summer of 1939—to help pay for the groceries at home.

I was always intrigued by the idea of radio. My father built himself a radio set when I was a kid. It ran off A and B wet-cell batteries. He had to send away to England for vacuum tubes. It was a large, elaborate, cumbersome affair, with headphones. By the time I reached second grade it had sprouted a huge speaker, dangling high above the set like a mechanical question mark. Now the whole family could hear.

"That voice is coming from Cincinnati," my father would say. I was impressed. In fact, I could hardly believe it. Here we were in Lima, Ohio, one hundred and twenty miles away. At that age, I probably didn't grasp what the distance meant. I just knew it was nowhere nearby.

I must have been only three or four when my father rigged up two spoons on a string tied to the legs of the dining room table. I was sitting on the floor. He sat down beside me, jiggled one spoon, and looked at me expectantly.

"See how the other spoon jiggles too?" he asked.

He was trying to get across to me the idea of wave transmission. Later on, he showed me how to make a simple mechanical voice-transmitter, using paper cups and a string stretched between them, like a small diaphragm microphone with attached speakers. Still later he came out with a more advanced model: tin cans and a long length of wire tied between them.

Before I was ten, I was playing with a little do-it-yourself telephone transmitter. It had two graphite sticks, the insides of lead pencils, which when crossed and connected to a current made a diaphragm vibrate with your voice, and another diaphragm vibrate to reproduce the same voice at the other end.

My father's contagious interest in voice transmission may have led to my lifelong fascination with the idea of professional broadcasting. When I first went on the radio in 1939 at the age of eighteen, the medium wasn't much older than I was. The first commercial radio broadcast had taken place on KDKA in Pittsburgh in 1920. The first regularly scheduled radio programs were broadcast from WWJ in Detroit—where I later worked for a time—beginning in 1921, the year I was born. In fact, the modulated wave that allowed voice transmission was only a couple of years older than I.

The kid who ran the newsstand in the public square downstairs from the Lima station was absolutely awestruck by radio. He used to wander in and hang around the studio to soak up what he could of the glamour. He wanted so much to be a part of it all. One day I asked him, "How much do you make at that newsstand of yours?" He looked a little glum and said, "Hell, I don't make more'n fifteen dollars a week." I didn't have the heart to tell him he would have had to take a major pay cut to take my glamorous radio job.

It might have been partly by accident that I stopped by the station that day, but I had long felt there was something terribly mysterious and compelling about it—talking into a microphone alone in a studio and having all those people out there listening to you, people you couldn't even see. It gave you a sense of power, of being at the center of things, of having an amplified voice.

But my first days in broadcasting were also frightening. At the end of a piece of music, when I was supposed to say something, my knees would shake uncontrollably. My pulse and respiration went up. Fortunately, the fear never showed in my delivery, but it did in my hands. If I had to hold copy, the paper would rattle. As a defense, I learned to lay copy out flat on the desk, or, if standing, to grab my lapels along with the copy, so the paper didn't move with my hands.

I sat at my 250-K Consolette, an RCA arrangement with a

row of faders, two of which were connected to turntables. Then I put the records on and opened the mike to say something. I became absolutely terrified. This syndrome is more common among professionals than one might imagine, and is known in the trade as mike fright. Howard Donahoe, my program director at WLOK, stood behind me one day, amazed at my anxiety.

"A year from now you'll look back and laugh at how scared you were," he said.

"A year from now I'll be dead."

Why did I do it? Why did I stay with it? Why was it so important to me to overcome that debilitating fear and go on broadcasting? The late thirties were a dismal economic era, and it might seem that I stayed with it because of a countervailing fear of failure and an overwhelming fear of not finding any other decent job. But there was a more mysterious force at work that had nothing to do with a job or money. Maybe my father was right: I never got a "job." I was a *broadcaster*, and it was unthinkable that I would quit. The last vestiges of that mike fright didn't go away entirely until I'd been in the business ten years. (To be followed, of course, by camera fright when television began.)

As a staff announcer I introduced programs and signed the station on and off. If it was a package program, I said whatever was necessary around the recorded material. At a bare minimum I would announce the call letters and breaks, and the commercial announcements. Between two network programs there was always a "chain break," when the network would ring chimes. This gave me less than twenty seconds to make my announcement. During music programs, I would usually say something after every song played. I never played a whole block of songs without commercial interruption, the way deejays do today.

If there was news to read, I read that too. Frequently, I was the only person at the station. Every month there was an official sunset hour by which we had to be off the air. That little station in Lima originally just broadcast during daylight hours. Many of the smaller, non-network stations couldn't even get a license to operate after dark.

On AM radio, the airwaves become more crowded at night. Even when we finally won a twenty-four-hour license, we stayed on only until midnight. Not enough people would have tuned in after that to make a full nightshift worthwhile. There was a joke among the staff that an announcer had only two jobs: to keep the FCC logs up to date and to sweep out the station at night.

Before World War II, the two networks ran a number of sustaining programs, for which there were no regular sponsors. NBC and CBS did all their own productions. ABC did not even exist. Years later, NBC's Blue Network would be sold off, under pressure from the FCC, to Edward Noble, the man who invented Life Savers. He turned it into the American Broadcasting Company, but despite the grand-sounding title, it took years to mount any real competition to CBS or NBC.

NBC broadcast its famous big band remote pickups without any sponsors at all. The network made the money back on big blockbuster variety shows, like Jack Benny and Fred Allen, broadcast out of New York or Hollywood on Sunday evenings. Jack Benny and Fred Allen's famous feud, during which they traded insults by the week, stimulated enormous interest in both programs. Both men, of course, remained good friends. People would tune in just to hear which new insult each comedian would hurl at the other. Fred Allen originated the "Jack Benny is so cheap that . . ." jokes that became staples for a generation of comics.

I look back enviously at how *Amos 'n' Andy* dominated the airwaves in the days when you could walk in the early evening through the streets of any small town and not miss a word of the program as it came wafting through every screen door. Movie theaters would interrupt their regular features for fifteen minutes to play *Amos 'n' Andy* over their sound systems. This public service was advertised right on the movie marquees. Film exhibitors knew if they didn't post such an announcement, no one would have gone to the theater at that hour.

At WLOK, we produced our own public service programs, such as a farm show every morning. We played mostly recorded band music, interspersed with occasional regional commentary. One day a farmer stopped by the station to see where the show he tuned to every morning came from.

"Where's that band play?" the farmer wanted to know. On one side of the control room was a fairly large studio. On the other was a smaller studio, hardly bigger than a news booth.

"Now that there's a pretty big band," he said sagely. "You probably have to put 'em in that big room."

"Actually, they're playing on a record," I said. He looked skeptical. I showed him the big transcription record with the name of the band printed on the label.

"Oh, I get it," he said. "You probably have to stick 'em in both rooms to fit 'em all in."

"No," I said, "the music actually comes off this record. They recorded the music a long time ago."

No matter how hard I tried, I couldn't get him to believe that we weren't broadcasting all our own music live, from right in downtown Lima.

In the early thirties, millions of Americans were still listening by coal-oil lamps to radios running off the old wet-cell A and B batteries. The sets had headphones or crinkle-finish speakers resembling tubas driven by headphone coils. By the mid-thirties, Atwater Kent was making a radio with regular paper cone speakers, vacuum tubes, and gang tuning condensers, that ran off ordinary household current.

Rural electrification was a major New Deal program, and by the end of the thirties most Americans had access to electrical power. Federal subsidies and rural co-operatives made it possible for more people to afford electricity—and radio. By the end of the decade people were lining up to buy waterfall-front veneer radios with Bakelite knobs and a booming bass capability that contrasted wonderfully with the tinny sound of the question-mark speaker. After a while, the bass was so overdone that it was called the jukebox thump.

Throughout the Depression, one of the most popular shows on radio was *The Smilin' Ed McConnell Show*, sponsored by Aladdin Lamps. In spite of government programs, whole sections of the country were still without electricity, and people would listen to their battery-powered radios by the light of Aladdin kerosene lamps. Smilin' Ed would sing hymns, and was dearly beloved throughout the Midwest. He was also known for hitting the jug—not just the bottle, an actual jug. He kept a large gin jug up on his piano, but his drinking on the job never seemed to hurt his broadcasting.

When electrification became more widespread, Aladdin could no longer afford to underwrite big-time radio programs, so Smilin' Ed, a versatile character, quickly bounced back with a new sponsor, a major paint company. On the live premiere of his new program, with a crew of ad agency executives listening from the control booth, Smilin' Ed took a few hefty swigs from his old gin jug, then started the show.

By his first station break, Ed was so far gone that he launched into a commercial for his old sponsor. When he realized what he was doing, the wheels turned quickly in Smilin' Ed's head.

"Some of you out there might be wondering why I'm doing an Aladdin Lamp commercial on my new show brought to you by a paint company," he started out. "But the reason I'm doing it is a good one. As you all know, for many years Aladdin Lamps sponsored my program. But the reason Aladdin Lamps are such a fabulous product is that they light up all the corners of every room in your house to show you just where you need paint!"

Smilin' Ed had shifted gears as smoothly as if oiled with Aladdin Lamp fuel instead of gin. And he had saved his job.

We had our problems on little WLOK, Lima. Besides Howard Donahoe, our program director, we had one other announcer, Jim Hoskins. Jim made it clear to anyone who would listen that he wasn't happy in Lima, or with radio announcing, and wanted to leave. He finally got his wish, leaving only Howard and me to mind the station. One of the five stations the Fort Industry Company owned was in Atlanta. After I had been at WLOK about a year, they asked Howard Donahoe to become program director in Atlanta. This was clearly a major market and a significant step up in the business. Howard accepted.

With Howard now gone, I was the only one announcing in Lima. The station manager, Don Ioset, offered me a deal I couldn't refuse.

"We are now licensed to go on the air full-time," he said. "If you're willing to become program director, we'll let you hire two more announcers. But you still have to take care of some of the announcing until we can hire a third."

I would have taken the job under any circumstances, but he doubled my salary. I shot up to $25 a week. I have never been quite so wealthy since. I certainly never again doubled my income in a single increase. I can remember actually thinking, "What am I going to do with all this money?"

I was living at home and my expenses were low. I contributed to the food fund at the house, but all I had to buy was an article of clothing here and there and an occasional phonograph record. I can remember going out on a date with only a dollar. In those days, with a dollar you could take a girl to the movies, buy a couple of hamburgers and milk shakes, and come home with change in your pocket.

Earning $25.00 a week made me feel like a millionaire. I now knew what it was like to be rich. The experience introduced me to the idea that wealth is not an absolute value, but a ratio of income to needs: a person earning $1000 a week who needs $1500 is poor. But a man earning $500 a week who can get by on $400 is living on top of the world.

My grand new position conferred not only money, but power. In a short time I had not two but three announcers on staff, all older than I. This was hardly surprising, since I was only nineteen. One of the new men was in his early twenties. The other two were in their mid-twenties—obviously approaching middle age. Concerned about maintaining my new-found authority, I agonized over how to prove to them that I really should be the boss, that my position of power was not just a fluke.

One night I was working late and two of the new men had

stayed through the late shift. We were all hungry after signing off the station at midnight. I offered to take them to dinner at the Milano Cafe, the closest thing to continental elegance Lima had to offer, and the only eating place open at that hour.

Over some good pasta and a fair number of drinks, the conversation turned to girls, and the relative merits of amateur versus professional women. Part of this discussion, I remember, examined the terms "lay" and "professional," with the seriousness that only alcohol can produce. We pondered the likelihood that a professional girl could really be a better lay than a "laygirl," and whether if we were indeed "laymen" we would wish to give up that status for any degree of "professional" skill. I believe we agreed we would not.

It was a subject I knew something about, though only from a distance, and only by accident. The summer after my sophomore year in high school, I had taken a job in an auto-parts shop winding armatures for generators, alternators, and starters. I would wind the cable, paint the armatures with shellac, and bake them in an oven, all for fifty cents a day.

It was not exactly an exciting occupation, but directly across the back alley from the garage was a house of ill repute run by a locally famous madam named Nettie. Nettie would come over with various appliances and ask us to fix them. The shopowner would invariably roll his eyes, but every time he would relent and do the repair job. We usually got the sweeper or refrigerator motor working some way or another, and, in the process, got to talking to Nettie.

Here was my trump card. That night, at the Milano, I decided it was time to put this worldly experience, secondary as it was, to some practical use.

Putting on my most sophisticated voice, I suggested turning talk into action.

"There's always Nettie's right over there . . ." I said, allowing the sentence to dangle enticingly.

They practically fell off their chairs with enthusiasm. But I was getting chills. The last thing I wanted to do that night was go to a whorehouse. I had a girlfriend and had never under-

31

stood the idea of buying sex. But having made my offer, there was no turning back. Not without looking like a total fool.

We strolled over to Nettie's, cutting across the back alley I remembered so well. The madam glanced at me curiously when she opened up her front door.

"Hi, Nettie," I tossed off. "I've got two more customers for you."

This first-names exchange raised their eyebrows even higher. These two older fellows were sure they were in the presence of an old man of the mountain. We sat down in the seedy parlor while Nettie fetched us drinks. I was desperately seeking some face-saving device to get myself out of this predicament, but I also needed to maintain my hard-won prestige.

The girls filed in. A couple of them were attractive. First names were awkwardly exchanged. As we talked, I came up with the solution. I offered to foot the bill for whatever arrangement my buddies managed to work out with the house. This strategy possessed the advantage of making me seem both generous and jaded at the same time. In my most patronizing manner, I waved both men upstairs, as if I had done this so many times I was tired of it. I sat downstairs and drank some more, and talked appliances with Nettie.

Though that evening cost me more than a week's salary, it was a bargain. From that night on, my newfound authority at the radio station in Lima was secure.

I might have stayed on in Lima for years and become a fixture on the local broadcasting scene, but I was still living at home, and much as I enjoyed my new prosperity, I yearned to be out on my own. As a full-fledged program director and staffer after my first year on the air, I had gained confidence in my abilities as an announcer. In fact, I might even have become a little swellheaded, something not hard to do at twenty.

My sights became fixed on New York City, that enduring mecca of broadcasting. I took a brief break from WLOK and hopped a train east. There was a man I wanted to see in New York.

Milton Cross was NBC's senior staff announcer. Cross did most of his work on the Blue Network, which had a highbrow, cultural cast. He was a classical music expert, handling the network's Walter Damrosch concerts and hosting the Saturday Afternoon Metropolitan Opera broadcasts. To my delight, I succeeded in getting a private audience with Cross. To my disappointment, he didn't tell me what I wanted to hear.

Rather than urging me to leave Ohio behind for the golden avenues of Manhattan, he advised me to stay put for a while. It would be wiser not to try to make it in New York, he said, until I had more experience. Then, after still more years in some respectable secondary market like Detroit or Chicago, it would be easier for me to sneak into New York "by the back door," as he put it. "Let them send for you," he advised.

I knew perfectly well, in the abstract at least, that his advice made good sense. But I was young, impatient, and arrogant. In fact, I preferred to assume that Cross was telling me in some subtle way that New York just wasn't big enough for the two of us. I took the train back to Ohio, disgruntled with my small-town lot and disappointed in the great Milton Cross.

But within a matter of months, Cross's predictions mysteriously began to materialize. It would take some time, but I would indeed be summoned to New York to accept a job Manhattan-based rivals would have killed for. I would, in fact, end up sneaking into Manhattan by the back door instead of storming the gates. But that would take place fifteen years in the future. I wanted results right now.

Within months I discovered that Cross had been right about one thing: the competition *was* far friendlier out there in the provinces. People were willing to give each other a leg up.

The grand old man of Lima broadcasting was an announcer named Gordon Shaw. While still in college, I saw him do a man-in-the-street interview and was enthralled by the sight. By the time I joined WLOK, Shaw had moved on to better things, as an announcer at WWJ in Detroit, the second-oldest and one of the best radio stations in the country. When he found an even better job at WJR, a rival Detroit station, he called me up and asked if I wanted to take a crack at his old job at WWJ. If I was interested, he would be happy to refer me. He wanted to do a favor for someone from his hometown. I was quite touched.

I was senior announcer and program director back in Lima, but Detroit would be a giant step up. It also meant a quantum leap in broadcasting power from 100 to 5000 watts. WWJ was run by the Detroit *News* as a promotional arm for their newspaper, and they always acted surprised that it made money. It was a well-run station, with six full-time announcers working rotation. At the outset, of course, I would be low man on the totem pole. But with three other radio stations, all in close competition, Detroit presented a great opportunity. Just as Gordon Shaw had moved from one station to another, I might be able to employ the same strategy, improving my position each time.

In a state of high tension, I took the train to Detroit to audition for Mel Wissman, program director of WWJ. When I finished reading, he stepped into the studio to ask me one question: "How long will it take for you to move up here?"

"About a day," I said.

I wasn't kidding. I had nothing to move but myself, and nothing to hold me in Lima. But I was more surprised than anything else by the fact that I had won the audition despite the fact that I did not have the distinctive "radio voice" of that era.

At the time, young announcers often tried to imitate the steel-edged, stylized sound of Westbrook Van Vorhies, who did the famous *Ma-a-rch of Time!* broadcasts. His deep Shakespearean tones resonated with authority across the nation. But I talked like an Ohioan, relatively accentless, somewhat quietly, hardly stylized. As long as I stayed in Ohio, it was no problem. But if I really wanted to go places in broadcasting, I assumed I'd have to learn to speak more like a Van Vorhies, or at least like Lowell Thomas, or Peter Grant, or Paul Sullivan.

I agonized over my voice throughout my radio career. Everything, of course, hung on that personal sound. That was all we had. I was constantly clearing my throat, trying to make my voice clearer, always afraid it would fail me, always afraid of my own inflections.

But whenever I found myself gripped by that familiar panic, I tried to remember Howard Donahoe's classic advice: "Forget your voice. Just concentrate on what you are saying." This notion was something like Zen Archery. When I did stop paying attention to how I sounded, my voice would miraculously improve. The change came with a subtle shift from "how" to "what." It was mainly a matter of relaxing into it and trusting in my natural abilities to get the message across.

But Howard's idea of good broadcasting contrasted sharply with what many others then believed. From the beginning of radio, an announcer was supposed to have something called a "microphone voice." Since the old microphones distorted your natural tone, you were expected to compensate by artificially enhancing your voice. Like many bright ideas, this notion went beyond useful reality. The sad result was the destruction of many a fine natural voice. Even singers felt compelled to compromise their normal tone patterns on the air.

The radio audience heard a stylized, edgy, high-pitched tone of voice, not relaxed in the least. Though this eccentric pattern of speech was popular, some of us, particularly in the Midwest, thought announcers should speak the way real people did. Luckily, Howard Donahoe and Mel Wissman, the first two program directors to hire me, were of the more naturalistic school. Of course, people from such states as Ohio and Nebraska tend to speak an unaccented English anyway. This put me squarely in among the "normals," unless I planned to compete in vocal gymnastics.

Not surprisingly, a severe backlash to all this voice emphasis set in. Since broadcasters were obviously selected for voice, it seemed equally obvious that someone with a pleasant voice must have been picked only for his sound and not for other merits such as intelligence.

This backlash—stressing content, not style—brought a number of very strange voices to the forefront in radio news commentary. They were not theatrical voices like Van Vorhies or the ponderous "microphone" voices of early radio. These were odd voices, even bad voices, sometimes abrasive, occasionally even impaired. The most famous examples were Gabriel Heatter and H. V. Kaltenborn, the most prominent news commentators of their day. The prevailing psychology went something like this: "That guy's voice is so bad they must have him on only because he's a real expert."

Still, radio needed all types. If you were blessed or cursed, as the case may have been, with a natural voice, you still won some auditions. I never tried to force myself to speak any differently. I simply spoke like a small-town Ohioan and did my job as well as I could.

Detroit: 1940. The end of the Depression, the beginning of a new decade. I was now up to $40.00 a week, which seemed like a fortune, even if I had to start paying my own rent. I lived at the Sigrid Apartments on Second Avenue, along with Mike Wallace, who was on staff at WXYZ in Detroit. Neither of us realized we both lived in that apartment building until years later, when we were both working in Chicago.

At WWJ, I had to sign the station either on or off, because announcers with more seniority were rewarded with cushier hours. Though I worked every weekend, I got two days off during the week. This felt like an enormous, possibly undeserved, even unneeded, luxury. At WLOK, I had grown used to working six and sometimes seven full days a week.

I led the good life in Detroit for about a year, young and prosperous and on my own for the first time. I was working hard at the station, attending classes when I could at Wayne University to continue my education, and slowly working myself into a better position in the hierarchy at WWJ. Once again, I might well have stayed put at WWJ or switched over to a rival station to improve my position in the Detroit market. But, to use an old broadcasting phrase, "circumstances beyond our control" intervened.

December 7, 1941: news announcer Ben Grauer broke into

the Sunday-afternoon programming to announce the bombing of Pearl Harbor. Then the network went back to its regular program. Later that day, as events quickly developed, Grauer broke in once again to announce that war had been declared, first by Japan, then by the United States. At the first announcement, I thought it was a bad joke. My initial reaction was that a mike had been opened accidentally, and that an apology would follow. Three years earlier, Orson Welles had scared the public out of its wits with his realistic drama of invaders from Mars. No one was expecting war in 1941.

In retrospect, what stands out most about Pearl Harbor day was that the medium was not commandeered to present continuous news. The newspapers were still the primary news outlet. In radio, news was strictly a stepchild to entertainment. It would take World War II, and pioneers such as Edward R. Murrow, to change that.

Twenty-two years later, when President Kennedy was shot, I happened to be with the head of NBC News, Bill McAndrew, when the word came. Without any hesitation, he stepped into the hallway and shouted, "Cancel all regular programming!" For the duration of the crisis, all three networks devoted themselves to wall-to-wall news, virtually around the clock. As host of *The Today Show* at the time, I was both participant and witness to the prominent role television played in the course of those events.

By the 1960s, current events and broadcasting coverage of the news had become inextricably entwined. Some critics began to wonder whether this trend might not have gone too far, with disturbing implications for the future. But as the 1940s and the Second World War began, broadcasting had not yet matured as a news medium. The war itself would take care of that. Nearly every major news broadcaster who came to prominence after the war earned his or her stripes as a war correspondent. Though I would end up devoting far more of my broadcast career to news than entertainment, I am an exception to that rule.

After Pearl Harbor, I tried to enlist in the armed forces. But I was suffering from an impediment, even if it had never bothered me much. I am color-blind. After being turned down by the Army Air Corps, the Navy, and the Marines, I even tried the Coast Guard. But they didn't want a color-blind sailor either. I had just about resigned myself to spending the war on the sidelines when the Army drafted me. They didn't seem to care whether I was color-blind or not. The only color the infantry cared about was GI olive drab.

After a long interrogation about my professional radio background, they put me in the heavy weapons company of an infantry division. I was sent to Fort Lewis, Washington, for basic training, where they tried to squeeze twelve weeks of training into five weeks of time. I can vividly remember running up a hill with a full pack on my back, finally reaching a point where my legs simply stopped working. An officer came by and asked me why I wasn't moving. I said my legs wouldn't work.

"You'd better hop into that vehicle that's taking a whole bunch of you back to the dispensary," he said. I did what I was told, as soon as I could.

A whole squad of us ended up being honorably discharged, on the grounds that we had been broken down by excessive overtraining. They called it a field-accident disability and simply left it at that. As far as I know, there was no investigation of the incident. They simply got rid of us all, probably to relieve themselves of any potential embarrassment.

I was a little dismayed, but also relieved. I had started out bitter in the first place because they wouldn't let me enlist, but simply drafted me when they needed more volume. Then a certain degree of guilt set in. I was out, but that didn't end the war. It didn't get my brother out. He was in Germany and would go through the Battle of the Bulge before he got home. It didn't get any of my friends out either.

I was also a little concerned that I might be permanently disabled from my short but excruciating stay in the Army. After all, on that hill everything quit on me in a rather frightening way. As soon as my discharge papers came through, I went to see a civilian doctor.

Everything looked fine to him. Whatever the effects of the physical abuse, they had apparently been only temporary. This eased my mind.

"You know," the doctor said, "I probably could arrange to get you back into the service."

I doubted he could get me into the Navy, and I had no desire to go back where I had been. "Thanks, but no thanks," I said.

I left military service in May of 1943 and returned to Detroit, where I found myself in the mood to tie up loose ends and perhaps to conquer new horizons. I broke up with a girl in Detroit to whom I had given a ring and went to Chicago to audition for NBC. I had a number of friends in Chicago I wanted to see, and I decided if I could work things out, I would stay there. WWJ was Detroit's NBC affiliate, so I had a remote connection with the network.

NBC Central Division Headquarters in Chicago didn't need any full-time people, but they could use some vacation relief. They offered me a temporary staff position with a guarantee of only three months. I would be hanging on by a thread, but I was in a mood to take a chance. I quit my job at WWJ and set off for the second city.

My reasons for moving were perfectly sound. This was an opportunity to go with a network. Chicago was the division headquarters, with a local station, WMAQ, attached to it. WMAQ was an "O and O," which meant it was owned and operated by the network. As network announcers, we would do our broadcasting out of WMAQ studios, but a good deal of that original production would be fed to NBC affiliates all across the country.

I had just turned twenty-two. This made me the youngest staff announcer hired by a radio network, even if the appointment was temporary. For all I know, that record may still stand.

Proud as I was, I was traumatized by my youthful status. As a junior member of the team, I felt inadequate. Whenever they asked me to do something new, the first thing that came into my head was, "Am I old enough to do that?"

Strangely, that attitude has stuck with me to this day. I am now one of the oldest people working full time in a major slot on the air. But there are still times when I think to myself, almost by reflex, "Maybe I'll let one of the older people take care of that."

In Chicago, I did a five-minute network news broadcast, but the important network newscasts came out of New York and Washington. They were done by the likes of Lowell Thomas, H. V. Kaltenborn, John W. Vandercook, Morgan Beatty, and Gabriel Heatter. NBC had dozens of affiliated stations across the country, but they did not all carry all the network material. Sometimes my five-minute network news was fed to only ten or fifteen stations at one time. My total listenership was frequently far less than that of WMAQ, our local Chicago station. But I could never shake the feeling—and the fear—that when I went "on the network," something grand and imposing was taking place. When I did exactly the same thing on WMAQ, I was less frightened.

For live musical programs, we always did our newscasts, commercial announcements, or announcing with written copy. There was almost no ad-libbing on the radio, in sharp contrast to today, when so much air work is plainly off-the-cuff. We even did scripted radio interviews, with questions and answers written out to be read. They must have sounded terribly stilted, but no one seemed to notice. Radio interviews sounded like radio dramas, except that they featured real people and were often badly read.

Staff announcing in the 1940s was no automatic path to either fame or fortune. It was basically an anonymous job unless you climbed to the very top of the profession. News commentators earned a certain degree of fame, and men like Milton Cross became well known when their names were linked to prestigious broadcasts. But the real stars on radio were always the entertainers, the comedians, the big-band leaders, the singers. I believe the main reason television linkmen have become famous is because all of America sees our faces.

As old NBC men drifted back from the war, they were restored to their former posts. Each time someone returned, I—as the most junior—stepped down the seniority ladder. But the thread I was hanging on refused to break, even though it sometimes stretched dangerously. Every few months I would get a new dismissal notice. But each time something miraculous would rescue me. The incident I best recall involved Charlie Lyon, a veteran NBC staffer who finally decided to live on the West Coast and host *Truth or Consequences*.

Although I didn't know it then, my true salvation lay in the impending death of Chicago as a major media center. In those days Chicago was still a great producer of original programming. Fifteen-minute soap operas were the bulk of the daytime business. Paul Rhymer, who wrote a popular soap opera called *Vic & Sade*, was a humorist on a par with Mark Twain, in my opinion. The show was fifteen straight minutes of pungent philosophy, far-out humor, subtle deadpan jokes, and fascinating characters. It had a devoted following, including Ethel Barrymore, Harry Truman, and enough people who appreciated Rhymer's unique wit to give the program decent ratings.

Rhymer's mother came out to Chicago one time to see *Vic & Sade* broadcast from the old *Amos 'n' Andy* studio. An announcer named Ed Roberts did all the Chicago commercials, but on alternate days the commercials would originate in New York. With the network feed, this was simply a matter of throwing a switch. Mrs. Rhymer, who was not well versed in radio electronics, sat in the control room, watching the program through the double glass wall between the control room and the studio. As the commercial came on, she could hear the announcer's voice but couldn't see anyone speaking. She peered around, then asked her son suspiciously, "Where is that voice coming from?"

"Well," he said, "on alternate days the commercials come from New York."

"New York," she said. "That's very interesting."

The next day she came back to the studio, this time with a friend.

When it was time for a commercial, Ed Roberts, the Chicago

announcer, stepped up to the microphone and started reading the copy.

With an air of great authority, Mrs. Rhymer turned to her friend. "See that man standing there reading the commercial?" she asked. "He's in New York."

Paul Rhymer fell over laughing.

I can remember a woman who understood just about as much about broadcasting having a fierce argument with my mother about originations.

"How is your son in St. Louis?" she asked.

"He's in Chicago," my mother said, "with the National Broadcasting Company."

"Oh, no," her friend said. "He's in St. Louis. I was just there last week, and I heard him on the radio."

Radio was kind to me. It gave me a life's work, and my life's love. My wife-to-be, Ruth, and I met in Chicago in late 1943. Ruth worked in the transcription department of NBC. There was an early Saturday radio program sponsored by Skelly Oil, produced by NBC in Chicago but sent only to KOA in Denver. I was the announcer. She was the director. I started the job early one Saturday morning after working the nightshift. I didn't appreciate being there, and I don't believe Ruth liked the hours any more than I did. I think we both secretly blamed each other for having to be there at that hour. For the first six Saturdays we never spoke, going about our jobs in chilly silence. Definitely not love at first sight.

One day I stopped by the transcription office to see a girl, Flora, whom I was dating. I had gone golfing the day before and had nearly broken my kneecap. A ball had come right off a driver head, sliced badly across the rough, and whistled straight into my fairway. I tried to get out of the way, but it hit me squarely on the kneecap. I went to a doctor, thinking I must have fractured it. I hadn't, but it was still very painful.

As I came limping into the NBC offices, I saw Ruth sitting there by herself. I didn't even say hello. Just asked her where Flora was. Flora had gone out to lunch.

"You're limping," Ruth said.

I told her the story of the errant golf ball, then mumbled, "It almost broke the kneecap."

"Well, it's a good thing it didn't hit any harder," she said sympathetically.

But I heard, "It's a good thing it didn't hit any *higher*."

I looked at her somewhat askance, not exactly sure how to respond.

"Yeah," I said, "I guess you're right." I limped out, a little puzzled, but curious.

"What kind of a girl is Ruth Shaheen?" I asked Flora the next time I saw her.

"I don't know," Flora said. "How do you mean?"

"I mean morally," I said, thinking about her comment of the day before.

"Oh, she comes from a very good family. Why?"

I said I just wondered.

It wasn't until after Ruth and I were married, six months later, that I told Ruth what I thought she had said. She was shocked.

Under the existing network rules, two family members could not work at NBC at the same time. So the day we got married, Ruth went on leave of absence and never went back. We like to think she's still an NBC employee on extended leave.

As my months at NBC piled up, I remained a network relief announcer. I was working full time and pulling my weight along with my ten official colleagues, but I had absolutely no job security. I could be discharged from my post on very short notice, and, when the last postwar dismissal notices finally came in, I was told that my time was up. I had four weeks to look for a new job. I started looking, but my heart wasn't in it.

I was about to head down to Wheeling, West Virginia, to see about a job possibility. Our son, Hugh Raymond—later known as H. R.—had just been born in Chicago. To be on the NBC staff in Chicago and then to run off to Wheeling to look for work seemed like a cruel exile. Jules Herbuveaux, head of NBC Central Division, was a very compassionate man. As a last resort, I decided to call him up and throw myself on his mercy.

"Well," Jules said, "there's got to be some way to keep you

43

on around here. You've got your new baby, and everything else. Just stick around," he said finally. "We'll see what we can do."

Unfortunately for both of us, Jules still had to answer to New York. New York didn't like its rules and regulations being stretched to do someone a personal favor. Bill Kephart, my immediate superior at WMAQ, soon got an angry note from the RCA Building at Rockefeller Center.

"Who authorized you to have eleven staff announcers when you've only been allotted ten?"

Kephart tried a classic stall. He wrote back to New York that he couldn't get by without eleven full-time announcers. Ten just wouldn't do. New York didn't like to be told what to do by Chicago. Their response was immediate and to the point: "You are budgeted for ten announcers. One has to go."

But Kephart kept stalling, hoping something might come up, like a last-minute commutation of a doomed criminal.

"I'm just not going to answer this right away," he told me. But the more Kephart kept stalling, the more New York kept pressuring him. Finally he said he would give me a dismissal notice, but he didn't say when. Five or six weeks went miraculously by without New York asking for anyone's head; then a senior staffer took off for a better job on the West Coast and I was named one of the ten full-time staff announcers. From then on I would enjoy some job security. I had been saved by the bell. Now it was up to me to do something with my good fortune.

I stayed with NBC in Chicago for eleven years, performing the whole gamut of announcer duties: news reading, music announcing, dramatic announcing, interviewing, narrating, commercials, variety show emceeing. I gradually worked myself up the totem pole, gaining more seniority. I started accepting a fair amount of outside work beyond my basic staff duties. This brought in not only added income, but a certain amount of public recognition.

I announced the University of Chicago Roundtable, a weekly gabfest of prestigious thinkers hosted by Robert Hutchins, then president of the University of Chicago. The Chicago and Northwestern Railroad sponsored an hour of classical music, which I also announced. Soon I was being offered the juicy assignments, the desirable shows.

But there came a time in the early 1950s when those lucrative outside jobs started to dry up. It was not because my work had deteriorated. The competition was a new kid on the block, making inroads into our business, chipping away at our bread and butter. Sponsors were pulling money out of radio, betting it on this new presence. It was called television and I hated it.

3

·

EARLY TV

September 1945. The tiny studio above the Balaban & Katz Theatre on State Street was lit up like a night baseball game. I sat facing a rack of lights so intense I might have been staring into the sun. Under the heat of those blazing lights I sweated right through my lightweight jacket in less than five minutes. The sweat probably kept it from catching fire. The broadcast itself was a government-sponsored fifteen-minute news break. I read a public service announcement about the Treasury Department and then the news.

My first appearance on television was over almost as soon as it began.

In those days, right after the war, film distributors were interested in developing television as an alternative to theatrical films. The experimental station WBKB was owned by Balaban & Katz, a major motion picture theater chain in Chicago. Fewer than four hundred television sets were operating in the entire city of Chicago, and most of those were in bars. I assumed I was broadcasting to a bunch of drunks and didn't take the job that seriously.

When I finished the newscast, I told the producer I'd never even seen a television program.

"We're off the air right now," he said, "but we'll be back on in forty-five minutes. There's a set in the lobby. If you want to wait, you can watch the next show."

I hung around the movie theater until the next program. I

don't remember what I saw, but I do remember a number of tiny figures moving around on a small, perfectly round screen. It was a thrill entirely different from watching a movie. With a movie, you know the action actually took place in the past. But on television, people were doing whatever they were doing at that very moment. In those days, live television was a genuine technological marvel, and it took years for the novelty to wear off.

I had never seen a television program, but I had seen a video camera and monitor at the 1939 New York World's Fair. My cousin Gar Hicks, a journalist with the New York *World Telegram*, managed to wangle a press pass for me to the fair. I stuck it in the band of my hat, the way journalists did in the movies, before setting off to see the exhibits designed around the theme of A Better Tomorrow.

Behind Billy Rose's Aquacade, Les Brown and His Band of Renown were playing on a large bandstand. The vocalists were Jack Haskell and Doris Day. As I strolled beneath the sweeping archway of the RCA exhibit, I saw a crude representation of myself reflected in a primitive monitor. With a start, I realized a camera was perched high above me, recording my every movement. So this was television, the electronic wave of the future!

As a professional radio buff, I was intrigued. It would take World War II research to perfect the electronic scanning beam, permitting television to become a commercial reality. Before the beam, prototype television sets used a mechanical scanning disk, perforated with holes set in a spiral pattern, a system far too cumbersome for use in the home.

In Chicago, WBKB's postwar experimental television broadcasts were produced under the supervision of an electronic genius known as Captain Eddy. Captain Eddy was hard of hearing but too vain to wear a hearing aid. Instead, he rigged up a hearing aid tucked away in a pipe bowl which he never lit. When he wanted to hear, he clamped the pipe in his teeth, and the sound traveled to his ear by bone conduction.

Captain Eddy was said to have worked with Vladimir Zworykin in developing the electron scanning beam. He had also served in the Navy, and was believed to have worked on a top-secret OSS plan for the invasion of Yokahama that would have involved sending unmanned boats filled with explosives into the harbor, using television as a guidance system. Now he worked for Balaban & Katz, intermittently broadcasting television programs to an audience of a few hundred barflies.

In the mid-forties, television was still something of a joke. Many otherwise intelligent people were convinced it was simply a fad. Who in his right mind would sit immobile in a chair to watch a television broadcast when there is so much else to do around the house? Listening to radio, a person could do other things. But to spend hours staring at a small screen, confined to your seat, seemed like an activity designed for the lazy, the bedridden, or the terminally bored.

Even when television started to develop as a serious rival to radio, many topnotch radio broadcasters refused to have anything to do with this obviously inane medium. The action was all in radio, they said, and would stay there for a long time to come. Television was an upstart medium, radio's poor relation.

For an NBC staff announcer like myself, getting into television from radio was really more of a drift than a jump. Television producers would come to us and ask, "How about coming down to the studio to do one of these television things?" It was entirely up to us. If we felt like it, we simply dropped by the studio, did the broadcast, and maybe made something on the side. There was no union, no schedule, no fixed fees. The American Federation of Radio Artists, originally called AFRA, would in time become AFTRA, the "T" for television. But that didn't happen until the early fifties, when the new medium finally became a true commercial enterprise.

Chicago had always been a major producer of big-time radio, a role it continued in early television. *Kukla, Fran & Ollie*, Studs Terkel's *Stud's Place*, the soap opera *Hawkins Falls*, and Dave Garroway's *Garroway at Large* were all pioneers in their respective categories. As an announcer, I worked on both *Kukla, Fran & Ollie* and *Hawkins Falls*. And I knew Dave Garroway and Studs Terkel, both of whom would eventually gain recognition far beyond the confines of Chicago.

When I first met him at WMAQ, Dave Garroway was a fascinating conversationalist, a brilliant broadcaster, and a wildly enthusiastic hobbyist. He rebuilt a Rolls-Royce practically from scratch, from a hulk he picked up at auction for a few hundred dollars. He did his own chrome plating in vats set up in a garage he rented in an alley near his uptown Chicago house. I would often drop by to borrow tools. I was building a telescope at the time, and he had a lathe and other specialized instruments I needed. He had a great interest in astronomy, and we used to talk about telescopes and stars and planets for hours.

On the fledgling NBC television network, Dave hosted a popular comedy and variety hour, *Garroway at Large*. On WMAQ, he headed a wonderful free-flowing late-night jazz-and-commentary show called *The 1160 Club*. Dave was a veritable encyclopedia of jazz, but he was also quite eclectic. For several weeks he insisted on playing a Bach two-part invention at the start of each program. His fans not only tolerated it, but accepted it finally as some form of classical jazz.

On those nights we worked a shift together, I would pay regular visits to his television show under the pseudonym of Fennimore Fuffner, using a disguised voice. Fennimore was an eccentric jazz buff who haunted unlikely night spots on the far South Side, and would report on various musical happenings, all of which were sadly out of date. I would make up names of obscure performers, or drop archaic ones like Paul Pendarvis or Anson Weeks. Fennimore appreciated second-rate and obsolete jazz, but his favorite music was so far out it was played on instruments that no longer existed. I'd tell Dave all about some exotic riffs I'd heard played on the bass ophicleide, or the keyed bugle. Fuffner became a popular fixture on Garroway's show.

Stud's Place attracted considerable attention, mainly because it was the first and possibly the last dramatic comedy show on television on which actors and others simply played themselves. Pianist Chet Roble, Dave Garroway, Cliff Norton, all appeared as themselves. Studs and his freewheeling cast would map out a rudimentary plot and play out the selected dramatic situations entirely ad-lib. *Time* tried to explain how this worked: "For example, Phil Lord, a crusty old actor, is played by Phil Lord, a crusty old actor." The show ran a half hour, twice as long as John Cameron Swayze's *Nightly News* or Liberace's musical show. It was so spontaneous that even the half-hour was usually too short. The format was imitated for a while by Billy Rose in a New York origination, but it failed.

Hawkins Falls, the first of the television soap operas, ran a half-hour, five days a week, sponsored by Lever Brothers Surf. The Drewers lived in the All-American small town of Hawkins Falls. Lona Drewer was played by the "Sade" of *Vic & Sade*, Bernadine Flynn, while Mr. Drewer was played by the actor Frank Dane. As the commercial announcer on the show, I witnessed an incident that would come to define the behind-the-scenes political intrigue now associated with soap operas.

Frank Dane was the male lead on *Hawkins Falls*. After a year on the program, he began to put pressure on the producer for more money, better hours, and improved working conditions. Bill Barrett, the writer, and Ben Park, the producer, were both young and talented, and they resented his constant demands. During rehearsal one day, Frank reacted strongly to a suggestion they offered about his delivery, and launched into a public tirade.

"Don't you guys tell me about my profession! I was acting on the legitimate stage when you were still in knee pants! I don't have to take this! Unless my demands are met, I won't be here for the next episode!"

Turning on his heel, he stormed out of the studio.

This performance was followed by an embarrassed silence, broken finally by Bill Barrett.

"Let's kill him," Barrett said softly.

Park nodded silently. They both shrugged as if to imply the lack of any reasonable alternative.

A few episodes later Drewer was sent off on a long business trip, and his plane was lost over the Irish Sea. Lona Drewer suffered tremendous grief over her tragic loss until a new love interest showed up in town, played by Jim Bannon. Frank Dane may have felt he was indispensable to the show, but he had set the stage for a policy that would keep soap stars in line for a long time. The procedure of writing a player out may even have been the model for the hit play *The Killing of Sister George.*

Early television out of Chicago was eccentric but often highly creative. One of the most unusual and brilliant television shows ever to grace the new medium was *Kukla, Fran & Ollie.* NBC brought the show over from the Balaban & Katz station WBKB, along with its creator, Burr Tillstrom. Burr was a good-looking man who rarely appeared on camera, and never during standard TV performances. The proscenium arch framing the puppet stage would reach only as high as his shoulder. During the show itself, which was shot live, Burr worked below stage level, manipulating his puppets while watching their movements in video monitors.

The world of *Kukla, Fran & Ollie* was peopled, or puppeted, by unforgettable characters. Ollie was a snaggle-toothed dragon of lovable flamboyance, while Kukla (Russian for doll) was gentle and stable and well-rounded, the quintessential Everyman. A delightful harridan named Buelah Witch, with scraggly white hair and a shrill voice and a high-peaked witch's hat, joined a whole host of peripheral characters, delineated with airtight personal integrity by Tillstrom.

Colonel Crackie, a Southern gentleman, took off in one episode and dominated the entire broadcast with a rambling but hilarious discourse about his high-school graduation, a "mizzable affair." After the show, I asked Burr why he hadn't followed the plan as it had gone during rehearsal.

He chuckled. "Colonel Crackie just wouldn't shut up," he said. "He took over the whole program."

Burr had a remarkable ability to compartmentalize his mind, almost like a split personality. A character might occasionally make a mistake, but Tillstrom never crossed a voice, the classic nightmare of the stage ventriloquist. During a private non-broadcast show at the Chicago Actors Club, Ollie came onstage quite drunk, weaving all over the stage, slurring words, splendidly and obviously smashed. This was hardly surprising, as Burr himself had been drinking. But Kukla was cold sober and kept saying in a disapproving voice, "You're going to have a big head tomorrow, Ollie. Don't come to me about it."

Burr might have made millions on his creations, as Jim Henson has done with his Muppets, but he turned down countless offers to license mass-produced Kukla and Ollie dolls. He was a purist, whose characters were utterly real to him and to everyone who followed them. He never would have been able to tolerate the mass marketing of creations that were dear to him and to all the children in his audience who believed in the magic of his invented world.

This sense of magic and reality intertwined was not completely understood by less imaginative souls. One day Burr showed up at the studio a little early, only to find his then-announcer wearing Ollie on one arm, working the puppet himself. As far as Burr was concerned, those puppets were asleep when his hands weren't in them. Burr didn't say anything at the time, but there was an immediate replacement of the announcer.

The next day I got a call asking me to audition to be the new announcer. Beulah Zachary, the producer—who later was killed in a plane crash in New York's East River—was worried that I wouldn't make it to the studio on time for rehearsal because of heavy midday traffic. My regular show, *Hawkins Falls*, was broadcast out of the old Studebaker Theatre on South Michigan Avenue. It was a twelve-minute ride up to the Merchandise Mart, where *Kukla, Fran & Ollie* was broadcast. I had about a half-hour to spare between the two shows, but Beulah didn't want to take any chances. If I wanted to do the show, she said, I would have to give up *Hawkins Falls*.

The trouble was, I liked doing *Hawkins Falls*. I pleaded with Beulah, promising her I would never be late, explaining that I didn't really rehearse much of what I did anyway. She finally relented, but laid down a firm decree. If I was ever late for an actual show, that would be the end.

There was only one solution. I hired a limousine service to get me from one location to the other. Day after day, I would pull up at the Merchandise Mart, lost in a classic Walter Mitty fantasy that someone from my hometown would be walking by just as I stepped out of my limo. But month after month I pulled up, jumped out, and no one ever noticed.

Finally one afternoon I spied someone I knew on the side-walk. It wasn't anyone from Lima, but it was a person I wouldn't have minded impressing. As my car pulled smartly up to the curb, my driver stepped around to open the door. I popped agilely out of my seat, clutching an important-looking sheaf of papers. Just then, my coat pocket caught on the inside door handle, tearing with a loud, ripping sound straight out of a Marx Brothers movie. I dropped my papers on the sidewalk, stumbled awkwardly, and wound up wishing I were dead. After that incident I forgot about making a real entrance.

Though the bulk of my early work in television was as an announcer on regularly scheduled series, I did do some spe-cials, or spectaculars, as NBC then called them. *The Story of Steel* was a documentary program in prime time, tracing the history of steel from Damascus to Toledo to Sheffield. After helping with research and scripting, my job was to narrate the program with demonstrations of steel products ranging in size from the movements of precision Swiss timepieces to large steel beams and girders. Since the show would be shot live, without commercial interruption, in prime time, and every-thing had to be memorized (there were no prompting devices), I was more nervous than I had ever been.

Larry Auerbach, the producer-director, wished me good luck before the show began. All the rehearsals had gone badly.

"Don't lose your sense of humor," he said. His phrase rang in my ears as we went on the air.

We opened with a sequence calling for a close-up view of the steel parts of a watch. For this tight shot, a propman had ar-ranged tiny pieces of a watch movement on a table draped in black velvet. As the camera dollied in for a close-up, the ped-estal hit the table leg and the lens-turret fell off the camera and onto the table among the watch parts.

The camera shots had been painstakingly worked out, using three cameras, but now we were down to two. Along with a tidal feeling of disaster, I felt manic laughter boiling up inside me. That phrase, "Don't lose your sense of humor," kept echoing in my mind. Somehow I got through those first few minutes, and the rest of the hour went reasonably smoothly.

Technical backwardness was not the only bane of live television. The medium was in a terrible state of flux. The first television commercial I ever saw was so naive it was positively heartrending. An actor sat behind a table, face-on to the camera, making an earnest pitch for some pots and pans.

"This saucepan here," he started out, holding the pan up but peering quickly off camera and shaking his head before plunging on, "This saucepan I have here . . ."

Letting the sentence awkwardly trail off, he ducked down behind the counter. When his head popped back up, his whole pitch had a new beginning.

"I'd like to tell you about this frying pan . . ." But then he had to start hunting around for the frying pan, which had somehow eluded him.

"Well," he said in exasperation, "this saucepan here holds four quarts . . ." He went lamely on, and at the close, the camera did a fast swish-pan from his face to a logo and lettered brand name. But the mike was still open.

"Where in the hell is that saucepan?" he hissed, before his fader was closed.

From the mid-forties into the mid-fifties, Chicago enjoyed a healthy decade of dominance in television, a legacy of its leading place in radio. But as creative and delightful as Chicago television was, by the mid-fifties an astute observer could see that Chicago was withering as an original media center.

The West Coast was drawing the Westerns and the action-oriented dramatic shows, because Hollywood offered vastly superior production facilities. New York maintained an effective monopoly in the news field, while churning out an impressive supply of highbrow dramatic offerings drawing on the talent of Broadway. *Playhouse 90* and *Studio One* were only two well-known examples of New York's rich contribution to the Golden Age of Television.

That left Chicago with only a few soaps and dramatic series.

In the beginning, television had begun to affect our livelihoods when it took proceeds away from radio. But the melting away of shows to both coasts was hurting those of us in Chicago even more.

I was hosting a fifteen-minute variety show called *The Bunch*, star-studded by Chicago standards and growing in popularity. We suddenly got a cancellation notice from New York. We were shocked. We went to our local network executives, curious as to what was going to replace *us*.

"Some pianist from Milwaukee with only one name," they said.

The pianist's name was Liberace. We watched his first program, candelabra and all. It was only fifteen minutes long, but it was destined to become wildly successful.

Early in 1954 Milton Cross's prediction from prewar days started to gain reality, making Chicago the perfect jumping-off point for any New York career. NBC New York was desperately combing the provinces for someone to announce a new program called *The Home Show*, starring Arlene Francis. Arlene had been an actress on Broadway, but she was best known as a panelist on *What's My Line?*, one of the longest-running quiz shows in television history.

NBC had run through a large number of worthy people in New York, everyone from Ben Grauer to Gene Rayburn, before deciding it might be more glamorous to import someone from "outside"—someone fresh and, at the same time, able.

Jack Rayel, NBC's line producer in New York, flew out to Chicago to talk to Ben Park, our head producer. Ben acted as if he were my agent.

"Well, I don't know," Ben replied when asked if he had anyone who might fit the bill. "Of course there's always Hugh Downs. But I don't know if you could get him."

That intrigued Rayel. "Why not?"

"Because I doubt he'd want to leave Chicago. He's too successful out here."

On his return, Ben told me what he had done. He knew

perfectly well I would have given my eyeteeth to break into New York.

"Don't act too eager," he said, "because I've set it up so they're really going to have to sell you."

I met with Rayel and did my best to play indifferent. Rayel took Ben's bait. He asked me to come to New York immediately for a rapid round of auditions. They had to see me on the set, he said, because they didn't want "just another announcer." Aware that the radio categories were fast becoming outmoded, they wanted someone who not only could come across on television, but who could ad-lib. They wanted to test my ability to explain material extemporaneously, using graphs, charts, and props.

I did have a few reservations about the possible move to New York. It would mean giving up the security of a staff position. As a network staffer in Chicago, you enjoyed the best of both worlds. You drew a steady salary, but you were free to do outside jobs as long as they didn't interfere with your regular duties.

The Home Show, by contrast, would be a free-lance job. My fortunes would be riding with that one show, and I would be under contract to it. I would no longer be an employee of the network, even though the program would be broadcast on NBC. It seemed like quite a gamble, particularly since there were still people who seriously believed television would not last out the decade.

Fortunately, I had little time to weigh my options. They were going into rehearsals in New York without waiting to settle on an announcer. I flew out three days before the premiere and was immediately put through an elaborate series of tests and auditions. I knew a number of other candidates were undergoing the same process. I was convinced they would end up picking one of them instead of me.

The show was due to air the first Monday in March 1954. Sunday night, less than twenty-four hours before air time, they still hadn't reached a decision. They were rehearsing segments they planned to air the following morning when I walked up to

Pat Weaver, president of NBC and creator of *The Home Show*. Weaver was standing in the middle of his elaborate set, on an enormous sound stage, directing the action.

"I think I ought to know whether or not I should be going back to Chicago," I said as meekly as possible. "I'm due back there Monday morning if you're not going to use me."

Weaver just stood there for a moment, looking right through me.

"Oh, why don't you stick around," he said. "I guess we'll use you."

That was the casual way in which the decision that changed my life was made. I called Chicago and told NBC I wasn't coming back. Then I called my wife to tell her to close the house and bring the kids to New York.

The Home Show was one of the three stars in the Pat Weaver galaxy: *The Today Show*, *The Tonight Show*, and *The Home Show*. Eventually I would do all three. Weaver had launched *Today* starring my old radio friend, Dave Garroway. *The Tonight Show* in its current conception was still a few years down the line. But Weaver had high hopes for *The Home Show*, which he insisted would pull millions of intelligent women viewers from their bland diet of soap operas and slick magazines.

Sylvester "Pat" Weaver was truly one of the seminal geniuses of television programming, as important in his own way as Zworykin had been on the technological front. A 6' 4" brash redheaded Ivy Leaguer and a notedly natty dresser, Weaver balanced on a "Bongo Board" in his office while making weighty decisions. He had come to NBC in 1947 straight out of Young & Rubicam, the big radio ad agency. Having produced Fred Allen's successful *Town Hall Tonight* series for Y & R, he became supervisor of all Y & R radio programming while still a very young man.

At NBC, he was recruited to counteract CBS's strong surge in the ratings, brought about by CBS Chairman William Paley's daring commando-style raid on NBC's talent roster. As president of the network, Weaver pioneered the ninety-minute spectacular and created the concept of selling ad time on television in blocks. The participating sponsor idea eliminated pressure from the single sponsor on the content of a program. Before working up *The Today Show* and *The Home Show*, he had created *Your Show of Shows* in 1951, starring Sid Caesar and Imogene Coca, possibly the greatest comedy program in television history.

Pat Weaver had a passion for futuristic, high-tech sets, full of up-to-date hardware. When Dave Garroway first saw *The Today Show* studio in Rockefeller Center, he echoed Orson Welles's famous comment about a Hollywood film studio: "This is the biggest electric train set any boy ever had."

The set of *The Home Show* was equally advanced, with revolving turntables that moved entire sets, automated camera read-outs from closed captions to subtitles, rear projection screens, and state-of-the-art communications equipment. Dave, who was one of our first guests on *Home*, shook his head at the mechanical complexity.

"A year from now you won't be using any of this fancy stuff," he said. "The only things that will be moving on this set will be the people."

Dave was right. Arlene and I found the complex hi-tech set distracting, and hardly ever used its more advanced features.

When the show went on the air, I opened with this line: "Good morning and welcome to *Home*, the Show for Today's Homemakers . . ."

Our variety of guests often strayed far afield from the original show concept—as a televised home economics class. A prominent rabbi, Marc Tannenbaum, for instance, came on one morning to discuss Jewish religious ceremonies as they applied to the home.

One component of the high-tech backstage apparatus was a sophisticated intercom system by which directors could tell stage managers such things as "Strike the kitchen set and go to the patio." During rehearsal, Rabbi Tannenbaum finished his segment and was about to step offstage (but not quickly enough to clear the next shot) when the director pushed the wrong button. He barked over the PA system, "Strike the rabbi!" Rabbi Tannenbaum looked stunned, as though he had already been struck. Then he grinned, as he realized what was meant.

The owner of a rare musical instrument store in Greenwich Village, the Village String Shop, once came on to display a number of priceless medieval string instruments. They were rigged on catgut lines suspended from a horizontal bar, the catgut running beneath the scrolls. For union reasons, the stagehands insisted on tying the instruments to the bar themselves. They were to be hung about five feet off the ground and flown upward out of camera range when the segment was completed.

The owner of the Village String Shop kept asking them if he could inspect the suspension himself, but the stagehands wouldn't let him near the rigging. When the instruments were finally flown, the master horizontal bar broke and they all came falling straight to the floor. I'll never forget the expression on that man's face when his priceless instruments turned into kindling before his eyes.

When Buddy Hackett agreed to come on *The Home Show* to plug a new series, the segment producer asked, "Buddy, while you're on, if you could do a comedy routine for us that would be great."

"See my agent about how much that might cost you," Buddy said.

"But we're plugging your new show."

"I'll come on and talk as long as you want," he said. "But if you want me to do what I do for a living, that'll cost you."

During this discussion, I happened to be rehearsing a segment in which I had to jump off a ladder. Buddy wandered over to watch what I was doing.

"They got you covered for this?"

"I don't know," I answered.

"You getting any extra for this? Hazardous duty pay?"

"I don't think so," I said. I had never thought of that.

"Are they taping your ankles and wrists? Is there a doctor around?"

I was impressed with Buddy's street smarts. But then Buddy explained where he had learned this practical toughness. He had had a tough row to hoe when he was a kid, and had developed a strong distaste for exploitation of any kind. His father had been an upholsterer. One day Buddy went with his father up to a large resort hotel in the Catskills to do a job.

The hotel had agreed to pay them $75.00 for the day, re-upholstering a lobby sofa. It was winter and very cold. They weren't allowed to go inside, and when lunchtime came they couldn't get lunch. At the end of the day, the hotel manager said, "We're only going to pay you forty-five dollars." Buddy's father was upset because the $30.00 loss meant a negative profit for their efforts.

"Why don't you just finish quickly and do a lousy job?" Buddy asked him.

"I can't do that," his father said. "I wouldn't know how. I either do it or I don't do it."

Years later, Buddy was booked into that same hotel and a price was set of $10,000 for one night.

Buddy said "No. Ten thousand and thirty dollars."

"I felt I owed it to the old man," he reported years later on the air.

I stayed with *The Home Show* for about three years, from April of 1954 to August of 1957. Arlene Francis and I were in the RCA building when Robert Kintner, a successor to Pat Weaver as NBC president, offered us a ride uptown in his limousine. He confirmed the rumor that *Home* was going to be canceled. After dropping Arlene off at her home, he asked me if I might be interested in anchoring the seven o'clock news. I told him I certainly was interested, but I never heard anything more about it. We later got word that a two-man team was coming on to go up against CBS's Walter Cronkite: Chet Huntley and David Brinkley.

At the time, I was going after everything, following my Chicago habit of always doing more than one show. I was only doing *Home* in New York, and I felt somewhat uneasy about having all my eggs in one basket. Shows came and went, and I was no longer an NBC staffer. I was a free-lance announcer, so I auditioned for everything. I found myself competing against all the bright young men in broadcasting. To appear studious, they all wore large horn-rimmed glasses. Just to distinguish myself from that crowd, I refused to wear glasses even though I was nearsighted at the time.

In the fall of 1956, I finally struck broadcasting pay dirt. I was asked to announce *Caesar's Hour*, Sid Caesar's new show, designed to follow his first great success with *Your Show of Shows*, which starred Caesar and Imogene Coca.

Produced by Max Liebman, it had been in the grand tradition of *The Milton Berle Show* and *The Ed Sullivan Show*. Live comedy variety shows were the foundation of prime-time entertainment, and nighttime television was like a modern vaudeville revival. *Your Show of Shows* came on once a week, Saturday night, and television comedy was never the same afterward.

When I first met him, Sid was in his middle thirties. He had been a brilliant onstage improviser ever since his nightclub years, but his strong suit as a comic broadcaster was his unique grasp of television. This was at the time when we were all frantically trying to adapt the basic elements of radio to a visual medium. Some entertainers made the transition without a hitch, others had trouble, some never made it. Jack Benny went right from radio into television and never looked back. Benny instinctively knew a television joke from a radio joke, but Fred Allen could not adapt to the new medium.

Sid Caesar topped them all as an original television talent. He was a bull of a man, who really did once dangle Mel Brooks out the window by his heels. But he did wild things only when he was drinking. Sober, he displayed an excessive courtesy stemming, I believe, from an enormous reservoir of basic insecurity. On rare occasions when I spoke to him in his dressing room, I would knock softly. He would invite me in, jumping up and shaking my hand as if I were the King of Persia instead of just his announcer.

Playing himself, Sid was timid. Playing a comic character,

Sid knew no fear. He only felt fully alive when he was on the air. But without the protection of a character, he was nearly incapable of uttering his own name on the air. In the beginning, Sid would come out onstage and say simply, "Hello, I'm Sid Caesar and welcome to *Caesar's Hour*." But he said it with the stark, evident terror of a kid in a high-school play. I started handling that introduction, and gradually all the introductions to the various skits.

I remember saying to him, "Why don't you just imagine yourself becoming a character that happens to be called Sid Caesar?"

"But who would I play?" he asked.

Once he had put on the comic mask, he was unstoppable, effortlessly switching roles from mad German rocket scientist to obsessive concert pianist. In one skit, Sid appeared as a piano soloist with a symphony orchestra. He banged out a fiery piano opening and then moved into a lyrical passage. Pianist Earle Wilde was providing the actual audio. Sid hit a terrible clinker, stopped, then started again, hit the same clinker again, and became so upset he slammed down the lid and turned toward the audience, sulking splendidly.

The conductor rushed out onstage and managed to wheedle him back to the keyboard. Sid sat down, composed himself, raised both arms, and slammed down both hands for a massive chord. Unfortunately, he hadn't lifted the keyboard cover. The sketch ended with Sid clutching both his hands as if they had just been broken and he would never play piano again. It sounds corny in reconstruction, but on live television in the 1950s, that comedy had a voltage no similar program has achieved since.

Every night I would announce the show and do the setups for the sketches. I'd say, "Here we see so-and-so coming home from work," and Sid Caesar would play the role. I was the link to reality, while Sid would explore strange worlds through his adopted character.

Occasionally I participated in skits. Carl Reiner and Howie Morris and Sid and I did a skit called "Layering," a takeoff on the ponderous introduction to a prestigious program of the time. An actor-announcer introduced an actor-host, who introduced me. I came on and introduced Carl Reiner, and he introduced Sid as program host. But there was no program. It was just one long introduction.

People were terrified of Sid, but he was terrified of himself. Above all, he was a realist. In the 1956–1957 season, after his enormous success began to wane, he took a voluntary pay cut from $25,000 down to $15,000 a show.

Caesar's Hour was canceled by NBC in the spring of 1957, after just one season. I did two shows more with him on ABC the following fall, but NBC interpreted my contract as exclusive. Sid was out that season, and was then dropped by ABC. That was the last regular television he did. When Sid Caesar went off the air, he vanished so completely, retreating into booze and pills, that he later wrote a book called *Where Have I Been?*

It might have been called *Who Have I Been?* Caesar had his ups and downs and has now made a spectacular comeback. More than any other comic, he was the prime symbol of the originality of early television.

That period had been good to me. I started as a successful but relatively obscure young announcer in Chicago and wound up on network television. But I never suspected that within a short time I would be thrust into the national limelight as the professional sidekick of the high-strung comedian who virtually invented the modern television talk show.

4

THE TONIGHT SHOW

After forty years in television, I think I've achieved a certain visibility. I like to think much of this is due to my persistence and a natural talent for the medium. But I have to admit that my genesis as a television "personality" dates back to the Jack Paar *Tonight Show,* and particularly to one extraordinary night, twenty-six years ago.

It was 8:15 on a Thursday night, February 11, 1960. The old *Tonight Show* had a curtained stage. As José Melis struck up the band, I stepped out from behind the curtain to make my announcement. After billboarding the show and guests, I said, "Now here's Jack!"

I just said it straight. Not like Ed McMahon, who strings it out: "Now he-e-e-e-re's Johnny!"

The house was packed to the rafters that night. And not with the usual out-of-towners. Practically every gossip columnist, newspaperperson, and media expert in New York was there. The halls were jammed with overflow media people and company lawyers. They were waiting, in a state of extreme suspense, to see what was going to happen.

All during the day Jack Paar had been intimating to various press people that something was indeed going to happen. Something unprecedented in television. Something dramatic. Something newsworthy.

For nearly four years now practically everything Jack Paar did or said on the air had been hot copy. Media attention, particularly from the print press, had put the national spotlight on him. A good deal of that spotlight had naturally spilled over onto the rest of us in the show, including myself. But if Jack garnered the most attention, it was Jack who suffered the most.

Jack Paar had an unerring instinct for the "natural reaction" that would have maximum impact on camera; what would later be called theater of the real. But to say Jack was theatrical does not mean he was fake. In fact, Paar was possibly the least fake person ever to be seen on a television screen. People still ask me, "What was Jack Paar really like?" The secret behind his remarkable on-air success was that his "act" was no act.

Between 8:15 and 8:30 P.M. we taped a portion of the program to be sent out to a limited number of stations in the network lineup—about eighty in all—to air from 11:15 to 11:30. At 11:30, the full two hundred and some came on for the rest of the show. Jack often waltzed through that first quarter hour, waiting for the full station lineup before bringing on any important guests.

At 8:30 on the dot the spotlight again swung my way. I gave the big hello for the second time: "Now here's Jack!"

I retired to a chair beside his desk. Instead of the usual round of applause, there was a definite, palpable hush. The main event was about to begin. He blinked hesitantly out toward his audience. At first everything seemed perfectly normal. He launched into one of his personal, often frankly confessional, opening monologues.

"If you read some of the papers yesterday," he finally said, "you'd think I committed some terrible obscenity."

Whether he had committed an obscenity or not had become the issue of the moment. The night before, Jack had told a story which by today's standards would be considered perfectly harmless. But in 1960 his joke featuring a WC, a water closet, had caused nationwide consternation, particularly at NBC.

A young network vice president ordered the offending initials bleeped out of the tape. The first Jack knew about the censorship was in watching the program from his house. He was incensed that he hadn't been told in advance. Bleeping out words on television was new back then. It had never happened on *Tonight,* mainly because the show had been live and we had been taping for only one season.

If the network's action was a bit unusual, the flap in the newspapers was not. All the columnists knew was that Paar had been bleeped. Until they checked with network officials, they had no idea what had been taken out. But imaginations ran riot.

By now the *Tonight Show* audience had grown used to Jack's opening sallies, striking back at the newspapers for nasty things they printed about him. Jack loved to attack newspaper columnists. And they loved to attack him. It was a love-hate relationship which promoted them both. The fact that Jack was always hot copy seemed to impress our broadcasting industry even more than his millions of viewers.

Now an uncomfortable silence hung in the air, a sense of waiting for the next move. "The newspapers said what I said was obscene," he went on. "But I thought it was all very funny." Jack smiled wanly, an expression at once strained and sincere.

"I've been thirty hours without an ounce of sleep. I've been wrestling with my conscience all day. I've made a decision about what I'm going to do."

He waited a few moments more. For what? He had the floor. His shoulders twisted with visible tension.

"Only one person knows about this. And that is Hugh Downs. My wife doesn't know about it. But I'll be home in time to tell her. I'm leaving the *Tonight Show.*"

He reached for a cup of water and took a long sip.

"There must be a better way of making a living than this," he said, seeming to be struggling with his emotions. "There's got to be a way of entertaining people without being always involved in some form of controversy."

With that, almost tenderly, he turned to the studio audience, lowering his voice nearly to a whisper.

"You've been pretty peachy to me always."

That remark caught me off-guard. More than anyone I knew

in show business, Jack Paar hadn't always felt that way. His feelings toward his audience were sometimes as guarded as toward the newspaper press. Once, in a frank moment I had given my opinion to a reporter from *Newsweek*.

"Jack has genuine warmth. He also has more reserve and hostility toward an audience than anyone I've ever known. Sometimes I think if he were a lion tamer, he'd turn his back on the cats and aim his whip and chair at the house."

The day the article hit the newsstands, I was summoned to Jack's dressing room. He sat there looking angry and wounded.

"I read what you said about me in *Newsweek*." He glared at me reproachfully. "That comment you made really hurt."

Then he smiled, almost sheepishly. "But Miriam explained to me what you really meant, and I think I understood."

His last look told me I was forgiven. Naturally, I was grateful to Miriam, who is something of a saint. I think that Jack, who is a fundamentally honest person, always appreciated honesty in others, even when it hit him where it hurt.

Which is not to say that Jack couldn't be paranoid. We were standing in a bar one night after the show when a bottle crashed loudly behind us. When something like that happens to me, my reaction is so lethargic that it's all over before I even get out of the way. But Jack immediately leaped up, looking wildly around, sure the bottle had been directed at him. His attitude toward the public was the same—flavored by suspicion. *Time* called him "a sensitive, often defensive man, who shoulders a sizable chip."

"I have been hurt and betrayed by more people than anyone I know," he once said. That sense of betrayal was part of his self-image as a long-suffering soul, an image which was surely helpful to him in show business. And it was an image I think he favored. It gained him so much attention, both good and bad.

"Jack in all his work let his own quirks, neuroses, suspicions . . . play freely on the surface," said Dick Cavett, one of his former writers. "There was always the implied possibility . . .

he would explode one day . . . and you might see a live nervous breakdown viewed from the comfort of your own bedroom."

"Jack has no armor," was how a former agent once put it. "You can pierce him with a Kleenex."

Because his armor was so thin, he often struck back defensively at those he felt had hurt him. Gossip columnists usually led the list.

But tonight the lion tamer was taking a different tack. He was thanking his audience for what they had done for him. One measure of his fame was the public's enormous and natural curiosity about him. For five years, as I've said, a question had been so commonly asked in public, particularly to me, that it became something of a cliché.

"What's Jack Paar really like?"

If there was any answer, it was that the Jack Paar you saw on the small screen was the real Jack Paar. People are used to performers performing, actors acting. The Pagliacci performance syndrome demands that the clown has to laugh even when his heart is breaking. When Jack Paar came along, everyone thought his directness was just another stunt. His dropping of the mask made people think he had developed the most elaborate disguise of all. He was so real he had everyone fooled.

Jack was honest, sometimes brutally so. Basically a kind-hearted man whose bluntness often got the better of him, he wasn't smooth like Carson, who exudes control. He responded straight from the heart and right from the hip. If something made him cry, he'd cry. If something made him laugh, he'd laugh. And if something made him mad, he'd get mad, right on the air.

That night Jack Paar gave a hungry public yet another indication of what he was like. He reached for my hand and shook it warmly. Before I could respond, he strode straight off the stage.

It's true that I knew he was going to leave. An hour before taping, he told me in his dressing room. But I thought he was going to spring his surprise at the end of the program, not at the beginning. For the briefest moment, I felt like a vice president must feel when the president is about to leave or be removed from office. I knew I had to say something.

"Jack frequently does things he regrets," I ventured to the national television audience. "But I'd like to think that this is not final—and that Jack will be back."

Whether he would be back or not, I was forced to take over *The Tonight Show* that night. Only then did I fully understand why Jack had come to me an hour before air time. He asked if there were any guests I might want to have on the show that evening, people we could get on short notice—good talkers. It had been his way of letting me know I was going to have to handle them on my own. But I had missed the point.

Jack himself would later write: "Hugh Downs was nearly speechless. . . . His eyebrows haven't come down yet." But I, more than anyone, couldn't help but give credit where it was due. Jack was nothing if not a master of the unprecedented. Everyone at the RCA studios in Radio City that night, and millions more viewers at home, had been eyewitnesses to a television first. The highly paid host of *The Tonight Show* had just walked off his own show.

Jack's own explanation for what he had done was revealing: "I might have been throwing away a half million a year, but America had to be taught a lesson."

He later wrote, "In less than an hour it would be the birthday of Abraham Lincoln, the man who freed the slaves. So I emancipated myself from the program. . . . Having been fired any number of times by the network, I finally fired the network."

The lesson Jack was trying to teach was a hard one for success-driven Americans to accept. A man earning half a million dollars a year—a super fortune in 1960—seen by millions of Americans five nights a week, whose face had graced the cover of *Time*, whose actions were debated in Congress, still felt like a slave to his job.

Now I had a whole show to get through. Orson Bean was the

first guest. It was a perfect opportunity for someone as out-spoken as Bean to take a stand. He stepped straight up to the box.

"NBC is utterly dehumanized," he began, striking out at the most likely target in that strange situation. "They are no better and no worse than other million-dollar operations. They are all dehumanized. They have no loyalty. I don't know if they're going to run this tape. They probably won't. They don't have the guts. They handled this in a rotten way."

That certainly was one man's opinion.

I hosted the rest of the show without ever moving into the host's chair. And I wound up pronouncing a plague on both their houses: I criticized Jack for telling a tasteless joke, and I chastised the network I had been associated with for over twenty years for unnecessarily cutting it out of the program.

By 1960 the show was taped in advance. But when we were still going out live, there was a nightly potential for anything to be said on the air, whether libelous, objectionable, scurrilous, blasphemous, or simply stupid. It was dangerous for the net-works, mostly because of the legal minefields, but it was exhila-rating precisely because it was live. Every night, people who loved Paar—and people who hated him—tuned in to see what this unpredictable man might do next.

Arthur Murray's wife came on one night as a guest. Jack asked her how she managed to keep her excellent figure. Her answer: "Jack, destiny has shaped my end."

I did most of the commercials myself in those days. Jack threw the line to me. I sailed right into my prepared copy: "Friends, no matter what size or shape can you have, the Al-liance can opener can open it."

I was unable to stop laughing, as was the audience. Later, I worried that the Alliance company would be upset. But, rather than ask for their money back, they sent me a gold-plated electric can opener. They said that one spot did a great deal for their business.

Then, by the end of the fifties, the new technology of vid-eotape offered a convenient escape hatch from the risk of live television. Network legal departments were among the first to push for the change. To retain some of the precious quality of spontaneity on programs like *The Tonight Show*, the networks devised a policy of "live tape." This meant the tape would be shown as shot and could be altered only under truly exceptionable circumstances.

The move to live tape struck a compromise between live television and the canned variety. Live tape was supposed to retain some of the sense of immediacy, of cameras recording the event before a live audience, in real time. If it was not truly live, it was still more spontaneous than moviemaking. Live tape managed to keep some of the essential rawness of live television by refraining from alteration unless a guest (or the host) said something deeply objectionable on the air. This was the beginning of the telltale bleep you now hear on so many talk shows.

In early 1959 we switched over to tape. We moved from the shabby old Hudson Theatre on Forty-fourth Street into a windowless studio in Radio City. The move was partly a gesture to Jack, who wanted to go home at night and watch the show from bed like everyone else. But, unlike everyone else, Jack was in the habit of taking notes as he watched. We would start taping at 8:15, three hours in advance, to go on the air at 11:15.

Taping had another advantage: the audiences were more alert at that earlier hour, more like a theater audience. The old eleven o'clock audience had been more of a nightclub crowd. Some were full of booze. Others were half asleep. A few were pretty obstreperous.

The advent of videotape also presented the chance for sponsors to try to reshoot or alter their taped commercials. But this was something I tried to resist. On one taped show, I did a commercial for a small electric organ company. I was supposed to play something on the keyboard, but when I touched the keys, no sound came out. There had been an electrical mixup in the studio. While they were trying to get the power back on, I turned to the camera and said, "It does work, but not when it isn't plugged in. Which just proves, I guess, that it really is an electric organ."

72

After the taping, the stage was crowded with angry ad-agency people. They insisted the commercial had to be done over in time for air. I said to myself, "Wait a minute. If I let them establish a precedent like that, we'll be here every night doing take after take to please these people."

"You'd better get hold of my agent to find out how much it'll cost you," I told the reps, in the distant hope of dissuading them.

The network executives soon grasped the idea that if they allowed this to happen it would mean an awful lot more work for the same money. So a policy was established. If you wanted to be a television sponsor, you paid your money and you took your chances. Sponsors were given the right to cancel a commercial under certain unusual circumstances. For example, if between the time of a taping and the scheduled broadcast there was an airplane crash, an airline had the option of taking its spot out and replacing it with a public service announcement. They would get a makeup slot some other time. Otherwise the tape held and that was that.

Jack Paar's *Tonight Show* was a little like riding a bronco. You never knew what was going to happen, whether on the commercials or with the unpredictable host. This racked up a lot of extra ratings points, but it made the network nervous.

NBC got what it feared most that February 10, 1960. It all began with that hoary old joke about the WC. The story was told to Paar by a friend, who had been told it by his thirteen-year-old niece, who had heard it from her junior high school teacher. The teacher had even distributed copies of it to her class of eighth graders as an example of "cultural confusion."

The joke did possess a bit of charm: A proper English lady visiting Switzerland asks a local schoolmaster to find her a room. He writes to say he has found one. She writes back inquiring whether the place has a WC. Not entirely sure of his English usage, the schoolmaster consults the parish priest. The priest concludes the initials could stand only for Wayside Chapel. The Swiss schoolmaster replies to the English lady:

I take great pleasure in informing you that the WC sits nine miles from the house you occupy, in the center of a beautiful grove of pine trees. . . . It is capable of holding 229 people and is open on Sundays and Thursdays . . . I would recommend that your ladyship go on a Thursday when there is musical accompaniment. . . . It may interest you to note that my daughter was married in the WC, and it was there that she met her husband. . . . I shall be delighted to reserve the best seat where you will be seen by all.

There was more along the same lines, but I'm sure you get the idea. When Jack heard the bleep on the tape, he became utterly incensed. He was troubled not only by the network's action, but the opportunity it gave his sworn enemies—the newspaper columnists—to run stories suggesting he had told an "obscene" story on the air.

Jack demanded that NBC air the tape the following night, "to let the viewers decide." When NBC refused the request, Jack decided to walk.

That night, Shelley Berman was my second guest. As one of Jack's most successful discoveries, he felt he had to pay tribute where it was due. "A lot of performers are going to suffer because of this," Shelley said, shaking his head sadly. "Jack did so much for them."

It was a point well worth making. A large part of Paar's talent as a talk-show host lay in his ability to uncover talent in others. Many of his finds went on to fame and fortune in show business. A list of the beneficiaries of his generosity read like a comedians' Hall of Fame.

Carol Burnett. The Smothers Brothers. Bob Newhart. Shelley Berman. Phyllis Diller. Flip Wilson. Don Rickles. Joey Bishop. Nipsey Russell. Mort Sahl. Nichols and May. Bill Cosby. Woody Allen. Jonathan Winters.

Jack loved comics and show business people, but he also found time for serious guests such as Harlow Shapley, the famous astronomer. Most of all, Jack admired "just talkers," those like himself who could make his stage "living room" the place where the best and the brightest had just happened to stop by for a chat.

In pursuit of this Platonic ideal, he introduced the likes of Noel Coward, Oscar Levant, Peter Ustinov, and Robert Morley to American television audiences. All were brilliant entertainers in their own right. But it was Jack who put them on TV to talk.

Time hailed Jack in a cover story entitled "All the World's Straight Man" as "one of an all new class of TV-age entertainers . . . the just talkers." He made an obscure writer by the name of Alexander King famous overnight. King would banter on, with remarkable insight, about his personal problems, including his one-time narcotics usage. Like all people truly interested in conversation, Jack loved the witty, spontaneous moment. Most of all, he prized the off-the-wall, off-the-cuff comment. Particularly if it rang true.

As a straight stand-up comedian, working from scripted material, Jack could be pretty good. But he was the first to admit his timing wasn't the best. There were countless comics in show business with better delivery. His real strength lay in the ad-lib, the mark of a true wit.

One night, when the show was being broadcast from Hollywood, the studio at Sunset and Vine was so badly soundproofed that we could hear a siren outside. Cocking his ear, Jack interrupted his monologue and said, "Oh, they're taking Oscar Levant to dinner." Levant had gained a certain renown by having himself driven to a Hollywood dinner party in an ambulance.

Now all that magic seemed to be over. Jack had just pulled the ultimate ad-lib. He had walked off his own show. One question being asked all over the country that night was, Has success spoiled Jack Paar? Or has Jack Paar spoiled success? The reference was to a Broadway hit of the period, *Will Success Spoil Rock Hunter?*

The next day I flew to Chicago to do an educational project for the Ford Foundation. Within minutes of stepping off the plane, I found that my visit had made national headlines:

75

DOWNS FLIES TO CHICAGO. DOWNS GONE TO CHICAGO. Everyone naturally assumed my trip to Chicago had some mysterious connection with the events of the night before.

In fact, I had no idea where Jack was. No one knew where Jack was. Everyone figured I was the head of some secret delegation to the host-in-exile, trying to persuade him back into the fold. It was another example of how everything Jack did was turned into national headlines. We were all enormously famous back then, in a "hot copy" sort of way. I couldn't generate headlines like that today if I landed headfirst on the moon.

As it turned out, after a day or so of being blockaded by reporters at their Bronxville, New York, home, Jack and his wife, Miriam, were spirited by friends to an uncompleted motel complex on Florida's west coast. They spent most of their time in an unfurnished room watching television. Jack was never so depressed in his life.

Miriam, worried about Jack's terrible mood, called NBC. A worker at the motel had already recognized Paar and called the Miami *Herald*.

By complete coincidence, Robert Sarnoff and Robert Kintner, NBC's two top men, happened to be attending a conference of NBC affiliates in nearby Boca Raton. They drove over to the motel and suggested Jack take a little rest for a while, off in some quiet spot, somewhere he wouldn't be recognized.

Jack suggested Havana. He had already interviewed Castro there, the source of yet another controversy. "Oh, no," the frightened NBC brass responded. They had a different destination in mind. They handed him a pair of plane tickets. The Paars had just won an all-expense paid trip to Hong Kong. All Jack had to do was promise to return to *Tonight*.

The Tonight Show, as a time slot, was born in the summer of 1950 under the unlikely title of *Broadway Open House.* The first hosts were a public relations man and his ex-Miss America wife—Tex McGrary and Jinx Falkenburg. Tex and Jinx were eventually replaced by a rotation of hosts: Wally Cox, Jerry Lewis and Dean Martin, and Morey Amsterdam.

But the program never attained real popularity until it was regularly hosted by the comic Jerry Lester and his vivacious sidekick, an awesome-chested lady named Dagmar. Jerry was short, and spent a fair share of air time staring straight at Dagmar's chest, which hung prominently at his eye level. This remarkably unsubtle sight gag somehow never lost its punch.

But *The Tonight Show* as an institution came into its own with Steve Allen as host. He lasted three years, until the fall of 1956. His was not really a talk show, but more of a comic variety program, with an oddball supporting cast of characters including singers Steve Lawrence and Eydie Gormé, Don Knotts as a nervous "man on the street," Tom Poston as a man who couldn't remember his own name, and Gene Rayburn as the announcer and part-time "newsman" who broadcast from a "newsroom" in the basement of Broadway's shabby old Hudson Theatre.

They say Steve Allen saw the late-night *Tonight Show* as a dress rehearsal for his grand entrance into prime time. It was Steve's ambition to take on the mighty Ed Sullivan, but he never really got the chance. Still, he was widely reported to have spent his happiest moments with the show at his own farewell party.

NBC canceled *Tonight* in late 1956, when the network fired Pat Weaver, the show's brilliant creator and president of the network. Weaver was replaced by Robert Sarnoff, son of General David Sarnoff, the founder of the company. *Tonight* was replaced by *America After Dark,* featuring prominent newspaper columnists from several cities around the country. Supposed to capture the "excitement of late-night America," it ended up putting America to sleep.

In the summer of 1957, NBC decided to give a relatively obscure comedian named Jack Paar a shot at the show. They offered Paar an unusual twenty-four week contract instead of the more typical thirty-nine weeks. Taking a look at the calendar, Jack noticed that his twenty-four weeks would bring him right up to the last week in December. He knew what that meant. If things didn't work out, NBC would drop him at the end of the year. They could, of course, drop the show even earlier.

Like myself, Jack was born in Ohio. But he grew up in Jackson, Michigan. He was being interviewed by a local radio correspondent as a "typical kid on the street" when he suddenly found his true calling. Once handed a microphone, he had trouble giving it back. At sixteen he was sweeping out the local radio station at night and trying desperately to lick a persistent stammer by speaking with his mouth full of buttons. The slight remnant of that stammer was one of his most effective and endearing foibles, especially when he became excited.

His career as a comic blossomed during World War II. As a serviceman, he successfully exploited anti-officer sentiment, performing for war-weary GIs in the South Pacific. A war correspondent by the name of Sidney Carroll caught his act on Guam and wrote an admiring profile of Paar for *Esquire.* Jack found himself in the strange position of being a famous comic as soon as he got back to the States, even though he had yet to perform to a full house of civilians.

Jack was handsome and was quickly snapped up by RKO as a romantic lead. He was given matinee parts in a blissfully short string of B movies, "each one worse than the last," as he put it. One of them, a turkey called *Love Nest,* costarred the then equally obscure Marilyn Monroe. Jack didn't think much of Marilyn as an actress, but he didn't consider himself much better.

One Hollywood producer, trying desperately to sum up his elusive screen appeal, described him as "Kay Kyser with warmth." Kyser, a Southern bandleader, was not exactly Jack's idea of stardom. Jack and his wife made preparations to return to New York, and to his first love: comedy.

He landed a job as a summer fill-in for Jack Benny, a comedian whose style had a strong influence on Paar. Benny, in turn, had a great respect for Paar's talent. Paar did a short stint as host of the CBS *Morning Show,* replacing Walter Cronkite. He was supposed to provide competition for NBC's enormously popular *Today Show,* hosted by the colorful Dave Garroway and featuring J. Fred Muggs, a volatile chimp. But as Paar would later recall, "With the number of people watching us it would have been cheaper to call them on the phone."

When NBC decided to give Jack his big break, they weren't quite sure what to do with him. The former *Tonight Show*, starring Steve Allen, had focused on straight entertainment. Conversation provided only the mortar between the performance segments. At first NBC wanted to split the program into three separate half-hours. Jack was to host three different game shows during the period. Fortunately, that idea was put to rest. Left largely to his own devices, Jack invented the talk show as we know it today.

"I take little credit for suggesting and finally insisting that the only answer was to invent the conversation show," Jack later wrote. "So my claim to fame is that all I did was rearrange the furniture and introduce the davenport." He described his concept for the program as "one hour and forty-five minutes of people sitting around trying to change the subject."

I was picked to be what was called the network announcer. Jack had seen me on *Caesar's Hour*, the successor to *Your Show of Shows*, starring Sid Caesar.

When NBC asked Paar whom he wanted as his announcer, he said, "How about that guy from *Caesar's Hour*?"

When I found out about my new job, June Lockhart and I happened to be substituting for Tex and Jinx, the old hosts of *Broadway Open House*. Tex and Jinx had a local NBC show in New York, broadcast live out of the Peacock Alley at the Waldorf-Astoria. I called Jack not only to thank him, but also to ask him if he'd come on my show to talk about the new *Tonight Show*.

My first inkling of Jack's fundamental oddness came with his response.

"Sure, that'd be fine," he said. So far so good. But then he switched gears, without warning, and started talking about what was really on his mind at the moment.

"You know I just can't seem to keep leaves out of my swimming pool," he said.

He made the statement as if this were one of the more pressing issues facing mankind.

"I've used rakes and scoops and poles," he went on. "Nothing seems to work."

Not only was I unable to offer any advice on the swimming pool problem, I was now a little concerned about how this strange man might conduct himself on my program, and how I might fit into his. He was clearly used to saying whatever popped into his mind. He seemed to have no internal censor. But Jack came on and was a great guest.

The first *Tonight Show* went out to only a handful of stations on Monday evening, July 1, 1957. We had only two sponsors, Polaroid and RCA. Since RCA owned NBC, their participation could hardly be described as a commercial coup. At 11:15, for the first time, José Melis struck up the band and I stepped out from behind the curtain of the old Hudson Theatre.

"Welcome to *The Tonight Show*, starring Jack Paar, with Helen O'Connell, Stanley Holloway, and Franklin Pangborn! Now here's Jack!"

I stepped back behind the curtain. There was scattered applause. Jack came on and did an opening monologue. But the show didn't exactly take off from there. After it was all over, Jack was not pleased with the results.

He gave me his own gloomy assessment. "In three week's time they'll be running old movies." But even that first show had a special tentative quality about it, a sense of anxious reality, which became its first and most lasting asset.

Most early television tended to be pretty stagy. But the Paar show had a feeling of spontaneity, of eavesdropping on a roomful of people just sitting around talking, never entirely sure if what they were saying was interesting. It made a compelling scene, but we didn't see that at first. As I later confided to one interviewer, "I gave it a fast four weeks." They were turning over pretty fast in those days.

As the "network" announcer, my role was not large. I was supposed to introduce the show and the guests and do some commercials. In fact, my opening announcement was originally supposed to be voice-over, off camera. But the first night, one of the stage managers said, "Well, as long as we have the camera here, why don't you step out from behind the curtain."

I stepped out into the spotlight and never really stepped back.

Another man was then filling the role I would later assume. Jack's first sidekick was a character actor named Franklin Pangborn. Jack would later describe him as "that little guy who plays desk clerks and florists or hairdressers in the movies."

Pangborn was an unusual man. Though he had a flamboyantly camp manner on stage and screen, in person he could be pretty scary. He had a license to carry a gun and was convinced people were after him. He had a habit of patting his pocket, where he kept his gun, and glancing behind him suspiciously.

The first time Jack asked me over to talk with him, I think all he wanted was a little company. I was standing in my invisible announcer's position, off in the wings. He asked me a question, and I answered it—from where I was.

The next week he asked me over again. I wasn't sure what to do. I walked over to his desk, talked to him for a few seconds, and retreated to my assigned announcer's place on the sidelines.

That night the producer stopped by and said, "Don't go over to the panel again. You're supposed to stay over there—where you belong." I assumed I was getting some sort of indirect cue from Jack to stay off his turf.

This back-and-forthing went on for a couple of weeks. Jack would call me over. I would cross over to his desk. I would answer his question and then retire to my station. Sometimes I'd carry on a little dialogue with him from where I stood. I thought Jack was playing some sort of game with me. He thought I was putting the shun on *him*.

One of the first times we ever talked off the air, he asked, "How come you never join us at the panel?"

"They told me I shouldn't."

"Who said that?"

Not wanting to get the producer into hot water, I mumbled, "Well, some of the production people thought it would be kind of pushy of me to be over there."

"Forget all that," he said. "Anytime you want to come over, please join us."

It was all perfectly gracious. I felt as if I were being given an invitation to a private party. In a way it was like that. One of the reasons the show worked so well was that Jack treated his set just like his own living room.

I remember the first time I ever sat on Jack's famous davenport. I found myself squeezed in between Pangborn and Slapsie Maxie Rosenblum, a veteran boxer with a wry sense of humor. Rosenblum told us about a new police policy of arresting jaywalking pedestrians. He was jauntily jaywalking one time when he felt a policeman's hand on his shoulder. The first words out of his mouth to the cop were, "How fast was I going, officer?"

Franklin Pangborn didn't last long as Jack's foil. He was an actor, not an ad-libber. He worked well from a script, but he couldn't say much on his own. After a few weeks he disappeared, and I inherited his role.

The guests on the old *Tonight Show* were brought on to talk as a group. In that sense it was more like a party than Johnny Carson's *Tonight Show*, which is more like a sequence of controlled conversations than a spontaneous gathering. The focus is always on one guest at a time. Everyone else fades into the woodwork. Occasionally Ed McMahon might throw in his two cents, or one of the other guests might interject a witty comment. But with Paar, it was a verbal free-for-all. I think Jack's emphasis on the group stemmed partly from insecurity. He didn't want to be forced to carry the ball entirely on his own.

The first regular guest to help Jack handle his heavy load was a seventy-four-year-old spinster named Elsa Maxwell. Dubbed by *Time* "the Popocatepetl of party-givers," she wrote a society column for the Hearst papers. Jack fondly called her "the tugboat Annie of the international yachting set," and once said she "looked like Ernest Borgnine in drag."

A large part of Elsa's appeal was pure shock-value. It was always a little unsettling to hear an endless stream of cutting remarks from someone so old, so fat, and so plain. Hermione Gingold carried on a constant feud with her onstage. "Oh, that Elsa, she's just another pretty face," Hermione once snipped. But it was Elsa's sheer outrageousness which struck sparks on the show.

Jack paid Elsa special attention. When she came on, the two of them would sit in chairs in front of his desk. They would banter inanities between themselves. She was given to making shocking confessions such as, "I've always wanted a falsie more than anything else in my life." On another occasion she confided in Jack, "I'd just love to have a baby." Jack winced noticeably but recovered quickly enough to murmur, "Our first exclusive."

Elsa loved the power Paar gave her. Before they went on, Jack would ask, "Do you want to go after anyone tonight?" Elsa would whisper, "Ask me about so-and-so." Jack would comply. Elsa would start in.

"Elvis Presley is a menace to society."

"Princess Grace is awfully boring."

"Cleveland Amory . . . Who is Cleveland Amory?"

Jack later called her "a harmless old fraud." But she was not always entirely harmless. Her little arrows occasionally caused major eruptions, dragging Jack into prolonged gossip-brawls because of her loose tongue.

One of Elsa's finest moments came when Jack took a long-look at her voluminous legs. "Elsa," he said, "your stockings are wrinkled." Without batting an eyelash she shot back, "I'm not wearing any."

Elsa's prominence on the show was another example of Jack's fondness for genuine "characters." Not movie stars or famous people or beautiful people, but "real people" whose oddness stemmed from their natural funniness, not from a clever script.

Dody Goodman was a redheaded dancer with a manner so unbelievably scattered that Jack could hardly buy it himself.

When he first interviewed her, he asked her point-blank, "Are you for real or just putting me on?" Dody shrugged and sighed coyly before admitting, "Well, a little." Dody became a regular on the show.

A typical Paar-Goodman exchange would go something like this:

DODY: Jack, you've got something on your eyelash.

JACK: Is it out now?

DODY: No, I don't think so . . . Oh, my goodness, it's on my eyelash!

Dody Goodman became so popular so fast, she was perceived by some as an exception to the rule that Jack never resented any of his discoveries. *Time* thought Dody was trying to upstage Jack on his own show.

After a year of "playing Pygmalion to the professionally addled Galatea from Ohio," as *Time* put it, Paar "began feeling more like Frankenstein and less like Pygmalion." Jack appeared to interpret her every move as a calculated affront to his position. "You notice how she fiddles with her skirt?" he asked *Time*. "That's her method of competing. . . . My mistake was to let her rise. . . . This was the greatest overbuilding job I've ever done."

Jack carried on his conflict with Dody right on the air, not behind the scenes. After she effortlessly translated a poem from the original Latin, he finally blew his top.

"Dody, I know you're going to try to take over a show, but why does it have to be this one?" Jack told the press he was "beginning to feel like the announcer on the Dody Goodman show."

John Lardner of *The New Yorker* praised *The Tonight Show* because there was so much "low-key aggression in plain view." But at the time, I felt differently. "I think there's a tendency to air too many grievances out in the open," I told one reporter. "These things would be better off handled backstage."

In retrospect I was wrong. The secret of Jack Paar's *Tonight Show* lay in the fact that it was so uncontrived. Errol Flynn came on once to enormous applause. He strode up to Geneviève, a young French singer with fractured English—another one of Jack's finds. He bowed gallantly over her, kissed her hand in his most polished Continental manner, and murmured *"Enchanté."*

Paar laughed out loud at this performance.

"Enchanté? You've been talking to her for the last twenty minutes backstage!"

Jack never Hippodromed anything. (This is show business talk—to pretend that something spontaneous is taking place when it is really contrived: "Now here we are at the Hippodrome," when you are nowhere near the Hippodrome.)

Instead of asking a leading question and reacting with feigned surprise, Jack would lean forward to urge a guest, "Tell them what you just told me backstage." Jack's honesty and emotion were the real secret behind the intensity of the spotlight.

Before we knew what was happening, *The Tonight Show* caught on. From 62 stations and two sponsors, the station tally rose to 76 and nine sponsors within the first few months. "Before long," Jack later wrote, "we had 154 stations, 30 million viewers, and so many sponsors I felt guilty when I interrupted the commercials with the program."

For me, the hard part was not the ad-libbing. It was doing all those commercials. If I had to do a mop advertisement, they'd roll a piece of linoleum flooring out on the stage and I'd wet the mop as the camera moved in and I'd clean the floor with the mop. Sometimes they let me have help. On the O Cedar mop spot, I did half the ad, and Paul Lynde did the other.

Tuck Tape was one of our clients. They wanted me to demonstrate that the tape was so strong that it wouldn't break off a roll on a spindle. Before going on air, I spent quite some time trying to break that tape by yanking it off the roll as hard as I could. The sponsors seemed safe in their claim. It resolutely refused to break. But as soon as I went on the air the tape, following Murphy's Law, broke.

"This proves that this demonstration is honestly run—because I tried my hardest to break it—and did," I said.

Occasionally someone else would do a spot or two. José Melis, our bandleader, usually did Realemon. Their slogan was, "We Squeeze, You Pour." Realemon liked the way José said it, "We Squiz, You Porrre." But I had to do every sixth Realemon spot myself. The client felt that if I didn't do any, it might look as if I didn't like the product.

This had happened. A "high-density" vinyl floor tile called Sandran gave me a good deal of trouble. I began to get complaints from viewers who had put Sandran on their floors, saying that nailheads were coming up through it. It was a high-density vinyl, but the vinyl part was so thin that the density hardly mattered. The rest appeared to be tarpaper. I knew I had to do something, so I started to blue-pencil their copy. I took out all the superlatives. But finally I received so many complaints that I decided I couldn't do the commercial at all.

Interviewed by *Newsweek* on the ethical issues involved in doing commercials, I cited Sandran as an example of a product that raised difficulties for me. I couldn't be a testing laboratory, I said, so I wasn't qualified to pass scientific judgment on specific claims. But, based on what I could learn and the viewer response I was getting, I didn't feel I could be a spokesman for this product. This was printed in *Newsweek*, and Sandran threatened to sue.

After all the attendant publicity, I assumed my career as a commercial spokesman had come to an end. In fact, it turned out to be more of a beginning. When it became known that I would do commercials only for products I believed in, my effectiveness as a spokesman was enhanced. It was almost like an implicit endorsement if I was willing to do a commercial at all.

I've done commercials on the air from my first days in radio up to 1978, when I started on *20/20*. Though I have had problems with certain products, I cannot join those who condemn advertising in general as an unwholesome influence. Nothing can be fairer in a free society than to urge a public, on a commercial basis, to try a new product or service. That public is free to go back to Brand X, ignore the message, or try the product. But I am in agreement with standard network policies prohibiting people in news positions from acting as commercial spokespersons or becoming involved in advertising of any kind. News is the most important activity broadcasters engage in, and any appearance of commercial influence undermines its credibility.

By the end of our first month, the pure spontaneity of *The Tonight Show* had made it a coast-to-coast sensation. The main reason for this success was that Jack wore his emotions right on his sleeve. The wild Irish poet and playwright Brendan Behan was enormously attracted to that quality in Jack. In Luchow's restaurant one night, Behan said to me, "You know, I trust Jack. But I don't trust you."

I was not at all offended. I knew just what he meant. Brendan had no idea what I was thinking, because I didn't let him know it. I take the poker player's approach to life. My basic defense is not to let the world know what I'm thinking, particularly if I'm offended. To let people know they've made me angry gives them some satisfaction. I've never felt I should allow anyone that satisfaction at my expense.

Jack was not that way. His feuds and his fights and his frictions were famous and highly visible. There was constant conflict between Jack and his guests; between his guests and those they attacked on the air; between Jack and the world.

"At seven-thirty," crowed the New York *Post*, "the show might be a national scandal. At eleven-thirty, it is something of a national vice." On New Year's Eve, 1957, when Carol Burnett came on and sang, "I Made a Fool Of Myself Over John Foster Dulles," it made headlines in Washington. Not just newspaper articles, but actual headlines.

But after twelve superheated months, the real Jack Paar was getting tired. He had done 450 grueling hours on air, and was threatening to go on strike. First, he wanted to cut an hour out of the show. NBC refused.

"This grind is killing me," he complained. He wanted better working conditions. NBC agreed to move the show to studios in Radio City and begin taping at 8:15. Jack was somewhat mollified by these gestures, but he still felt abused by the pressure, even as he kept seeking it out. The feuds were exacerbated, I think, by the mounting pressures Jack felt to stay on top, to stay in the spotlight, to stay controversial.

His first major feud was with Ed Sullivan, a gossip columnist who by 1957 had become a nationally famous television star second to none. As much of a TV "personality" as Sullivan was, he still clung to his position as a powerful columnist for the New York *Daily News*. When Sullivan started out on TV, his guest talent came on the program without any fee, solely in return for a mention in his column.

But by 1957 he was being forced by the unions to pay $7500 a night for each act. He was enraged to learn that Jack Paar was getting away with paying his guests only minimum union scale, as little as $320. Sullivan declared that anyone who appeared on Jack's show for $320 would get the same from him. Jack was forced to point out that his show was a talk show, not a variety show. But it was all the same to Ed Sullivan.

The Sullivan feud finally simmered down, only to be replaced by a more serious fight with Walter Winchell. Taking on Winchell was something few people in the entertainment business were willing to do at the time. He was the most powerful columnist in the country. By the time television became truly powerful, Winchell was getting old, but he had enough clout left to destroy someone's reputation.

As Jack became increasingly famous, he seemed eager to prove his own power, and the power of his young medium. Winchell made a perfect target, particularly since he had made Paar a target.

At thirty-nine, Jack was like the young gunfighter riding into town to see if he could unseat the old gunslinger terrorizing honest citizens. In this case, the citizens were innocent performers, many of whom Jack knew.

Winchell made the first move. He wrote a string of nasty

cracks about Jack in his column. Rather than simply retaliate in private, Jack decided to pit the power of network television against the power of the syndicated press.

It was May of 1958. Jack and Elsa were exchanging pleasantries in front of his desk when Jack leaned forward to confide something to her. About seven million viewers were casually eavesdropping.

"Elsa, Walter Winchell is after me."

Elsa picked up the cue without much trouble.

"Why, Jack," she responded, "that man has never voted and never registered. Is that a good patriotic American or not? He is phonier than we are."

The year 1958 was not a good time to call someone as powerful as Winchell a questionable American. Winchell leaped into the fray, referring to Jack and Elsa in his column as "Dulsa and Jerque." The affair continued to escalate, with most of America happily resigned to spectator positions. "Mr. Winchell's high, hysterical voice must be caused by too tight underwear," Jack announced on the air. First Winchell's patriotism had been questioned. Now his masculinity.

Unfortunately for Jack and Elsa, the clever dig about not voting turned out to be false. Winchell produced a photograph of himself voting in the last election. NBC suggested Jack retract that particular charge. Paar dutifully showed the photo on the air, but used the retraction to slip in the last word: "The moral of this story is, it's easier to speak the truth than write it. . . . And the only way to kill a lie is to pour truth on it. . . . I have done that tonight. . . . Mr. Winchell lets his lies grow. . . . And any farmer can tell you what makes things grow."

Jack considered the affair a moral victory. "I think I am living proof," he said to the press, "that Walter Winchell has lost his power. . . . He can't hurt us. . . . Walter Winchell is a heel. . . . What worries me is the hole in his soul."

It was a strange situation. When Jack first took on Walter Winchell, many people said, "Well, that's the end of Jack." But by most accounts, Paar came out on top. He was among the first to fully grasp the enormous power of his medium. He got print publicity simply by virtue of the heat of his personality. He didn't need plugs in the gossip columns to stay in the public eye. And when the publicity was far from accurate, as was often the case, Paar would demand retractions, retribution, revenge. Many of us around him wished he'd stop crossing swords with every newspaperman that happened to offend him that week. We felt he was just feeding their fire, bolstering their fame. But Jack loved to keep the pot boiling.

Jack took what the columnists wrote about him personally. But he also saw his conflicts with them as a one-man crusade against a fundamentally unjust system. The columnists ruled the roost in show business, and he resented it. He hated their arrogance and their power, even if it was waning, and even if he was a symbol of the end of their dominance. Jack says it was Joe Kennedy who finally persuaded him to lay off Walter Winchell, not because it was hurting his son Jack, but because it was helping Winchell.

In Winchell's case, I had trouble feeling sorry for him. In 1954 I had interviewed him on NBC daytime television. He was promoting the Damon Runyon Cancer Fund, his pet charity. Toward the end of the interview he said, "Tell 'em they should send all contributions directly to me, Walter Winchell, because nobody knows who Damon Runyon was anyway."

Damon Runyon, of course, was quite a famous writer, author of the short stories on which the hit musical *Guys and Dolls* was based. His tragic death from cancer led to the foundation in his name of a charity devoted to cancer research, to which many people in show business contributed.

When the interview was over, I walked Winchell out to the sidewalk, where his car was waiting. As we were standing at the curb, a drunk ambled over. "I know you," he said. "You're Walter Winchell."

Without batting an eyelash, Winchell decked him, knocking him right into the gutter. Then he stepped into his waiting car and was driven away. I helped the drunk up, but neither of us had any idea why it had happened. Every time I heard Jack lash into Winchell, I couldn't get that image out of my head. As far as I was concerned, anything Jack said about Winchell was fine with me.

As the show progressed, my role as second banana grew more important. After Jack asked me to sit at the panel on a regular basis, I became a nightly guest, in effect. We would often engage in a little warm-up banter before the first guest came on. From there I became his frequent replacement as host. The end result was that some of the intense national spotlight on him inevitably spilled over onto me. I became, in a limited sense, famous.

I was used to a certain moderate level of celebrity by then. When I first worked in radio, a few people recognized my voice, but it wasn't until I became regularly associated with particular radio programs that anyone recognized my name. By the time I went on television, people started to respond not only to my voice, but to my face. Physical visibility, I learned, is a hundred times more powerful than name or voice recognition.

By then I had learned that much of the worth of adoration lies with the adorer. I can well remember getting the autographs of people I admired when I was young, like Artie Shaw at Indian Lake, or Lawrence Tibbett at an opera in Cleveland. I discovered that simply being in the presence of people who were famous was an enormous thrill.

At the time I can remember thinking, "What a thrill it must be to the person who gives out his autograph!" But the first time a young girl asked *me* for my autograph, I felt a different emotion. In the second before I wrote my name, I reacted with a sort of horror. What could she possibly want with this signature—*my* autograph? The whole situation struck me as faintly absurd. All the pleasure of fame turned to ashes in my mouth.

Still, nothing I had ever done prepared me for *The Tonight Show*. All of us became more famous then than we could have ever thought possible. It's hard to conceive of the persistent attention, the glaring headlines, the constant request for opinions on things we knew very little about.

In 1959 my agent persuaded me to act in summer stock in Ohio. We did a comedy called *Under the Yum-Yum Tree*. I was clearing over $10,000 for a one-week appearance in the Packard Auditorium in Warren, Ohio. That same week James Mason was reportedly paid under $2500 to star in a play on Broadway.

I can remember reflecting that something must be out of joint here. I knew perfectly well we were filling that hall because people knew me from *The Tonight Show*. I wasn't suffering from any illusions about my talents as an actor. I saw the discrepancy in pay between myself and James Mason as a rather sad comment on our cultural values.

Still, sensitive as I was to the injustice, I didn't feel like giving the money back. I'd started out in radio in Lima, Ohio, at $12.50 a week. Now I was finally being rewarded, if somewhat excessively, for my decades of work. But I knew I was being paid more for visibility than talent.

I've never minded recognition. Frankly, I enjoy visibility. But I think the main gain is commercial. Visibility, like time, can be considered to have monetary value. If I could calculate the value of mine for all the future and were free to make the choice, I'd cash in my visibility for money in an instant. Fame is not my oxygen.

But because of Jack Paar and his unique approach to his job, I became a television "personality." If I ever had any doubt about it, and my agent wasn't able to convince me, I could have seen myself so identified in innumerable articles and books of the time. One such source, *The Hungry Eye*, by Eugene Paul, described my evolving role on *The Tonight Show* this way:

Hugh Downs, Jack Paar's announcer and frequent replacement, developed into a "personality." . . . A personality is someone who does not do any particular thing well, but does everything weller than most people. He knows more about music than most, more about astronomy, psychology, skin diving, you name it. . . . He gives the impression of being able to say honestly what he thinks, although he usually shuts up unless pushed . . . then it comes out honest.

Jack once asked me, "Hugh, I don't embarrass people, do I?" "Yes, Jack," I said. "You do."

My role gradually evolved, through a constant give and take with Paar, into the part Jack himself found most amusing. I became Mr. Resident Know-It-All, otherwise known as Paar's Plato.

Jack loved to ask me questions. If I knew something about it, he'd respond sometimes with mock fascination; at other times with genuine interest. Part of the joke of course was that this was a "Can You Top This" contest. "Tonight," Jack intoned once, "Hugh is going to do a medley of famous Supreme Court decisions."

Roger Kahn, author of *The Boys of Summer*, one of the best books about baseball ever written, dubbed me the house intellectual. Red Skelton came on once and said, "Ask Hugh what time it is and he'll tell you how to build a watch."

Unfortunately, whole shows would sometimes go by in which I had nothing meaningful to contribute. So I'd keep my mouth shut and wait my turn. I didn't want to be the sort of guest who bites the microphone. At the end of a show like that, I'd grit my teeth and say to myself, "I'm not earning my keep. I sat there the whole time and didn't say a damned thing."

But I learned that just being there was part of my role. If a camera was on me while someone else was talking, and I had nothing appropriate to say, I'd occasionally nod my head sagely. I imagined the audience thinking to themselves, "Oh, Hugh knows all about that."

One time Jack had done some waterskiing behind a blimp. A blimp goes a lot faster than a towboat, so it can be pretty dangerous. Jack and I found ourselves immersed in a deep discussion about the fact that the faster you go on water, the shorter your skis can be. A man named Pope in Winter Haven, Florida, had actually succeeded in walking on the water. He skied behind a boat so fast he was able to skim on the soles of his feet. I launched into an explanation of how this was possible. I got into friction viscosity, the virtual incompressibility of water, and planing versus displacement flotation.

Jack listened patiently. When it was over, he said in exasperation, "Hugh, when you drown, you'll know the reason why!"

On another occasion he implied that in some sensitive areas my knowledge was not quite so useful.

"If Hugh Downs had been chaperone in the Garden of Eden, there would have been no world."

But all was not so comic in Jack Paar's world. After two years of unparalleled stardom and success, Jack started to take on serious issues and guests. In January of 1959 he flew down to Havana to interview Fidel Castro. His was the first filmed interview to be made after Castro's triumphant entrance into Havana. Jack had been told by the Catholic Archbishop of Cuba that Castro was not a Communist. The Hearst newspapers thought otherwise, and encouraged their most prominent gossip columnist, Dorothy Kilgallen, to go after Paar.

When Paar finally got his interview with Castro it did have its comic moments. He shot the tape in the Havana Hilton, where Castro was occupying a suite directly above Jack's. Jack told Fidel that he had visited the mansion of Batista, the Cuban dictator who had already fled to Florida. Castro offered to sell the house, lock, stock and barrel, to Paar for two million dollars. When Jack turned the offer down, Castro asked him if there was anything else he might like.

Jack thought a moment and said, "Well, I wouldn't mind the Norelco shaving concession down here when things quiet down a little bit."

That same year Jack interviewed another serious guest. Bobby Kennedy came on to talk about his work as chief counsel to the Senate Select Committee on Improper Activities in Labor and Management.

"Unless something is done, this country is going to be controlled by gangsters and hoodlums," Bobby led off. Then he named names. Jimmy Hoffa. Tony "Ducks" Corallo. And others. Most of them also had nicknames.

"Have you ever spoken so frankly before about this in public?" Jack asked.

Bobby reacted with some surprise. "I don't think I've ever been asked questions like this before."

"Well," Jack said candidly, "you're with big mouth now."

According to Pierre Salinger, then a top Kennedy aide, Bobby successfully tested and proved the political importance of frequent television appearances. We take this for granted now, but it was *The Jack Paar Show* that pioneered it.

In February of 1960, Paar walked off his own show. He returned in March. After giving my standard intro for the first time in weeks, the studio was deafened by applause. Jack was back. He started in right where he had left off, as if the intervening weeks had never happened. "As I was saying before I was interrupted, there must be a better way to earn a living than this. . . . Well, I've looked around, and there isn't. . . . Leaving the show was perhaps a childish, emotional thing. I have been guilty of such emotions in the past, and I may be again. I'm totally unable to hide what I feel."

That night, Bobby Kennedy came back on to resume his attack on organized crime. In June of that election year, his brother Jack paid us a visit shortly before winning the Democratic nomination for President. This was before the equal-time provision had been passed by Congress. The furor over JFK's appearance may even have hastened that bill's passage.

Once he had a taste of public affairs, Paar found he enjoyed playing the role. In September of 1961 he took comedienne Peggy Cass and a camera crew on a visit to the Berlin Wall. This was just after the Wall's completion, and relations between the superpowers over the Wall were tense.

Jack converted some of those tensions into mass entertainment. He made the background of one show the Berlin Wall. For another he showed film footage he'd shot in Russia. When Jack toured the Friedrichstrasse border crossing in Berlin to interview GIs, he ended up being attacked in the press and in Congress for his efforts. The newspapers claimed Jack had been given special treatment that had threatened to widen hostilities.

"It was the biggest turnout the American Army has ever made along the Berlin Wall," one newspaper sardonically commented. "All for Jack Paar." The incident filled eleven pages in *The Congressional Record,* and the Army colonel who conducted Jack on his tour of the Wall was severely reprimanded. So much for trying to show the "human" side of the Cold War.

After leaving Berlin, Jack flew on to Moscow, then came back to let fly at the press: "I do not intend to be pushed around by the U.S. Senate, or newspaper editors, publishers, or their henchmen, columnists, among whom are the worst rakes, deadbeats, bunko artists, and town drunks in our culture."

He quoted newspaper reports of Dag Hammarskjöld's safe arrival in Africa, when in fact Hammarskjöld's plane crashed on the way. Jack saw these as prime examples of the basic dishonesty and inaccuracy of the press. He pulled out *The Sunday Times Magazine* and displayed page after page of advertisements showing women in their underwear. How could they criticize him, he wanted to know, when this is the stuff of which newspapers are made?

He even tore into friendly Irv Kupcinet, the Chicago newspaperman whose "Kup's Column" has long been a fixture in the Windy City. Jack challenged Irv to question his own activities, seeing as he had once "been arrested for drunken driving with a woman not his wife."

That took me by surprise. On the air, I told Jack that his attack on Kup was uncalled for. Kup didn't deserve that. Besides, he had been cleared of the charges Jack brought up.

A Chicago newspaper later offered me $10,000 to sign an article criticizing Jack for his actions. They said nothing about my actually writing the article. That was one offer I had no trouble turning down.

Despite everything, I must say I had a ball on *The Tonight Show.* It was one of the most stimulating periods of my career. Unfortunately, I don't think Jack Paar was ever that happy with the show. He agonized over everything, often to the point of depression. If things went right he became troubled. He reminded me of Thomas Edison, who was suspicious of the phonograph he had invented because it worked right away.

It is confining to do five shows a week. After a while it wears on you. I felt many of the same constraints Jack did. I never got home before 1:30 in the morning when we were live. Even with tape, we still signed off after ten.

Still, I enjoyed myself on the show much more than Jack did. In fact, I had a wonderful time. The spotlight was shining nicely my way, and I didn't have the responsibility of hosting the show. I made contributions when I wanted or I'd keep my mouth shut and collect my money.

But Jack took it all terribly personally, and seriously. This was certainly understandable. It was, after all, his show. But I think his obsessive self-criticism came from the same part of his personality that made it impossible for him to wear funny hats or play roles in comic sketches. He had no problem showing his own emotions on screen, but he didn't like adopting some-body else's. Basically he was not an actor. He always remained partly the Presbyterian minister his mother had wanted him to be. One critic even likened him to be "a Protestant preacher after a couple of drinks."

I used to grieve for him. He should have been enjoying his stardom, but for whatever reason, Jack seemed in agony a lot of the time.

He seemed born to suffer. He reacted to everything that came his way with the most uncensored sort of response. Jack cried openly on the air at a time when it was highly unusual for any man to cry in public, much less on television. Paar himself penned the name "Leaky Jack."

To Paar, the whole experience was a constant strain. If he thought he'd been bad the night before, he had to do better. If he'd done the show about as well as he could, he had to top himself or face an inevitable sense of decline. When we finally switched over to tape, he'd rush home to Bronxville to watch the show from his bedroom. But being able to watch himself only increased his anxiety. Five nights a week he would fall asleep with that notebook in hand.

The enormous degree of exposure he thrust on himself during those fiery five years took a personal toll on the man. Jack Paar seemed to burn himself out before the concept of burnout became fashionable.

I think in the end what made the difference between us was that Jack was more conscientious about broadcasting than I. I can be serious about important things, but not everything is important. I remember saying that to an advertising man from Madison Avenue. I was talking about doing commercials on *The Tonight Show* and confessed that I lost little sleep over that sort of work.

This man was shocked.

"If you can't take that seriously, what can you take seriously?"

I thought for a moment.

"If I was cutting into someone's body as a surgeon," I said, "I think I'd take that seriously. Or contemplating a space voyage. But I'm not planning to get an ulcer over whether the box of aluminum foil is held at the right angle."

In this country, unfortunately, you always have to "be" what you do for a living. Which means how you make your living becomes your identity. In other countries you might ask a man what he does, and he might say, "I write poems," or, "I climb mountains." Then you find out he is a bank teller.

Somehow I've never been able to subscribe to the American notion that you are what you do for a living—and God help you if you don't like it. I realize it's important to care about your work, but I've found that in my line of work you also have to relax if you want to do it well. And you have to relax if you plan to stay at it for a while.

It is a business that can grind on a person in a very destructive way. Since there was nothing else I wanted to do, I built armor against the pressures and stresses of broadcasting. I began to take it less seriously and to try to have fun with what I was doing. (With the result that I began to do a better job than when I was so serious about it.) I came to regard the profession as a means to an end and not an end in itself. My young family was really the center of my life, and my self-identity embraced many activities outside broadcasting.

Broadcasting didn't come easy to me. As a young announcer in radio, I suffered through terrible bouts of mike fright. I finally recovered from that condition, only to subject myself to something even heavier—camera fright. After I outgrew that I learned how to relax, even on the job.

I was capable of going to sleep on *The Tonight Show*. If I was tired, and if whatever was going on was boring, I'd sometimes find myself drifting off, right on the air. On one occasion, during a desultory, low-key dialogue between Jack and the late Hans Conried, I woke up with a start.

"Oh, God," I wondered in some alarm. "How long have I been out?"

I peered around nonchalantly to see if anyone had noticed. Apparently nobody had. At least no one said anything. I sighed in relief and did my best to pay attention, like a sleepy kid in class. I knew if Jack had noticed, he'd have built a whole show around it.

I was supposed to be an island of sanity on *The Tonight Show* in the midst of imagined craziness. Everything is relative. Even Jack was thought by some to be unstable. I helped to dispel that notion on *The Merv Griffin Show* by quoting a staffer who said, "Jack is really mentally very stable. He's just a *carrier* of mental illness."

After five years of carrying neurosis to the very corners of the nation, Jack decided to call it quits. "I've seen what this pressure cooker existence has done to some of my friends," he said to the press. He was referring to our mutual friend Dave Garroway, the volatile host of *The Today Show*. Garroway's wife had committed suicide and he had suffered from severe bouts of depression and paranoia after years in the spotlight. Years later, Garroway too would take his own life.

The last *Tonight Show* with Jack Paar was taped March 29, 1962. The night before, Jack had laid into a prominent programming executive by the name of Mort Werner, who *Newsweek* said had given Paar his start in the business.

"Hugh," Jack said to me on the air, "I didn't know Mort Werner was a programming genius. I thought he was just an ordinary guy. Did you know he was a programming genius?"

"Look, Jack," I said, bringing him down to earth one last time. "You may be leaving, but I still have to work with these people."

On the final night of the show, I stepped out from behind the curtain as José Melis's band struck up *The Tonight Show* theme.

"Welcome to *The Tonight Show*, starring Jack Paar, with Robert Merrill, Buddy Hackett, and Alexander King! Now here's Jack!"

Jack stepped out to a standing ovation, lasting nearly two minutes. After crying a little, he apologized.

"I cry when I take the Coca-Cola bottles back to the A&P. It's a weakness."

He couldn't resist getting in a last stab at the newspaper press.

"Now that I'm leaving, I know they'll start in, because I won't be around to hit back."

I couldn't resist injecting one last sober note of reality: "Well, it's not the end of the world, or even the end of television."

Then like an old soldier reviewing past campaigns, Jack briefly recalled his old fights with Ed Sullivan, Walter Winchell, Dorothy Kilgallen, Walter Annenberg. He quoted a survey which indicated the waning influence of the print media and the growing power of television.

Toward the end of the show, I introduced a series of taped testimonials. It was certainly quite a roster, though only a small fraction of all those who had contributed to or benefited significantly from the show.

Shelley Berman, Robert Morley, Danny Thomas, Charles Laughton, Nipsey Russell, George Burns, Tallulah Bankhead, Joey Bishop, Bob Hope, Billy Graham. Richard Nixon. John Kennedy.

Because it was an election year, we had both Kennedy and Nixon make tapes; I suppose to grant them equal time.

"I bid you goodnight," Jack said at last.

He exited crying.

Then he was gone from *The Tonight Show*. This time for real.

5

THE TODAY SHOW

Jack Paar left *The Tonight Show* in March of 1962. His climactic departure kicked off an awkward interim period, and we ran through an endless procession of substitute hosts. Meanwhile the network was holding off appointing a successor to the King of Comedy. Since Jack himself had never designated a rightful heir, NBC decided to generate a little public suspense.

Jack Paar was a hard act to follow. Who was going to be given the chance? Joey Bishop was handed a week as host, though he wasn't a serious contender. Merv Griffin? Johnny Carson? Perhaps even me. Hugh Downs as host of *The Tonight Show*? I confess I entertained the idea at some length. I thought I was in the running, because over the five years I had filled in as host more often than any other substitute.

Tradition is a fickle force in our upstart medium. But it does play a role, and this time it nixed any chance I had to succeed Jack Paar. Tradition dictated that the host of *The Tonight Show* should be a professional funnyman. I have always found the networks' preference for comic talk-show hosts to be misplaced. True, a host on this type of program is supposed to be funny. But he is not *there* to be funny. He is there to bring out the humor of his guests and show it off to its best advantage. The great part of Paar's genius lay not in his own formal comedic talents, but in his native wit and knack for enhancing the wit of others. When Jack was funny, his show was funny. But when Jack and his guests were funny together, that show really *soared*.

A great host on television is more like an orchestra conductor than a musician. It can be a plus, when a conductor plays an instrument. But great orchestras don't hire instrumentalists when what they need is a conductor. In the same way, networks shouldn't always be hunting for comics when what they really need is a host.

The talented comic Jack Carter proved this point. During this interim period, he was given a shot as guest host. Carter was brilliant, spitting out jokes like a comic machine-gun. He did amazing impersonations and had the studio audience in stitches most of the time. A very hot personality.

But he practically killed himself doing it. At one point, in an act of absolute desperation to get that one last laugh he snatched up a paper cup. He flattened it out, jammed it in his mouth, and with the edges of the cup protruding over his lips, proceeded to do a hair-raising Al Jolson imitation. I watched from my safe place on the panel with a shifting mixture of awe, laughter, and pity. I thought to myself, "If there isn't a station break very soon, this guy is going to collapse right here on the floor."

Jack Carter is a marvelously inventive comedian, but he would have been a rotten host of *The Tonight Show*. On the few nights he hosted, his hijinks and rapid-fire personality intimidated his guests instead of encouraging them, as did Jack Paar. If Paar took five years to burn out as host of *Tonight*, Jack Carter burnt himself out in five nights. Of course, Carter was not nearly as serious a contender for the host job as, say, Merv Griffin. But he was a prime example of the type they were looking for. Fortunately for NBC, cooler heads prevailed at the top. Johnny Carson was picked for the job.

A great many people were surprised when NBC picked Johnny. Like Paar before him, Carson had come out of relative obscurity into the bright spotlight of *Tonight*. Unlike Joey Bishop, or even Jack Carter, Carson was not a household name. He had been the host of two daytime game shows on CBS: *Who Do You Trust?* and *Can You Trust Your Wife?* Successive decades have proved that NBC made a superb choice with Carson. But not because Carson was a great comedian. Johnny Carson just happens to be a great host.

Unlike Jack Paar, Johnny is a cool personality. And like most cool personalities, Johnny wears well on the tube. He has what we call "legs." It's hard for a hot personality not to wear out his welcome when invited into the nation's bedrooms five nights a week. Johnny also manages to do some things Paar preferred not to do. He happily wears funny hats and costumes, and plays silly roles in comic skits, while still sustaining an unflappable image as the consummate host. Johnny's genius lies in his ability to combine the roles of both comic and host, without losing the best of either world.

Though I did not think of myself as a comedian, when I filled in for Jack I did an opening monologue just like the other guest hosts. But I didn't try to tell jokes. I worked up a series of personal observations, mainly based on incidents I had experienced or witnessed, or read about. With the help of the writers, I sharpened them. I tried to make the monologue a reflection of my own personality, which seemed to work. At least the studio audience didn't boo me off the stage, and no one from the crew came in from the wings with a hook. At the time, I thought I was entertaining. Surveys indicated the viewing audience thought so too, which may prove how easily they can be pleased.

When NBC finally picked Johnny Carson, I couldn't help but be disappointed. But I can't say I was surprised. I wouldn't have seriously considered staying on as Johnny's second banana, and in fact was not offered the opportunity. Ed McMahon had been Johnny's announcer on both his daytime shows, and hiring Ed may even have been a condition set by Carson.

One happy result was that at last I was through with announcing. If I took on another show in addition to *Concentration*, the daytime game show I had been hosting since 1958, it would have to be one of my own. I thought perhaps I might be able to work more normal hours than I had with Jack

Paar. But NBC had something different in mind. Something at the opposite end of the clock from *The Tonight Show*.

On *Tonight* I had signed the network off five nights a week. Now NBC wanted me to sign it on at 7:00 A.M., which really meant waking up at 4:00 A.M. Very few prospects would have made me go on the air regularly at that ungodly hour. I had no compelling desire to become a chronic undersleeper. In fact, I love regular hours and a good eight hours of sleep. But destiny arranged things otherwise.

I was to be the new host of *The Today Show*. That is, if I wanted to be. When they made the initial approach, I knew it was an offer I could hardly refuse. Above all, it meant moving from the Programming into the News Department. As host of that morning news show, I would be moving away from the performing end of the business into the reality elements of broadcast journalism.

It was an ideal assignment at that point in my life. *The Today Show* had a reputation for intelligence and dignity, and, despite its strange hours—7:00 to 9:00 A.M.—it had a good audience—professionals, politicians, and executives getting ready for their day. If that meant getting up at four every morning, so be it.

Part of the deal was that NBC would be providing a limousine. It was hardly the luxury most people might think. If you've ever tried to catch a cab in Manhattan at that hour in the morning in marginal weather, you know just what I mean.

John Chancellor had been hosting *Today* for about a year, but was now headed back into hard news, which he considered his real beat. Until a few years before, John had been NBC's number-two man in London, then became the network's correspondent in Moscow before coming home to host *Today*. After a difficult year on the "dawn patrol," he made it clear that he preferred working in the field.

I had known Chancellor since the mid-forties, when we were both on staff at NBC radio in Chicago. He was called Jack Chancellor then. He was a newswriter, which meant he stayed in the newsroom writing copy to be read by announcers and news "personalities" who did little of their own writing. In earlier, more primitive situations, a staff announcer such as myself would take copy direct from the wire service machines and read it almost verbatim, flavoring it with whatever style or nuance we felt was appropriate. In those days, Chancellor himself never went on the air, but his ability to translate print-news copy into news script was such that I simply read what he wrote without question. On one occasion that level of trust tripped me up.

Jack always had a mischievous sense of humor. One sleepy Sunday morning I was scheduled to do a five-minute newscast to the network. A thick Chicago fog lay low on the ground, and I had turned my lights on as I drove into downtown. I parked on the apron of the Merchandise Mart and ran upstairs into the studio. I was on the air reading the newscast when Chancellor slipped me a new piece of copy. Without looking through it first, I started reading it on the air.

"The owner of a 1948 Packard parked in front of the Merchandise Mart is going to be awfully surprised to find his battery dead. He left his lights on." Of course I had to explain the whole prank to the network audience.

After accepting NBC's offer to be Chancellor's replacement on *Today*, I had lunch with him at the old Forum of the Twelve Caesars in New York. His first words of advice were deceptively simple: "If you ever feel too tired to go on, just tell 'em you want to take a day off."

At the time I thought that a sensible suggestion, but I really don't know whether he ever followed it himself or not. People in our business are constantly offering each other good advice they never follow themselves. During the next nine years on *Today*, I missed one broadcast because of a flight delay, and a few others because of injuries. But I never took a day off because I was tired.

Television morning news is a strange business. Like any other form of "magazine" show, it needs to find its own mix, that mélange of factors which will bring people back to the screen. But the formula for success is very different from a prime-time news magazine or the nightly news. In the morning, news and entertainment must be carefully balanced to hold the attention of a distracted and busy audience. While large numbers of Americans watch morning shows, they are also trying to get up, get dressed, shave or put on their makeup, eat breakfast, get to work, or try to get the kids off to school. Too much fluff can seem silly when the viewer is trying to get a handle on the day. On the other hand, too much hard news demands a level of attention most viewers are not prepared to offer when so much else is going on.

The networks' longstanding confusion over how to handle such shows—which are in cutthroat competition every weekday morning—is demonstrated by their choice of on-camera people. Over the years, the faces have changed, but the basic conflicts have stayed the same. News divisions push for solid broadcast journalists with hard-news backgrounds. Meanwhile the pressure for ratings points creates a demand for pretty faces, show-biz talents, and a breezier style. Occasionally some talent surfaces who combine the best of both. But more often, on-camera people are pulled in opposing directions. After a brief stint at the early-hour desk, they are rotated into other, less demanding time slots.

An example of this miscasting took place in 1954, when CBS replaced Walter Cronkite as host of *The Morning Show*. They brought in Jack Paar. Clearly, CBS didn't know whether it wanted a serious newsman or a comedian to handle that thankless job. As it turned out, neither Cronkite nor Paar was successful going up against Dave Garroway and *The Today Show*.

More recently, CBS News hired Phyllis George, a former Miss America, to co-anchor *The CBS Morning News* with Bill Kurtis. That selection prompted protests from some within CBS News that she lacked strong journalistic credentials. Unfortunately, such credentials alone have never guaranteed success on a morning news show. Neither, it turned out, did Ms. George's beauty and charm.

The mystery of early-morning news has been with us for decades. But in the beginning there was no competition to

Today. When NBC's brilliant young president, Sylvester "Pat" Weaver, launched *The Today Show* in January of 1952, the early-morning news field was wide open. CBS didn't try to compete for another year, when they created *The Morning Show* with Walter Cronkite. ABC stayed out of the ball game altogether for years, until launching *A.M. America*, which in a year became *Good Morning America*. Last out of the starting gate, it now frequently finishes first in the ratings.

Today met with dire predictions, but Pat Weaver—who also created *Tonight*—believed in pushing television into time zones where it wasn't supposed to be. At 7:00 in the morning, and at 11:30 at night, America was either snugly in bed or about to get in or out of it. Certainly not proper times for people to be watching television. Weaver set out to prove these beliefs wrong.

Like most television news debuts, *The Today Show* was not a critical success. New York *Times* critic Jack Gould called it "excessively pretentious and ostentatious . . . unreasonably confusing and complex." One pundit put it more bluntly: "Do yourself a favor, NBC. Roll over and go back to sleep!" But Weaver dismissed this sniping as the work of frightened, competitive print people. Newspapers understandably felt threatened, for television was moving in on their traditional monopoly of providing news in the morning.

Weaver was a showman, not put off by hyperbole. He proudly billed *Today* a "Window on the World." The studio was dubbed "The Nerve Center of the Planet." Dave Garroway, *Today*'s first host, was expected to hold all this together.

Like many of us, Garroway had first made his name in radio. During World War II, he hosted an unconventional free-form jazz and commentary show broadcast from Hawaii to war-weary sailors. After the war, he came back to Chicago and established the *1160 Club*, an influential popular music program, then moved to television with a Sunday-night entertainment program called *Garroway at Large* on the fledgling NBC television network. That show was also broadcast out of Chicago.

Garroway at Large had just been canceled by NBC when Mort Werner, *Today*'s first producer, flew out to interview him for the host job. Pat Weaver had been leaning toward Hughes Rudd, but finally agreed with Werner that the relaxed, offbeat Dave Garroway was just the man the nation needed to wake them up gently at 7:00.

The show had its shakedown problems, but from the start, Garroway was superb. Like Paar, he exuded a sense of pure spontaneity. Still, *Today* took time to catch on. Some say it never really became popular until January of 1953, a year after its debut. Len Safire, brother of New York *Times* columnist William Safire, discovered the perfect early-morning foil for straight news material, an obstreperous chimp named J. Fred Muggs. In the 1980s, such an animal-clown act would go down like a whiskey sour at 7:00 A.M. But the fifties were a looser era. The chimp was an instant hit.

During the coronation of Queen Elizabeth II later that year, J. Fred got himself and the show into hot water. Just as the NBC camera was covering, at close range, the setting of the English crown onto the royal head, the rear end of Mr. Muggs could be plainly seen impudently clearing a sofa back in the New York studio. Garroway, never one to miss a bet, compounded the original monkeyshines by solemnly asking J. Fred, "Don't you ever wish you too could be king in a far-off land where you originated?" The ensuing uproar in the House of Lords is said to have delayed the introduction of television to the British Isles by several years.

When I came on as *Today* host, I had plans for a somewhat different kind of show. The hijinks of a chimp were clearly dated. But the pace of his successors—my predecessors—the hard-news men, had not been working either. Within a short time the show began to lose viewers and sponsors. Neither Chancellor nor Ed Newman, as veteran broadcast journalists, were prepared to do commercials, as Garroway had done.

After a year of declining ratings and revenues, NBC dropped the hard-news approach. First Newman was let go. Then Chancellor let it be known he wanted a change. By then it was clear that *Today* needed one as well.

*　　*　　*

On Monday, September 22, 1962, I had to get up at 4:00 in the morning to be at Rockefeller Center by 5:00. My wife had laid out my clothes for me the night before. This is something more than a sign of wifely devotion. As I mentioned, I happen to be color-blind. Some years back, Ruth came up with a partial solution to the problem, and had numbers sewn into many of my clothes. If she can't be around to help, I can match them up by myself—mathematically.

As my NBC limo cruised through the pre-dawn darkness, I went over my notes for this first show. My guests were actor Dick Powell and the gregarious ballplayer Joe Garagiola. Though I wouldn't have suspected it then, Joe would eventually replace Jack Lescoulie on *Today*. That morning I was looking forward to my return to live broadcasting. After years of taping *The Tonight Show*, I welcomed the challenge. Going live, I felt, would help produce the feeling of casual immediacy I wanted.

I stepped out of the limo at Fiftieth Street and headed for "30 Rock," the RCA Building. In Dave Garroway's early years, *The Today Show* was broadcast from a storefront in Radio City featuring RCA's latest television sets. Crowds would gather out on the street at dawn to watch Garroway and his crew doing the show. When they finally retired from that storefront studio into the anonymous depths of the NBC building, the program lost its distinctive local flavor. If *The Today Show* was going to provide a window on the world again, I wanted to have a real window.

I headed for the State of Florida Showcase on the ground floor of the RCA Building. The State of Florida people took down their posters, pictures, and mannikins dressed in Day-Glo clothing and loaned us their place from 7:00 to 9:00 every morning. When we were through, everything would go back up—an arrangement we carried on for three years.

At 5:00 that first morning, Bernie Floreman, our propman, asked me if I wanted something to eat. I asked for some bacon and eggs. With just an hour before going on air, I decided I'd better go off someplace where I could be alone, eat my breakfast, and go over my material. Bernie brought me my breakfast.

I retired into a dark, windowless room in the back. One small bulb hung on a wire down from the ceiling, shedding not so much light as shadow. I was feeling a bit nervous. Now I was spooked by the general atmosphere. The ghostly presence of the mannequins stored in the room had an unsettling effect. Suddenly a loud, scratchy voice boomed out of the darkness:

"My name is Jungle Jim!"

My hair stood on end. I slowly rose out of my chair. It turned out the Florida folk had left a talking bird back there with a cloth over his cage so he could sleep. Jungle Jim, obviously a light sleeper, had been awakened by my rattling around.

My future sidekick, Joe Garagiola, had recently published his first book, *Baseball Is a Funny Game*. The hardball stories he told that morning were ample proof of his own personal spin on the national pastime. Dick Powell, on the other hand, seemed unable to give the interview his full attention. When he answered my questions with shrugs and monosyllables, I assumed I had said or done something to offend him. His behavior seemed uncharacteristically rude. Only later did I learn that the previous day he had been told he had inoperable cancer. He had courageously gone ahead with the show because his visit had been booked well in advance. Powell died a few months later. It was an upsetting beginning for a first show.

There were limits on what I could personally do to change *Today*. We were locked in by contractual agreements between the network and the member stations. For example, the stations were given five "co-op" minutes at the end of each first half-hour to broadcast local news. We sent out a network feed for that segment, but few local stations bothered to take it. Member stations also had two minutes of "station time," twice in the first half-hour, to air local commercials. Our network commercials went in each second half-hour.

We were on for two hours, from 7:00 until 9:00 A.M. But our research told us that hardly anybody watched straight through the entire program. The result was an emphasis on short feature segments and a good deal of repetition. We also had a time-zone problem. The show was live, but it was also taped and sent out to Mountain and Pacific stations for airing between 7:00 and 9:00 local time. In the Central Zone, stations carried our second hour live and followed it with the taped first hour!

Because of this time reversal between New York and Chicago, I could never say "Hello" or "Goodbye" to the audience. I had to say, "Have a good day," or, "If you're leaving us now . . ."

I had hoped to come up with all sorts of new ideas for the show, but it wasn't easy to do anything that hadn't been tried before. Fortunately some old ploys could be repeated. Since many male viewers watched us in the mirror while shaving, I suggested we transmit some on-screen messages addressed to them in reverse mirror writing.

"That sounds great," said Jack Lescoulie. "But we tried it before, back in 1953."

That didn't stop us from doing it again. I now knew how hard it was to come up with something really new.

My image of our audience was a husband with his hat on, getting into his coat, gulping down a cup of coffee while watching us, one eye cocked to the screen. Or a woman about to dash out the door to catch the bus to work. And of course, kids being packed off to school. Millions of viewers were also going to be dressing, shaving, eating breakfast, and talking while watching the show. But that mental image of the typical American household, going about its morning business while I spoke to them from my desk, never disturbed me. In fact, I found it reassuring. They were not a captive audience, and might even be more tolerant and less critical of the show.

At 7:00 o'clock sharp every weekday morning, for nine years, the red "tally" light mounted above the main camera would flash on, signaling the presence of millions of viewers.

"Good morning," I'd say, whether it was good or not. "This is *The Today Show* in New York. And I'm Hugh Downs."

When NBC asked me to become host of *Today*, they said, "We're thinking of bringing in Al Morgan as producer."

I said, "That sounds great."

I'd known Al Morgan a long time. He had been a writer on the old *Home Show*. I liked Morgan, and I thought he seemed very capable. I gave him the nod without question.

At the same time, NBC asked for my creative input. Bill McAndrew, head of NBC News, said he wanted me closely involved in developing the new show.

In Dave Garroway's day, *The Today Show* had been produced by the NBC Program Department. On entertainment shows, when stars become galactic, they usually end up calling the shots. Jack Paar, after becoming a star, virtually controlled *The Tonight Show*. The same holds for Johnny Carson today. In both cases, star status elevated the hosts to the powerful position of producer-packager. When Garroway was host of *Today*, he also ruled it with an iron fist, hiring and firing people at will, from the lowliest gaffer up to the producer himself.

But when Dave Garroway left, the show was taken over by NBC News. Different rules apply in the news department. On-camera people do not control, produce, or package network news shows. On the other hand, news anchors are sometimes given the status of "editors" of their broadcasts.

Unfortunately for both me and my producer, Al Morgan, no one at NBC was sure whether *The Today Show* was a news show or a programming show. It was produced by the News Department, true. But as a straight news show it had been a flop. Al and I were going in to split the difference between Dave Garroway and John Chancellor. Neither of us had a news background.

I could appreciate that NBC had gotten itself into an undignified posture with Garroway and Jack Paar, both of whom had capitalized on their star status during stormy negotiations with management. I could see why NBC would not want to get into a similar position with a new *Today* host. But when I was hired, the network paid lip service to the idea that, as host, I would and should have approval of key production decisions. It was important to me.

Al and I both wanted to restore the show to the best of the

Dave Garroway years while keeping some of the news format of Chancellor and Newman. We both felt we shouldn't put anything on the air that didn't have a news hook of some kind. We weren't going to fall back on fluff just to be entertaining. But we also agreed that doing the show as a straight news broadcast would not work.

Al and I both worked under Pat Weaver on *The Home Show*, the third jewel in Weaver's famous triple crown after *Today* and *Tonight*. Weaver's greatest contribution to programming was that he understood how news could be engaging without losing accuracy or integrity. We had seen how news and entertainment could be happily blended, and in the true spirit of Pat Weaver, we realized that *The Today Show*, if properly done, could be serious without being dull.

But we also had our problems. As producer, Al Morgan apparently needed a degree of creative control I had never been asked to submit to before or since. His perception of the relation between producer and anchor was not at all in line with mine. He once remarked that the on-air people of *Today* were his "stable of performers."

I have always felt strongly that what I say on the air has to come from me, even if it is something I have learned only the day before—or something put in the form of a script by a writer, researcher, or producer, and fine-tuned by me and others, including company lawyers. In the end, I need to assimilate and process those words and ideas, to make them my own, before trying to communicate them to an audience.

This conflict with Al Morgan lasted six years, with both of us trying to compromise, but never able to resolve it. It finally came down to a basic philosophical difference. Was *The Today Show* a largely spontaneous production, with real personalities reacting to interesting events, or a tightly scripted "production" run along show business lines? If Al felt I had that kind of acting ability, he was flattering me. I could never have carried it off, even if I had been willing to try. I believe in the end the broadcast ball always comes back to the on-camera personality. And as far as the public is concerned, that's where the buck stops. But Al felt that television is basically a producer's ball game.

It was ironic that we couldn't make it work, because in a sense, it *is* a producer's ball game, at least in a news department context. I had no trouble from the outset accepting the network's policy that the company has the final responsibility for what goes out over its facilities. And the producer, as the company's agent, must execute that policy. In every other situation and broadcast project I've been involved in, there has been an understanding that (a) a network is not obliged to allow me to say anything on air or present any material that contravenes policy and (b) a network cannot *require* that I say anything or project material that my conscience or comfort could not live with. Only on *Today* was there ever any trouble with this understanding.

The first inkling of a major problem came in choosing our Today Girl. Al Morgan felt that the presence of a woman again would add something desirable to the show, and I had no disagreement with that. The first Today Girl, former Miss America, Lee Ann Meriwether, had been primarily a weather girl. But the post had gradually evolved into a featured female role and an important ingredient in the mix of the show.

Al Morgan wanted to hire Pat Fontaine, a weather girl from St. Louis. I knew nothing about her, so he suggested I meet with her in person before we made a deal with her. Over lunch, Pat let slip a revealing fact—how grateful she was to Al for locating a house for her in the New York area. It turned out she had been hired some days before. As it happened, Pat Fontaine didn't work out, and left after about a year, but it was a hint of the friction to follow.

Before I left for vacation, I specifically asked Morgan not to hire a replacement for Fontaine right away, and I thought we had agreed. But when I came back from vacation, I found he had hired Maureen O'Sullivan as the new Today Girl. This time he hadn't even gone through the motions of getting my input.

O'Sullivan was a mature, accomplished actress, then playing to wide acclaim in a hit Broadway comedy, *Never Too Late*. She was also well known for her role as Jane to Johnny Weissmuller's Tarzan in a string of Tarzan movies. But after six months on the job, it became clear that she wasn't right for the show, and vice versa. The fact that she was such an accomplished stage and motion picture actress, I believe, ended up working against her on television.

For all her problems, Pat Fontaine had possessed a kind of rough competency as a broadcaster. Maureen O'Sullivan, by contrast, was a lovely lady but a lame broadcaster. One morning we were in the Florida Showcase about to do an "on-the-street" piece. The usual crowd had gathered beyond our plate-glass window.

Maureen was asked to step outside with a microphone to interview some of these people. After that, she was supposed to cut to a station break. The cue to break was a sign-off phrase: "We'll be right back. This is *Today*, on NBC." At that point local stations would run their own commercials.

The stage manager and I went over all this with Maureen. "When Eddie gives you the cue, just say, 'This is *Today* on NBC.' That's all you've got to do. You'll be off the air then, and you can come right back in." She seemed to be absorbing most of it, but I could tell something was still puzzling her.

From my desk in the studio, I could see her on the sidewalk, microphone at the ready. I said, "Maureen is outside the studio now, with a few of the people gathered out there. Let's see who she's going to talk to . . . Maureen?"

Eddie gave her the cue to begin. She said, "We'll be right back. This is *Today* on NBC."

All the stations dropped out. She never talked with anyone on the sidewalk.

Everybody wanted to be supportive of Maureen. She had a very appealing personality, and we all sincerely wanted to help. But Ms. O'Sullivan was an actress and couldn't develop a definite notion of how broadcasting worked.

Maureen would have been more comfortable playing a scripted role rather than being herself on camera—for some people the hardest role of all to play. Al Morgan had hired her, he said, because he wanted to bring a touch of Broadway to *The Today Show*. It wasn't Maureen's fault that this was precisely what he got.

Maureen was finally let go in 1964. I told her first, and it was later confirmed by Jerry Madden, the NBC executive in charge of the show. She was not pleased by the way it was done, and years later she told me she had always thought that I hated her.

"Maureen," I said, "I never hated you. I just didn't think the show was right for you, and vice versa."

In 1977 she appeared as a guest on my PBS program, *Over Easy*. All the old vagueness was gone. She was bright and crisp in her responses. She freely admitted, on the air, that during her time on *The Today Show* she had had a problem with legal, prescription drugs. For years, she said, she had been walking around in a terrible fog. I never had any idea that the vague quality I took as a personality trait had been chemically induced.

The Today Show put severe emotional and physical strains on its staff, both on camera and off. Dave Garroway had his "doctor," a powerful concoction composed of tranquilizers and amphetamines; Maureen her prescription pills. I don't think it was only the odd hours. Jack Paar had been right to dub the morning news the dawn patrol.

Television is rightly regarded as a man-killing business, and the field is certainly strewn with psychological and emotional casualties. Many thought Jack Paar would have become one if he hadn't quit *The Tonight Show* in time. The stress is real, and an on-camera personality can easily fall prey to it. I think much of the strain stems from an often lethal combination of visibility and responsibility. I don't claim to be impervious to professional pressure, but I have taken a few sensible steps to diminish its corrosive effects.

When I was starting out in broadcasting, I was often full of fear. I suffered from mike fright and then from camera fright; from fear of competition and fear of failure. But when I finally made what I felt was a successful transition to television, I started to relax. Above all, I tried to stop worrying about other people's jobs. But there was a time when if a light burned out on the set I was sure it must be my fault.

As a young radio announcer, I once had to ask a "man on the street" whom he planned to vote for.

"None of your goddammed business," he snapped into my open mike.

On later reflection I decided he was probably right. The problem was that he had *said* it was none of my *goddammed* business. In those days, words like that were media poison. I was convinced this horrible error meant the end of my broadcast career. It never occurred to me that since it wasn't my fault, I was not responsible.

In time I started to realize that it made more sense to mind my own business than to spend my time worrying about anyone else's job. Of course, if you are willing to trust others to do their jobs, you run the risk of being called lazy. Al Morgan once called me the laziest man in television. An NBC cameraman put it more kindly: "This guy makes Perry Como look like a nervous wreck."

But the calmer approach has always worked for me—in preservation of health, in audience acceptance, and in allowing me, most of the time, to do more than one broadcast series simultaneously. *The Guinness Book of World Records* has cited me as having done more network TV broadcasting than anyone else in the world, with just over 10,000 hours on the air, as of the publication date of this book. I'm proud of that record, and of the precautions I've taken to make sure I didn't burn out like many of my colleagues.

In July of 1962 NBC asked Jack Lescoulie to come back to *Today*. Jack had been with *Today* practically since its inception, and had proven an admirable foil to the garrulous Garroway.

He returned to the show feeling justifiably vindicated. When John Chancellor had been brought in, Lescoulie was pulled out. When I came in, NBC hoped to restore the show to the best of its Garroway days. Lescoulie was rehabilitated and came back with an understandably proprietary feeling about the show. He had been with *Today* since the beginning, and he was proud of his seniority.

Unfortunately, his attitude developed into a fierce quarrel with a unit manager who sought to keep the lid on expenses. I never understood why Jack allowed himself to get involved in this regrettable duel. On location in the Virgin Islands, Jack made a request for additional expense money. To his astonishment, the unit manager said no.

As soon as Jack got back to New York, he fired off a memorandum informing NBC that if he found this man on the set when he came back to work, he was not going on the air. He may not have fully realized that things had changed considerably around *Today* since Dave Garroway's departure. I remember trying to reason with him about it.

"Are you going to let someone like this, who has only been with the show a short time, push you off a show you've been with for over a decade?"

But Jack thought he was in the right. I don't know whether or not he really thought the company would back him up. In any case, he came in the next Monday morning to help me through a special three-hour broadcast. The unit manager in question was there, on the set. Following through with his ultimatum, Jack refused to go on.

Unfortunately for him, NBC had grown tired of being dictated to by its so-called stars, and Jack's bluff was called. We did the broadcast without him.

Joe Garagiola made a perfect replacement. He had spent eight years as a catcher, with the St. Louis Cardinals, Pittsburgh Pirates, Chicago Cubs, and New York Giants. He has a wonderful ability to ad-lib, and the frequent target of his best wit is himself. Joe once told me, on the air, about making a very rough landing at Washington's National Airport, in a two-engine DC-3. The wing tip had scraped the ground.

"Were you scared?" I asked.

"Well," Joe said, "I can't say I was scared. But I did get rope burns from my rosary."

When Maureen O'Sullivan left in the summer of 1964, a

search began for her replacement. Al Morgan's inclination, shared by the NBC brass, had been to hunt outside television for likely on-camera candidates. He particularly favored actresses, assuming they would be suitable for TV if given proper scripts and direction. This was a fine theory, but I never believed it worked in practice.

NBC News spent a lot of effort searching for the right show-biz personality to grace *Today,* but they overlooked the talent they had on their payroll. I didn't want this crucial decision to be made again without my full input.

"Why not develop our own personality right here?" I asked Morgan and Bill McAndrew. "Why not take someone who's grown up with television?" I felt television was now mature enough to develop its own talent.

"Such as?" they asked.

"Such as Barbara Walters."

"She's a writer," they said.

I argued that she was not just a writer, but a producer, and very bright. *And* good looking. Besides, she had been on the air several times.

Barbara's work as a writer-producer had always been of high quality. She had been assigned to write and produce a short biographical feature that welcomed me onto the program. Displaying her fine eye for detail, she dug up out-of-the-way facts about me and put them together in a light, pleasant collage. She even went out of her way to find childhood photographs and other memorabilia. It may have been a silly assignment, but she took it seriously. I was impressed then, and working with her later on the air, I was more impressed.

By this time Barbara was no novice at broadcasting. In addition to writing and producing for *Today,* and her air stint at CBS, she had done an on-air segment on the opening of the Playboy Club in New York. Besides, the original fluffy Today Girl concept had become outmoded. An assignment once suited to a weather girl now demanded a full-fledged broadcaster. Women of the 1960s were looking for a more serious voice in the industry. The Today Girl with whom they could identify had to be a Today Woman. Barbara Walters was a logical candidate.

Morgan agreed to give Barbara a try. We didn't plunge her into a full-time on-camera role. For a few weeks she came on two or three times a week, permitting us to test the waters.

This cautious policy made sense. The publicity surrounding these television "talent searches" can be irritating, distracting, even damaging to those involved. The barrage of publicity surrounding the recruitment of Sally Quinn to co-anchor *The CBS Morning News* was a case in point. She and Barbara were good friends, but the press made it into a competitive situation. Columnists kept writing about how Sally was going to murder Barbara on the air. The buildup ended up helping no one. Quinn might have evolved into a competent broadcaster, but the advance spotlight created an expectation that damaged her from the first moments on the air.

It was soon obvious that Barbara was a hot personality. Her broadcast range could be expanded far beyond the traditional "feminine features" with which she began. Barbara's first *Today* field trip as a writer-producer had been to cover Jackie Kennedy's trip to the Orient. It made an excellent segment. We had all been impressed by her professionalism during our special Saturday-morning coverage of President Kennedy's funeral, her first on-air assignment for *Today*.

I had anchored the program from NBC studios in Washington, while Barbara spent the whole broadcast, as producer, at the Capitol Rotunda, where the President's body lay in state. For a long time, as we waited for the White House entourage to appear, Barbara kept the story from sagging under its own tragic weight while fully projecting the sadness of the occasion.

On camera, she was a pleasure to work with. We found we complemented each other with a striking contrast of styles. I had always tried to make a guest feel as at home as possible, emphasizing diplomacy and a general approach to questioning. Barbara went after details and emphasized clarity, sometimes at the expense of tact. She is aggressive in her interviewing, but I've never known her to be hostile. What we have in common is that neither of us thinks in terms of an on-air personality. We are what we are, stand or fall.

If Barbara had become an official Today Girl, she would have been Number Thirty-Two. The number was that high because for a while there had been a Today Girl of the Week. But her joining the on-camera staff spelled the end of the Today Girl. It was a frivolous and sexist idea, one whose time had gone.

In the meantime, the behind-camera conflict between myself and Al Morgan seemed impossible to resolve. In spite of some compromise by both of us, something was chemically wrong. It was ironic that we had worked well as announcer and writer on the *Home Show,* but couldn't as anchor and producer of *Today.* I wish it were all his fault, but by the time things really became inflamed, I suspect I was half the problem.

Things were not right from the beginning. When NBC first approached me, they showed me a nice, comfortable office on the third floor of the RCA building. I liked it. When I finally finished *Tonight* in September of 1962, I went straight to *Today.* I found that a wall had been moved in my office to enlarge Al's already spacious office next door.

"Should I fight about this?" I remember asking myself. At the time, I decided not to.

Al Morgan had written a successful novel, *The Great Man,* based on his time working as a writer for Arthur Godfrey. I think it might have been his writer's perspective that led to his unshakable belief that the play is the thing in television, not the on-camera personality. He seemed convinced that a producer is a sort of ventriloquist, and that on-camera personnel are marionettes.

When it came time for me to sign my next contract in 1968, it had become more than a personality conflict. In my mind, it was a matter of saving the show. In the early days of Morgan's regime, he had been full of energy and ideas, and had done a lot to make the show work. But after nearly six years, he seemed to have lost interest.

I stayed on *Today* and Al left. NBC simply reassigned him and let his lucrative three-year contract run out. Stuart

Schulberg was immediately brought in as the new producer. Stuart was the brother of Budd Schulberg, author of *What Makes Sammy Run* and *On the Waterfront*. Their father was the well-known Hollywood producer Benjamin P. Schulberg, head of production at Paramount under the legendary Adolph Zukor. Stuart had directed a number of prize-winning documentaries for NBC, including *The Air of Disaster* and *The Angry Voices of Watts*. He was a highly literate, warmhearted man, and a fine television producer.

Stuart's arrival changed the off-camera atmosphere dramatically. Early on in the new regime, one of the writers asked Schulberg what I would think about a certain story.

Stuart said, "His door is right there. Why don't you walk in and ask him?"

The writer was shocked. Morgan had discouraged writers from discussing program matters with me, but I had not been aware of the extent of this intimidation until Stuart Schulberg came in. In the succeeding, blissfully trouble-free years, I was never once sorry I had persuaded NBC to make the change. During these years, *Today* reached heights in ratings and adjusted dollar revenue that I am told have not been surpassed.

Several months after he left, Morgan wrote an article for *TV Guide* about his stint as *Today* producer that highlighted events and personalities connected with the show. It was well written and accurate, and it recalled with affectionate detail almost everyone from on-air personnel to stagehands.

My name was not mentioned. Not even once.

Being a television personality is a wonderful way to observe history, sometimes even close at hand. But television can influence news as well as report it.

Early in my tenure at *The Today Show*, I was given a chance to understand how television coverage can serve the ends of political power. In the spring of 1963, at the invitation of President and Mrs. Kennedy, Ruth and I attended a state dinner honoring Robert Frost. The guest list was far too large for everyone to be accommodated at the White House, so an armory in Washington was commandeered for this state occasion. Ruth and I found ourselves sitting at the head table.

During dinner, a member of the Cabinet turned to Ruth and said, "You really ought to ask your husband to invite Adlai Stevenson on his program." He added, "Soon." Stevenson was then United States Ambassador to the United Nations.

Ruth asked the obvious question: "Why?"

The Cabinet member whispered, "I can't say why."

Later in the evening she relayed this strange message to me. I was intrigued. The next morning, I called Ambassador Stevenson's office at the United Nations and invited him onto the show. His secretary said he would love to come on Friday. We made the booking.

An hour later his office called back. The secretary asked, "Would it be possible for the ambassador to come on tomorrow morning instead?" I was somewhat surprised, but I said yes. We were able to reschedule a few guests at the last moment and block out a fair amount of time for him. I was sure he had more to talk about than the delinquent dues of the Soviet Union.

Later that day I found out what this was all about. A political conspiracy was afoot in Washington. Certain forces within the Kennedy administration had decided to oust Stevenson from his ambassadorial post. As a first step, the group plotting against him had planted a potentially damaging story about him in *The Saturday Evening Post*. The magazine was due out on the newsstands that week. This didn't give the Stevenson forces much time to rally. They needed all the help they could get. In desperation, Stevenson sidestepped the conventional channels of power and took his case straight to the people. That is, to the viewers of *Today*.

Adlai took full advantage of the time we gave him to make an eloquent defense of his performance as U.N. ambassador. At that stage of the Cold War, it was a very sensitive and difficult post. To close the interview I asked him, "Do you expect the administration to give you a vote of confidence?"

"I can't speak for the administration," he said. "But I certainly believe they will see the situation in light of what I have just described.''

The *Saturday Evening Post* piece hit the newsstands as expected. But the negative influence of the article had been effectively neutralized. The coup collapsed soon after, and Ambassador Stevenson kept his job. It was one time I felt truly a part of history, and not simply an observer of current events.

The Today Show was always popular in Washington. Lyndon Johnson was a regular watcher. He would occasionally call the studio to respond to positions taken by guests or just to comment on that morning's broadcast. He would ask, "Why in hell did you have to have that guy on?" Or he might praise something or someone he had just seen.

It was said in Washington that getting booked on *Today* was a faster way of reaching the ear of the President than sending him an intragovernmental memo. Surveys showed that a high percentage of the Congress also tuned in. During the Johnson administration, a large aerospace company—a defense contractor—decided not to purchase commercial time on the show on the ground that it might be seen as a form of lobbying.

My nine years on *The Today Show*, from 1962 to 1971, coincided with some of the most turbulent times in our history. Though the era has been called, for lack of a better term, "the sixties," the most difficult period actually stretched from President Kennedy's assassination in 1963 until Watergate in 1972.

If back in 1960 anyone had predicted the three assassinations of the Kennedy brothers and Martin Luther King, the antiwar movement, the ghetto riots, the marches on Washington, the endless demonstrations around the country, and the final tragedy at Kent State, we would have thought such a seer was seeing things.

From my vantage point it looked as if the country might really fall apart. The mood of the sixties was so tinged with outrage, fear, anger, and violence that it was a real demonstration of our national resilience that the country was not more badly damaged.

In the minds of many, the generation gap was either a cause

or a symptom of the turmoil. There is always a generation gap, but during that time it was unusually severe and seemingly unbridgeable. A society occasionally achieves a real rapport between generations. That happened among the so-called Founding Fathers. Many of them were barely old enough to be biological fathers; others were beyond normal child-rearing age. Young minds like Thomas Jefferson and Tom Paine worked closely with men old enough to be their grandfathers, such as Benjamin Franklin, who was over eighty by the time the Constitution was ratified. Together, they produced that brilliant blending of moderation and flexibility that is the glory of the Republic.

In the 1960s it was not rebellion against tyranny, but noisy dissatisfaction with orthodoxy that raised the level of social tension to where it began to tear the fabric. I remember when *The Today Show* covered the 1964 Republican Convention in San Francisco. There were demonstrators outside the hall carrying picket signs. These people were not yet hippies, nor were they really radicals. They were more like the rear guard of the "beat" movement. But they were a harbinger of what was to come.

One evening a woman high up in the Republican Party asked me a pointed question: "Couldn't you spend a little less time showing those unwashed, bearded people and focus more on Senator Goldwater, the children, and the flowers?"

"I've got to admit Barry and the children and the flowers might make a more pleasant sight," I said. "But you have to understand, we're supposed to be covering the news."

And we covered the news through those years, as it broke, not by sending out teams of correspondents, but by staying in our studio, for the most part, and inviting a constant parade of newsmaking guests onto our show. And they came on in droves, from poets to painters to presidents, from kings to congressmen.

Angier Biddle Duke was chief of protocol at the Kennedy White House when King Hassan II of Morocco came on the show. The king arrived, with an elaborate entourage, at precisely 7:19. Unfortunately, from 7:25 to 7:30 we had our "station" option time and would be interrupted if we started the interview before 7:30. Only a few member stations ran our network feed during this "co-op" period. We explained this, as simply as possible, to the king's retainers. But they seemed afraid to tell him that he might have to cool his heels for eleven minutes. His Majesty, it seemed, was used to having other people wait for him.

Since it was, after all, in his own best interests to wait, I thought I'd try a bit of personal international diplomacy.

"Your Majesty," I explained, "If we put you on now, we'd lose a hundred and fifty stations. But if we wait until seven-thirty, we'll have the full station lineup and time to talk uninterrupted."

He nodded agreeably, but within minutes had simply disappeared. His whole entourage was in an uproar. They were sure he had stomped off in a rage at my effrontery. It turned out quite the opposite. Somehow Hassan had managed to slip past his bodyguards and had taken an unescorted walk a block over, to Saks Fifth Avenue. He spent five minutes window-shopping and returned to the studio on Forty-ninth Street just in time to go on.

Despite his perfectly serviceable English, the king insisted on speaking French and using an interpreter. We conducted the entire conversation in French-to-English, rather than Arabic-to-English. I murmured a short phrase in Arabic as a courtesy to him. He smiled slightly but didn't respond. I think he thought he'd save me the embarrassment of having to continue in a language I obviously couldn't speak well.

Hassan II was eager to discuss his relations with the Moroccan Jews. He took great pains to explain that his opposition to the Zionist movement did not entail any prejudice against the Jews in his own country. "In our eyes," he said, "they are our subjects and we see them as protected by our laws." This was before the 1967 War, after which many Jews in Morocco fled to Israel, for fear of recrimination from their Arab neighbors.

After the show, Hassan had his men establish immediate

Hugh, at left, with three fellow seniors at Shawnee High School, Lima, Ohio.

Downs, in his radio days, takes a cue from the director. At twenty-two he was the youngest network announcer in America. *(Photo courtesy of Ellingsen Photos, Chicago)*

Hugh Downs with Dave Garroway, the eclectic personality who hosted *The Today Show* from 1952 to 1961. The show started the current trend of early-morning viewing. *(Photo by Raimondo Borea, New York, courtesy of Phyllis Borea)*

Downs in the Space Shuttle simulator at the Johnson Space Center. Hugh, who has been named head of the National Space Institute, was able to successfully "land" the shuttle twice after three failed training flights. *(Photo courtesy of Capital Cities/ABC, Inc.)*

Hugh Downs at the South Pole. As part of a *20/20* segment, Downs was chosen by the National Science Foundation to move the Pole thirty-three feet to its true location as measured by new satellite observation. *(Photo courtesy of Capital Cities/ABC, Inc.)*

Downs, with former *20/20* reporter Geraldo Rivera, examines an ancient Spanish cannon which they had just helped raise from the ocean floor in the British Virgin Islands. *(Photo by Tim Cothren, photo courtesy of Capital Cities/ABC, Inc.)*

Downs with a beard on the island of Moorea after a three-month sailing trip across the Pacific. Appearing as a guest on *The Tonight Show* on his return, Downs was not recognized by host Johnny Carson. *(Photo by H.R. Downs)*

Jack Paar and Downs on the old *Tonight Show*. As announcer and "sidekick" to Paar, Downs lent stability to Paar's high-strung style, gaining more notoriety than at any time in his lengthy career.

Joe Garagiola interviews Downs as he gets ready to drive a Scorpion Formula A racecar at the Indianapolis 500. As part of a *Today Show* segment he did a few laps in the car at 175 miles per hour. *(Photo courtesy of Dr. Robert Berman)*

The author climbing out of an Air Force jet at Andrews AFB after flying as copilot. Downs has flown several fighter jets and is licensed to fly single and multiengine propeller planes, seaplanes, gliders and hot-air balloons. *(Photo courtesy of the United States Air Force)*

Four generations of the Downs family pose for television. At left, Hugh's grandson Sadim Young (now sixteen and Hugh's favorite diving partner), son of his daughter, Dee Dee; Hugh; his son, Hugh Raymond ("HR"), a writer and television producer; and Hugh's father, now deceased, who was then eighty-three. *(Photo courtesy of KQED-TV/San Francisco)*

Downs and his co-host, Barbara Walters, on the *20/20* show. (© 1985, ABC, Inc.)

contact with Saks. He had been so impressed with their displays that he planned to return at a more leisurely moment. His aides arranged for Saks to stay open after hours so the king could shop without crowds. He bought $20,000 worth of merchandise. I later said to someone at Saks, "You really ought to give me a commission. If I hadn't kept him waiting ten minutes, you'd never have made the sale."

When Marlon Brando came on *Today*, he was concerned about American Indians. But he talked across a range of subjects, including little toy trucks that had commercial labels on them such as "Standard Oil."

"Can you imagine how children's minds are affected by this brainwashing?" he asked. "Once they play with this supposedly innocent toy, they'll grow up and see 'Standard Oil' at a gas station. They'll just sail right in and won't even know why!"

He then assailed a magazine article which had commented on his private life and his marriages in ways he felt were unjust and inaccurate. "I just don't think that's fair to my children, or to their mothers," was the way he put it. He seemed to want me to join him in deploring the journalism involved. Over breakfast after the show, he asked me why I hadn't backed him up.

"Marlon," I said, "I'm just the interlocutor. I give you the platform and you can say anything you want. It's not my job to be an advocate."

I told him about the Kinzua Dam controversy. In 1963 the Army Corps of Engineers wanted to put a flood-control dam on a river running through the Seneca Indian reservation. It would have destroyed the Senecas. I became so outraged by this disregard for Indian rights that I urged viewers on the air, to write to their congressmen to influence their votes on a piece of pending legislation. The Pentagon thereupon invited me to Washington and must have spent upward of $5000 on a presentation to persuade me that they weren't bad guys.

In order to build the dam, the engineers had to invoke the right of eminent domain and abrogate a treaty with the Seneca tribe dating back to 1792. The Indians were to be displaced by this edict, their ancestral homes destroyed. The additional cost of an alternative dam would have come out to about $.52 per person. I ended up stating on the air that the true villain of this piece was in fact the American people. Most legislators felt that if they had handed their constituents a bill for $.50 a person, they wouldn't be invited back to Washington.

NBC News was not pleased with my editorializing. They were particularly upset that I had tried to influence my viewers about congressional legislation not yet voted on. I understood their point, but I reserved my right to speak out, judiciously, about matters of strong personal concern. If I've mellowed in subsequent years, it is not so much due to fatigue or compromise, as to a better understanding of network news policy. A facility utilizing public channels and frequencies has no right of advocacy. As anchor of *Today*, I could present as guests advocates of opposing views. But to espouse a view on the air implied a network endorsement of that view.

The News Department also had an occasional bone to pick with me over my informal style. It was a habit I had picked up on *The Tonight Show*, and found difficult to shake. When Bobby Kennedy came on *Tonight*, I always called him Bobby, as in, "Good to see you, Bobby. How is Ethel?" Looking back on this habit, it does seem embarrassingly brash. But that late-night show was unremittingly informal, and the friendliness was sincere.

When Bobby came back to *Today* as attorney general, I was gently reminded by the network brass that he should be accorded proper respect. I understood, but on the other hand I didn't want to appear phony or come off as a stuffed shirt.

As polite as I tend to be on the air, my patience was sometimes severely strained. When Alabama Governor George Wallace came on *Today* in the early sixties, about the time he "stood in the schoolhouse door" to oppose integration, he said something so blatantly racist it made my skin crawl. He apparently felt, at least at that time, that if white children and black children were allowed to go to school together, somehow both races would be ruined.

An old saying came to me while I listened to the governor, who was appearing by remote from Alabama. "A fool points to the spot on the rug, while a wise man covers it with his mantle."

When Wallace finished delivering his views, I let a long beat go by. Turned into the camera, I stared out at the audience blankly for four or five seconds. Then, as flatly as possible, I said, "We'll go to a commercial now."

NBC News was not pleased. The public reaction, they felt, would be that I had somehow insulted Governor Wallace.

I pointed out that I had said nothing. But there is a section of the broadcasting code which states that an editorial can be the lift of an eyebrow or a pronounced silence. I had to admit I was guilty of committing a pronounced silence.

At the time of the Kent State shootings, James Michener came on *Today*. He had been doing some reporting on the subject and thought there were two sides to the issue. The National Guard men had been warned, perhaps inaccurately, about the possibility of a major uprising. This had thrown them into a state of panic, which helped to explain their behavior, Michener said.

I found it hard to see two sides to that question. I saw little reason to justify the act by armed men of firing into a crowd of unarmed students, whatever the rationalizations. But Michener felt there were reasons for their behavior which needed to be more fully explored. I have to admit I was a bit rough on him during that interview, though we have remained friends.

In retrospect, he may have had a more temperate and mature attitude than the rest of us. As television news people, we were taking a drubbing ourselves, and that put us on the defensive. At the 1968 Chicago Convention, the Chicago police were beating up television reporters along with the demonstrators. We felt we were being persecuted in the same way kings once punished their messengers for bearing bad news. There was a widespread feeling in conservative enclaves that if we just shut up, all the problems of the country would go away.

That feeling extended to network coverage of the Vietnam

War. Vietnam had an impact on *The Today Show* and possibly vice versa, but we weren't covering it directly. Still, our coverage, and TV coverage in general, had its effect on the national conscience. We reported the obscene body-counts and accounts of skirmishes, battles won and lost, over the breakfast table and around the clock day after day. I think this probably helped to turn the people against the war.

General Maxwell Taylor, one of the Joint Chiefs of Staff, came on the show one morning. In answer to my question about whether we were winning the hearts and minds of the South Vietnamese people, he made this curious pronouncement: "If the people of South Vietnam were opposed to their government, or to our presence in their country, the Vietnamese newspapers would reflect that."

He made that statement with a perfectly straight face. I pointed out that the newspapers in that country were completely controlled by the government. I was astounded that he could be so naive as to believe that South Vietnam had a genuinely free press. Who was making policy?

One morning during the Johnson administration, I asked Billy Graham, "When you preside over these prayer breakfasts at the White House, how much of that is talking to God, and how much is aimed at those present?" He was very frank. "You can do more good and amplify your voice when you are speaking at the seats of power than from an ordinary podium," he said.

"As a Christian minister, why wouldn't you advise a president against this war?" I asked when we were off the air.

"How do you know I'm not?" he shot back. "When you do things publicly you sometimes don't accomplish as much as in private council." It was an interesting answer.

During the sixties, many people came on *Today* to speak out on social issues. One of them was Dr. Martin Luther King. My contract with NBC provided that a car take me to all remote interviews, but this was one occasion where I had no desire to show up in a limousine. I interviewed Dr. King in a South Side Chicago slum dwelling where he had moved to rally support for legislation which would have given a tax break to landlords who improved their buildings.

My teenage daughter was with me at the time. We got out of the car and walked a half mile or so through an area of South Side Chicago that resembled postwar Berlin. Half the building sites were rubble or burned-out shells. For the first time in my life, I experienced what it was like to be in a minority. The environment was overwhelming.

When we finally reached King's apartment, he welcomed us and spoke with genuine eloquence about the deplorable conditions so many of his people were forced to endure. It was during this interview that I saw that this truly great man was working not just for the black race, but for the human race.

In addition to Marlon Brando, another outspoken guest during this troubled period was Dr. Benjamin Spock, the noted pediatrician, who had written what are still considered *the* books on child care. Many people criticized him, he said, for speaking out about the war in Vietnam and other national issues having nothing to do with child-rearing. But Spock maintained there was danger in our passive dependence on experts. Foreign policy experts, after all, had plunged us into the morass of the Vietnam War. He felt the average citizen not only had a right but a duty to try to influence policy. He was preaching old-fashioned Emersonian virtues of common sense and self-reliance.

We had any number of antiestablishment figures on *Today*, espousing various causes. But we also welcomed government spokesmen and other representatives of the establishment. I don't think the press of the time was deliberately slanting coverage of social issues, but I do think the press was perceived as insensitive to the views of conservative elements of our society.

There were a few times when I agreed with the Silent Majority's impatience with social gadflies. Dr. Timothy Leary came on several times to espouse his philosophy of "turn on, tune in, drop out." People said Leary burned his brain with acid, but I knew Leary before he experimented with it. I don't think it affected his brain much. He was always that way.

In retrospect it was remarkable that a man could appear live on a national network and say things like, "Hey, kids, don't pay any attention to what people say about the dangers of LSD. That's just a conspiracy on the part of the establishment to keep you in bondage."

"Tim," I said, "you've got to be kidding."

"No," he replied, "I'm absolutely serious."

But few people took him seriously. I think if anybody else advanced those views on the national airwaves, there might have been more of a flap.

Over the years, our guest list comprised artists, scientists, scholars, performers, and politicians, many of whom were intriguing. The English scientist Julian Huxley came on one morning and began his interview with a quote from an eminent British biologist J. B. S. Haldane: "The universe is not only queerer than we imagined it, but probably queerer than we *can* imagine it."

By this, Huxley explained, Haldane was expressing a basic characteristic of modern physics. When pushed to extremes of distance, speed, force, or temperature, "commonsense" ideas about the material world begin to break down. After Newton's laws were first presented, his Universal Law of Gravitation seemed universally applicable. Since it applied with only negligible error to the world as it was then known, there was no reason to believe it was not universal.

But in the twentieth century, Einstein discovered that those Newtonian laws work well at the scale of most human endeavor, but not for subatomic particles or large-scale structures such as massive stars or galaxies. If you tried to put up a building or a bridge the size of a galaxy using Newtonian principles, his so-called laws would break down. The theories of special relativity and quantum mechanics have set the world as we had formerly known it on its edge, turned it around, and then inside out. Huxley was particularly eloquent in explaining the profound effects of this shift. Through experiences like this, I came to realize that TV audiences can follow very deep material if it is not presented murkily or pedantically.

The great photographer Edward Steichen also paid us a memorable visit. In 1905 Steichen practically discovered photography as a genuine art form. Before him, many photographers simply thought of photography as a way to imitate painting. In his early years, Steichen's photographs did have a painterly quality, stemming from an "obsession with image." One of his earliest and best-known pictures is of New York's famous Flatiron Building, shrouded in an Impressionistic mist.

But as he matured, Steichen became a determined realist, with a finely tuned social conscience. He showed us wonderful pictures he had taken during the Great Depression of the people of the dust bowl. They evoked images of such extreme poverty and desolation that they strongly resembled contemporary pictures of suffering in drought-stricken Africa.

Toward the end of his life, Steichen, housebound, devoted himself to taking endless pictures of a single tree, much in the way Monet had painted various versions of a single haystack. In all weathers and seasons and times of day, he photographed this one object. He had come full circle, back to an obsession with image.

Carl Sandburg, who was Steichen's brother-in-law, always had a flair for the dramatic. On *The Today Show,* he read fragments of his own poetry or reminisced about his Chicago days. I once asked him if a story I had heard from a Chicago Symphony Orchestra musician was true. He confirmed it. As a struggling young poet, he had been invited to recite his work at a literary tea given by the wealthiest woman in Chicago, Mrs. Potter Palmer. Her husband had built the Palmer House Hotel and paved its barbershop floor with silver dollars.

On a hot summer day, Sandburg walked with his guitar all the way from his South Side home to her enormous mansion on the Near North Side. He arrived early, but was so overheated that he asked if he might take a bath. She showed him to an upstairs bathroom. The ladies assembled in the drawing room. Tea was served, but Sandburg didn't appear. Finally, Mrs. Palmer tiptoed rather tentatively upstairs, only to find the young Sandburg fast asleep on a bed upstairs, entirely nude, exhausted from his long summer walk.

Ian Fleming, creator of the James Bond spy series, paid us a visit one morning. Before we went on the air, he asked me to ask him why he drove a Bentley.

As a rule I didn't often cooperate with such requests. I've learned to phrase a planted question by starting off: "You asked me to ask you . . ." Or, "I've been asked to ask you . . ." But this time I merely inquired about his preference for the Bentley automobile.

He looked at me blankly. "I don't know what gave you that idea," he said. "I drive a Studebaker Avanti and a Mercedes."

I've never figured out what his motivation was. But he got in a plug for two cars while stepping on me to do it.

Believe it or not, I got taken another time in the same way. Clare Boothe Luce, the widow of *Time* founder Henry Luce and a brilliant woman who enjoyed several careers, asked the segment producer to have me ask if she intended to run for political office in the near future. She had been a congresswoman and had been appointed ambassador to Italy, but I thought she wanted the question straight, without a lot of extraneous background. When I asked her about a future in politics, she stared at me as if I were something distasteful she'd found on her salad plate.

"If you knew *anything* about history," she snapped, "you would certainly know that I ran successfully for Congress in 1943." As she went on to list practically every political affiliation she had had since birth, I found myself wondering how I had ever allowed myself to fall into this trap again.

My guests were entertaining more often than not. But my medium is never quite so entertaining as when things go wrong, as the many shows about bloopers have proved. For a filmed public service announcement against littering, I was supposed to wad up a piece of paper, give a little spiel about keeping your city clean, then throw the paper neatly into the basket. It sounds simple, but things kept going wrong. On about take four I crumpled up the paper, gave my pitch, and suddenly started to smell smoke. I looked down at the waste-paper basket, back at the camera, and said, "This damned thing is on fire!" The outtake has played on a number of shows.

One marvelous *Today* blooper that was never released took place during a commercial for Pacific Mills contoured sheets. Fitted sheets were brand new then. The focus of the ad was the ease of making a bed with them. The slogan was, "Makes Bed Making Easy as Child's Play." The spot featured a little girl happily making a bed with her mother helping. As I started the phrase, I committed a classic Spoonerism: "Makes Child Making Easy as Bed Play."

Before I got the whole thing out, I cracked up and practically fell on the floor. I hardly had time to reflect on the inadvertent profundity of my remark.

Long before the advent of Quantels and Dubners and other computerized electronic wizardry, we had a mechanical weather crawl on which the conditions for various locations were printed out on a long sheet of paper wrapped around a large wooden drum. During the two minute local commercial break between segments, a camera was trained on the drum, and a stagehand would manually crank it. Brief one-line weather reports for various cities across the country would crawl through the frame.

Stations that didn't sell their option time would be free to take the weather crawl: "Sunny in Seattle" or "Warm in Omaha." Someone (and we never found out who) took a brush pen and wrote "Shit" in there, somewhere between Seattle and Schenectady. It created something of a flap in those areas where it was seen. After that, a crew member was permanently assigned as security for the weather crawl.

Obscenity was the network's major worry about our "window on the world" facing Forty-ninth Street. They were afraid that demonstrators, or even some perverse individual, would hold up a sign covered with obscenities that would go out over the airwaves. People did hold up all sorts of signs, but they were typically of the inoffensive "Hello Dubuque" variety. In the three years we broadcast out of the Florida Showcase, no one ever held up an obscene message or flashed or mooned or streaked. For all the network's fears, that was one nightmare that never came true.

Personally, I was never concerned about inadvertent, or even intentional, obscenity. I suffered from a different form of on-camera nightmare. I used to worry about being held hostage by fanatics or terrorists. Being so exposed to the public every morning, facing busy Forty-ninth Street, I had visions of fanatics taking over our broadcast facility and threatening to kill everyone in the studio if their views weren't aired.

I don't think this concern was paranoid. Security at our storefront studio was not exactly airtight. A nut once slipped right past our guards, ran behind my desk, and started hollering some incoherent message to the world. The guards hustled him off, but I asked NBC to beef up security around the studio door. I didn't want to find myself staring down a gun barrel one morning.

We had some faithful and persistent members of the crowd outside the studio. Al Barney was a cashier at the Ham 'n' Egg Restaurant in Rockefeller Center. The great thing about him was that he was always there, rain or shine. He was a dapper, midlife Latin-lover type who wore an elegant pearl-gray Homburg and had a natty-looking upturned mustache. He'd stand outside the studio, peering in at us forlornly for the entire two-hour broadcast.

One day he showed up holding a portable television set so he could watch himself watch us through the plate-glass window. He seemed to have no other purpose than watching the *Today Show* in person. He would occasionally receive postcards addressed to Al Barney, *The Today Show*. They would be delivered to us and we would hand them over to him. He seemed admirably content with his lot, having achieved a strange form of fame as unofficial regular on *The Today Show*.

One of those mornings, two men turned up to deliver a piano to the studio before the show. They arrived in a truck, in their coveralls, with their bill of lading. They went through the whole procedure of having the floor manager sign a receipt for the piano. But when the floor manager asked, "Where's the piano," they didn't know. They looked at each other as though each thought the other knew. We asked them all the obvious questions.

"Did you stop off at the bank?"

"Why don't you retrace all your stops in your mind? Maybe you'll remember where you left it."

They couldn't remember.

On the air, I explained the situation.

"We were supposed to have a piano here this morning, but the deliverymen somehow mislaid it."

The audience response to this was incredible. For months I'd meet people on the street who'd say, "I think I saw your piano in a bar near my house." Or, "Maybe someone took it to Carnegie Hall and it got lost at a concert." We received mail suggesting every possible whereabout of the missing piano. The mystery was never solved, but it generated a lot of conversation.

The piano incident was one example of a peculiar media phenomenon—the unpredictable nature of audience reaction. For some reason, many in the *Today Show* audience found the lost piano incident absolutely riveting. Long after countless fascinating personalities had come and gone, the lost piano remained in the collective consciousness of our viewers.

The unexpected is often the most compelling. I can recall a few other occasions when certain statements I made on the air, which seemed utterly innocuous at the time, caused major reactions in the national audience.

On *The Tonight Show* I casually admitted that I had once slapped my wife. Jack Paar and I had been talking about marital stress, and he asked whether my marriage had been subject to this problem.

"Marriage is really a constant process of mutual adjustment," I said. "In our first year together, I just didn't know how to handle the tensions. It was mainly a difference in temperament. I have a phlegmatic Anglo-Scottish temperament. Ruth has a fiery Mediterranean temperament. I hadn't yet learned how to deal with that. So I whacked her. It was only that one time."

At the time I didn't think that I was saying anything so

unusual. But the reaction was sharp. While I think I was clear in my statement that there was no chronic physical abuse involved—something that would have made Ruth a battered wife—*admitting* to slapping your wife is about as outrageous a confession as one can make on live television. It was not, sad to say, all that uncommon an act. It was simply a very uncommon confession.

I naively assumed the whole thing would blow over in a couple of days. But Jack took to referring to me as the wife-beater. He never let me live it down. It was probably a sign of the times that a lot of the mail I received didn't criticize me so much for what I had done, as for being so open about it.

One woman wrote in blasting me for what I had said. She then went on: "My husband is a mild-mannered, softspoken man who'd never dare lift a hand against me and would never live to tell about it if he did."

I couldn't help but wonder if this woman's husband wasn't mild and softspoken only because he wanted to stay alive.

Some years later I had a similar confessional experience on *The Today Show*. In 1965 I shaved my head to start my Pacific voyage. When it slowly began to grow back, I noted with some horror that it was coming in unevenly. In fact, in a few places its comeback was distressingly sparse. I didn't need a lot more hair, but I did need to strengthen the scalplock area. I knew I could never make it on the air as a bald personality. Fortunately, Dr. Norman Orentreich had recently perfected his technique of banishing male pattern baldness by using hair transplants.

I saw Orentreich's doctors on seven successive weekends. In those sessions, they transplanted hair from places on my head where it grows thickly, to thinning areas. I never had any problems with the process, but I was told it gave a few of those early patients the willies. After they started drilling into one man's scalp, the patient shot up in the chair and announced: "Wait a minute, I just remembered something! I have to run out and put a quarter in the meter."

He ran out of Orentreich's office and never came back.

I was prompted to talk about the transplant on *Today* mainly because a New York *Post* gossip columnist had listed me as someone who wore a hairpiece. Since I did not wear a hairpiece, I decided to discuss why my hair looked better. I also believed it would be educational. I never expected the response I got from that one discussion. Years after, people would mention my talking about my hair transplant on *The Today Show*. I ended up starting a sort of chain reaction in the entertainment business. Joey Bishop went out and got a hair transplant, I was told, because I had done it. Frank Sinatra is said to have followed Joey. I hadn't intended to start a trend, but if I did, it's the kind of thing broadcasting can do.

On *Tonight*, I also told the story of having my tonsils out twice, once at nine and again at twenty-three. When I was twenty-three I came down with tonsilitis. This puzzled me since my tonsils were supposed to be gone. A doctor in Chicago took a look down my throat.

"You say you've had your tonsils taken out?" he asked suspiciously.

"Yes," I said.

He looked again.

"By a *doctor*?"

My tonsils had been taken out by our family doctor, who did not specialize in surgery. The operation took place in Lima, Ohio, on a kitchen table. The anesthesia was diethyl ether on a rag wrapped around a cone. Fourteen years later, the doctor in Chicago told me my soft palate looked as if I'd had polio. It was obviously a hatchet job.

He sent me to the hospital to have my remaining scar tissue taken out. I was in the recovery room in St. Elizabeth's, looking forward to going home within a day, when a priest came in and started to mumble something in Latin. Before long I realized with a start that he was giving me the last rites. The thought crossed my mind that there might be something the doctors hadn't told me.

"Father," I finally said, reaching up one hand in an attempt to stop him. "I think there's some mistake. I'm only here for a short time."

A sad look came into his eyes. "My son," he said solemnly, "we're *all* only here a short time."

Of course the priest had wandered into the wrong room.

Whenever I could, I did an extra assignment for NBC. In 1969 I got a particularly interesting opportunity, to host an NBC special that took me to Siberia. It was not only interesting, but as it turned out, threatening. For quite a few hours during that trip, I had reason to believe that I would never return home from the Soviet Union.

Our program was called "The First Americans," a title inspired by the scientific belief that the ancestors of American Indians—both North and South—came out of Siberia many thousands of years ago. They crossed the Bering Land Bridge into what is now Alaska, then migrated down the Americas as far south as Tierra del Fuego, at the foot of South America.

The idea of the program must have pleased the Russians, because we were welcomed by the Soviet Academy of Sciences. They encouraged us to film an archeological dig of these early Mongoloid people, an "elephant house" which dated back about 15,000 years. This find was near a little Siberian town called Ozerky, located about 140 miles northwest of the city of Novosibirsk.

Professor Vance Haynes, of the University of Arizona, an American Indian specialist, had told me about these houses, adding that he hoped to find the remains of a similar one in North America.

It was called an elephant house because the ancient relative of that animal, the mammoth, was the principal item in the economy of these Old Stone Age people. They ate the meat, dressed the hides, and used the bones for a variety of things, including the construction of their homes, which were something like modern Quonset huts. These early Indians used the large leg bones as upright columns, then arranged the ribs to arch over and span the house width. Finally, they covered the ribs with the hide of the animal.

When I visited the Ozerky dig, it was 66 degrees below zero Fahrenheit. I asked my host, Dr. A. P. Okladnikov, head of that branch of the academy, if the climate was this harsh 15,000 years ago. He said he thought it was. As I stared at the remains of these homes, I marveled at the resourcefulness of these ancient people. I was wearing the most modern arctic gear available, but I still would have been dead in a few hours without some heated shelter to get into.

After we filmed the houses, we doubled back down the narrow road to the Trans-Siberian Railroad. Our caravan of military vehicles churned through the snow to the same place we had left the train two days before. There was no depot, but the train stopped and we boarded.

No Westerners are allowed to travel on this section of the railroad in the daytime. Foreigners going between Moscow and Novosibirsk must fly at night. So it was a special privilege that Okladnikov had arranged. He asked only that we not take photographs from the train. I never saw anything that looked important, but those were the ground rules, and we obeyed.

When we got to Novosibirsk, which has an enormous railway station, I set my case down on a curb. We were waiting for the two minibuses which would take our entire party to Academy City, a few miles outside town.

My guide and translator, a short man named Yuri, was drunk. He had borrowed my last thirty rubles to buy vodka. I excused myself to use the men's room in the station before boarding the bus. But when I came out, Yuri was gone. My case was gone. The minibuses were gone.

It dawned on me that I was in something of a fix. I was in the far reaches of the Soviet Union. My passport and other identification were in my case. I had no money and no command of Russian. I couldn't work the phone to Academy City even if I had a coin, which I didn't.

I set out to find someone who spoke English. This took a bit of doing. For an hour and a half, I talked—in English—to people in ticket booths and behind what looked like information counters. But they only stared blankly at the gibberish I was mouthing. I began to despair. Finally, with sign language, a woman indicated that if I waited on a bench, someone would assist me.

After another lengthy wait, I sensed a presence. I looked up from my half-doze to find two men in light tan coats standing over me. I asked if they spoke English and the taller one nodded.

I immediately began to explain my situation, but he said only: "This is not a proper place to talk. Follow us."

We walked quite a distance to the far side of the station and up a flight of stairs. They had taken me to a police station. The man in charge asked me to be seated and immediately wanted to know where I had come from. I told him Ozerky. Twice he asked for my passport and twice I told him where I thought it was—on a bus on the way to Academy City. Twice he looked sideways at another official. His expression plainly said that he didn't believe a word I was saying.

What complicated the situation was that I wasn't supposed to be on that stretch of the Trans-Siberian Railway. The questioning went on for hour after hour, and at one point, I had the feeling they thought I had parachuted in—as in "American spy."

Apparently I was under arrest. I explained, again and again, that I was a guest of the Soviet Academy of Sciences. If they would get in touch with Professor A. P. Okladnikov, he would vouch for my legitimacy. But no one reached for the telephone. It was obvious that I was not getting through.

I really believed that I could be put in a labor camp and never heard from again. Funny phrases came to my mind. Like, "I'm the host of the *Today Show*," or "I insist on seeing the American Ambassador." But this was not Moscow. In this far reach of Siberia, I was just someone who had criminally ridden the Trans-Siberian railroad and had no passport. I was doomed unless they called Okladnikov.

Six hours had now passed, and I was truly frightened. Then someone, inexplicably, suggested that they call Academy City. I think they decided on this simple solution because they didn't know what to do with me. To assign me to a firing squad would have probably required filling out forms in quintuplicate. I don't think they wanted to be bothered.

After they finally got through to Okladnikov, the climate suddenly changed. They smiled, and were courteous and helpful. They not only arranged a taxi to take me to Academy City, but they gave me money for the ride. I thanked them, and all the way, I contemplated methods of killing Yuri.

It turned out that he had boarded the bus, too drunk to remember that I was in the men's room. The people on each bus assumed that I was in the other one and steamed off without me. When I learned that Yuri had to live with his parents for lack of housing, and had been unlucky in love, I forgave him.

I had never been so happy to see anyone as I was when greeted by Professor Okladnikov. I had almost disappeared forever into the vast land from which "The First Americans" had come.

The nine years of hosting *Today* were exciting, exhilarating, and exhausting. I was tired. I had settled into a state of numbness that would go away only when I went on vacation. After a few days of relaxation, I would remember what it was like to be really alive. As much as I enjoyed doing *The Today Show*, I couldn't help remembering Jack Paar's famous words, "Television is killing me." It wasn't exactly killing me, but it wasn't extending my life, either.

After nine years of chronic lack of sleep, I began worrying about the possible damage to my health. I had hoped to do the show for ten years, but in those days television had a fondness for three-year contracts. It was either going to be nine years or twelve.

When the 1970s began, I started thinking about making a change. I didn't want to retire. I simply wanted less time on the air. I knew if I left regular television, I was taking a chance on never being able to come back. But I also knew that if I didn't leave soon, there was a chance I would never leave, at least not in one piece. I decided to take the gamble that people would remember me, that television wouldn't forget me, and that I wouldn't miss the "amplified voice" that had been my companion for so many years.

Winston Churchill once said that taking daytime naps was the only way he could catch up on his sleep. The only way he could sleep during the day was to take off his clothes and get into bed. Following Churchill's advice, I went through a phase of trying to fight my tiredness by taking naps in the afternoon.

One winter day I took off all my clothes and fell into bed. I woke up with a start. I had no idea how long I might have slept. The clock said 5:30, an hour after my usual rising time. It was dark outside. I jumped out of bed in a fright and pulled on my clothes, wondering if I would make it to the studio by show time. My son, who was a little boy then, came into the room fully dressed.

"What are *you* doing up?" I asked.

He looked at me strangely.

"I just got home from school, Dad," he said.

Whenever I had second thoughts about leaving *Today*, I would remember that afternoon.

6

CONCENTRATION

Throughout most of my *Today Show* years and my last few seasons on *Tonight,* I moonlighted every weekday afternoon as host of the game show *Concentration.* Ever since my radio days, I never felt at ease doing only one show. Though some people apparently found my dual duties as host of *Today* and *Concentration* highly incongruous, I always found the contrast stimulating. I never minded straddling the fence between News and Entertainment, prepared to jump one way or the other as opportunities arose.

I hosted *Concentration* for ten years, from 1958 through 1968. I never once regretted taking that job. In fact, the only misgivings I ever had came at the very beginning, when game shows as a species became suspect and were threatened with virtual extinction.

In the 1950s America went wild over quiz shows. The airwaves were filled with them: *Tic Tac Dough, The Price Is Right, The $64,000 Question, The $64,000 Challenge, The Big Surprise, Twenty-One.* For little but the cost of studio overhead and a few buckets of prize money, game shows were able to draw enormous national audiences and enormous national attention.

Quiz show winners became instant celebrities. It was finally fashionable to be smart. If you didn't want to take your chances playing on a quiz show, you wanted to produce one. Every network, every producer, every host, every sponsor, everyone involved in the big business of television suddenly wanted his own quiz show, game show, or big-money prize show. But just as the

California Gold Rush produced more than its fair share of crooks, this modern media bonanza created its own form of mischief.

In April of 1957, *Time* set off the first alarm. It finally dared to pose the question being whispered all around our industry: "Are the quiz shows rigged?"

But, after asking the question of the hour, *Time* put on its kid gloves. "Producers of the big money shows know they cannot afford to risk collusion with the contestants," the report continued. "Charles Van Doren, *Twenty-One's* most famous alumnus, feels certain that no questions were being form-fitted to his phenomenal mind."

Dan Enright, of Barry & Enright, the house that produced *Twenty-One*, became indignant at the very mention of rigging. "Money has become a cheap commodity," he declared. "The game is the thing. Ours is a good one!"

The denials continued, but people with reason to wonder were becoming convinced that some game-show producers were controlling the outcomes as a means of building suspense. To enhance drama, to attract more viewers, to be more entertaining—wasn't that what TV was all about? In the name of meeting audience needs, all sorts of questionable stunts became not only conceivable, but justifiable.

Of all the quiz-show celebrities of the time, none was more celebrated than Charles Van Doren, a young instructor at Columbia University. The scion of a distinguished literary family, Van Doren became the toast of intellectual society with his frequent displays of wit and erudition as a contestant on *Twenty-One*. In early 1958 a New York *Times* reporter questioned him about this unprecedented string of victories as the reigning whiz of the quiz shows.

"I never get any kind of hint or help," he declared. "So far as I know, nobody ever did on the program."

Herb Stempel, the former star of *Twenty-One*, had honestly won $50,000 in eight weeks as a winner. After his defeat by Van Doren in the fall of 1958, Stempel publicly charged that Barry & Enright, *Twenty-One's* producers, had instructed him to lose to Van Doren. Van Doren had been fed the right answers and coached to enhance his delivery, Stempel charged.

Enright not only denied this, but Jack Barry, host of *Twenty-One* and Enright's partner in Barry & Enright, defended his show on the air. "The truth will out," Barry announced. "The audience's faith has not been abused."

The authorities became interested. A grand jury was convened by Manhattan District Attorney Frank Hogan, and a congressional hearing was called to look into the quiz shows. That week in September 1958, I went on the NBC network as host of *Concentration*. It was to be the last of the great game shows out of Barry & Enright.

Fortunately for all of us concerned, *Concentration* was purchased by NBC in a move to counter the bad publicity beginning to come out of the investigations. But unlike the big-money quiz shows, we were due to go on in the morning, five days a week. Unlike the questionable programs that went on in prime time, once a week, *Concentration* had been conceived as a simple game show more suitable for a daytime audience.

Still, the whole house of cards was falling, as more of the truth started to come out. We didn't even know if we would be allowed to launch *Concentration*. Only a few days before the premiere, I ran into Jack Barry, host and co-producer of *Twenty-One*, on the street.

"I think the contestants are getting the answers," he said. His expression was one of shock and disgust. "Damned if I know who's doing it. But I think they're getting the answers."

This was the most effective evasion I'd ever encountered.

Hogan released a damning brief, charging that "A national fraud is being committed, whereby television quiz shows have been misrepresented to millions of citizens as honest tests of the contestant's knowledge and skill."

Van Doren finally broke down and confessed before the U.S. Congress. He had been given, and had memorized, the answers to the questions on *Twenty-One*.

Van Doren revealed how he had been coached to make his responses more "entertaining." He would pause before certain answers, then screw up his face in apparent concentration before his delivery. He had been assured that the show was merely entertainment, and that giving help to quiz-show contestants was a common practice and merely a part of show business. At the end of his reign, the young Columbia instructor had pocketed $129,000, a hefty sum compared to his teacher's salary, but surely not enough to compensate for the destruction of his reputation.

In a matter of weeks, Goodson-Todman, the other major quiz-show producer and originator of *The $64,000 Question*, also fell under a cloud. Even President Eisenhower commented on it. "The fixing of quiz shows," he announced at a press briefing, "is a terrible thing to do to the American public."

Those were dark days in television. The ensuing uproar shook the industry to its foundations and did not subside for years. The network brass defended their ethics, while denying all knowledge of the independent producer's activities. The entire prize-show field came under intensive public scrutiny.

This was not the perfect time to be launching my own game show. Fortunately, *Concentration* was straight. It had a virtually unriggable structure and the tightest security in show business.

I had wanted to get my own quiz show for years. Night after night, before the bust, I would watch the hot young quiz-show hosts conducting their hit game-shows. I figured I could do as well or better. At the time, I had only a night job, from 8:15 to 11:15, five nights a week, on *The Tonight Show*. I was no longer a network announcer, but a free-lance television personality. I had to think about my future and about financial security.

If a show was canceled, as they were in those days at the drop of a hat, I had no base salary or benefits to fall back on. To be practical, I needed a fallback position in case *Tonight* went off the air. So I went around to all the companies involved in producing game shows to let them know I was available.

Game and quiz shows, by and large, were not produced by the networks. In the early days of broadcasting, two major networks, NBC and CBS, had maintained total control over program content. They produced nearly every program themselves, either as a network broadcast or as an original production by an affiliate.

But as television's national influence and power increased,

the FCC grew concerned that this might lead to a monopoly of the public airwaves, and pressured the networks to increase their purchases of programming from outside producers. The networks gave up a certain degree of control, but they ended up making more money. The outside packagers were better able to cut production costs, bargain with unions, and streamline operations.

At its peak, the new system worked wonders for everyone involved. From independent producers on up to the networks and affiliates, profits soared as more and more people became wrapped up in the quiz-show craze. Then the scandals hit. The FCC went back to the networks and told them, in effect, the opposite of what they had said before. "You should have more control over what you put on the air. You have a responsibility to the public because you use the public airwaves." The pendulum swung back the other way, and the networks ended up buying up all the shows they could and producing them themselves.

Barry & Enright and Goodson-Todman had been the titans of the game-show industry. They were putting out as much product as could be crammed onto the airwaves. Before the scandal broke, I learned that Barry & Enright had a new show in the works called *Concentration*. Bob Noah, a producer at B & E, had worked up the idea. It wasn't entirely original—the old card game Concentration had supplied the concept.

To play Concentration, you place a deck of cards facedown and turn two of them up. If the face value matches, you get to keep the pair. If they don't, you turn them back over and try to remember where they were. Then your opponent plays. If you can recall a position correctly, you can grab that card when a mate to it turns up. The side with the most cards at the end wins. The major skill involved is concentration. You try to remember where the cards are on the table.

As conceived by Noah, the playing cards became three-sided surfaces on the Big Board of the show. Contestants tried to match pairs of prizes corresponding to different numbers. If you asked to have a number turned over and it displayed a car, you had to try to find another car to make your match. Then came the tricky part. You didn't just win a car if you matched up two cars. Instead, a third surface would be turned faceup after each match. The prize would be credited to your account. Part of a rebus would then be revealed.

Norm Blumenthal, an artist, was brought in to devise and execute the rebus on which the program was based. In a rebus, pictures stand for words. Thus, Brigitte Bardot would be represented by a bridge, the word "it," a metal bar, and a chunk of dough. As matches were made, bits of the puzzle would start to be pieced together. More prizes would be chalked up to different sides of the game. The first person to guess the rebus won all the prizes posted on his or her side of the board.

That all sounded straightforward enough, and I agreed to audition for the job. I was not exactly thrilled to hear that the show would be on every day, during the day. I had been gunning for a prime-time, high-visibility, once-a-week spot. Something like *Twenty-One* or *The $64,000 Question*. When I heard from Jack Barry that they had been hoping to get Gene Rayburn as host, I assumed Rayburn was their first choice. But he was not definitely committed. They offered me a shot at the job.

When they asked me to audition, I began to worry. From my earliest days in broadcasting, I had never done well at auditions. Some combination of anxiety and poor luck. I didn't see why my luck should change now. Besides, I knew I wasn't right for *Concentration*. I wasn't the typical game-show type.

But I also knew I had never been right, in the conventional sense, for anything I had ever done throughout my career. For decades I had suffered from a state of mind I called the Ugly Duckling Syndrome. I always knew there was some other guy out there with a steelier voice and a punchier delivery who would get the job. Nine times out of ten I was right.

When I was a radio staff announcer in Chicago, *The Aldrich Family* was an enormously popular coast-to-coast radio drama. Dwight Weist was the announcer. The program was scheduled to come out of Chicago for a two-week period, and for some reason Weist couldn't make the trip. An announcement was

152

posted on the bulletin board at the NBC Central Division, inviting all NBC staff announcers to audition for this plum position.

The New York ad agency man came to the station on a Saturday. I got stuck on the El coming in to work. A few of the other staff announcers had seen the notice and shown up. But the agency man was furious when he found such a slim selection to choose from. When I finally turned up, late, the Chicago program director made something of a fuss, mainly to save face.

"You'll have nothing to worry about now," he said. "Here's young Hugh Downs. He's the best in the business."

I didn't figure on winning the thing anyway, so I read without my usual nervousness. When I finished reading, the agency man looked at me strangely.

"Can you be at the Eighth Street Theatre at six o'clock?"

"Sure," I said, utterly dumbfounded. "Why?"

"Because that's when rehearsals start."

It finally dawned on me that I had won this plum. But as pleased as I was, I thought it was a fluke. Looking back, it was probably for the best that I was never good at pitching used furs and plastic dashboard figurines. I never quite fitted the stereotype of pitchman or announcer. Nor was I a comic, an emcee, or an entertainer or newscaster. Having no discernible talent in any performance category, I never fell comfortably into any particular niche. The problem wasn't whether I could do the job; it was whether I could get the job in the first place.

It happened again when I tried out for host of *Concentration*. I read in my usual low-key delivery. I could see by Enright's reaction that I was clearly not right for the job. Poor Dan Enright had never seen such a cool audition. He was clearly not impressed.

"You've got to inject a note of *fun* into your voice," he insisted.

I tried to explain to him, as modestly as I could, my personal philosophy.

"If an element of fun comes up naturally while playing the game," I proposed, "I'll be happy to react to it. But I can't *tell* people to have fun. They'll just have to have it themselves."

I tried to explain that I was never good at auditions. I had to

153

get into the spirit of the thing when it was real, when it was happening. With an audience present and real contestants playing, I assured him I could have as much fun as Gene Rayburn or Bill Cullen. In my more high-spirited moments, I claimed, I might even approach the hysterical heights of a Monte Hall.

Enright looked doubtful. He obviously had his reservations about my style. But I was starting to make a name for myself on *The Tonight Show*, and a large part of that reputation rested on injecting a note of reality into my broadcasting. Though I was unaware of the problem at the time, Enright must have been thinking hard. To have one game show on the air in which reality reigned might not be such a bad idea. It might even look good for his troubled company. And at that time he knew how troubled it really was.

They decided to take a chance on me. I was even free to use my own delivery. But I didn't get my own way on a couple of other points. I wanted to dispense with the show-biz paraphernalia: the fanfare, the booming theatrical music, the flashing applause signs that are the trademark of most game shows. To be perfectly frank, all that magic and contrivance offended me. It distracted from the matter at hand, which was, after all, playing the game. Television had enough magic as it was, without adding more false reflections to the hall of mirrors.

But they were not prepared to go that far. They knew what formula had worked in the past, and saw no reason to change. The game itself, as good as it was, was just not good enough for them.

I had been a little flat during the tryouts, and I think I might have worried the producers at the premiere show. I was more subdued than they wanted. Actually, I was having trouble keeping all the game rules in my head, and had little time to be sparkling or witty. But somehow I got through it and gained confidence as we moved ahead. The show stayed on. And before long we were the number-one-rated daytime show.

Meanwhile, all the glamorous nighttime, prime-time, big-money quiz shows were dropping off the air. People had been dazzled by them, but when the rigging was exposed, it was like

Toto pulling the curtain away from the Wizard of Oz. Americans can be naive and gullible people, but they don't like to be tricked.

No one was dazzled by *Concentration*. It was just a fine game to play and a fun game to watch. Most of all, it was the *real* thing. Theatrics, dramatics, and histrionics were kept to an absolute minimum. Whatever emotion was displayed was genuine, not the result of coaching from behind the drawn curtain.

Most important, in that period of television fraud, our show had an underlying layer of trust. It was utterly rig-proof. We made sure of that. We also made sure that the show's integrity was well understood on all sides of the camera. Every morning the stagehands loaded the board in a restricted area which they couldn't leave until the show was over. And even if someone had been told a right answer, which was highly unlikely, it wouldn't have done much good. If a contestant blurted out an answer before racking up worthwhile prizes, he would go home with little to show for his trouble. If he waited until the rebus was nearly revealed, he took the chance of losing to the other side.

I myself never knew the answers until someone made a first guess. I had Norm Blumenthal give me a card with tape over the answers. When someone made a guess, I'd tear it off. "That's right!" I'd shout, and they'd win. Or, "That's wrong"—and the game would go on. Then the other side had a chance to guess. The guessing would go on back and forth until someone finally got it.

The structure and format of the game made *Concentration* virtually rig-proof, but the tainted atmosphere of the time made it imperative that we take no chances. NBC hired a former Scotland Yard detective to act as a security agent for the show. The network was so discreet that they wouldn't reveal the man's identity to any of us involved with the show. Meanwhile we had hired our own security agent. Before air time, one day, our security agent found the NBC Scotland Yard fellow snooping around backstage, near the off-limits area of the Big Board, and threw him out of the studio.

Despite our extraordinary precautions, I once thought we

had suffered a leak. It was during our first few months on the air, when a guest called out two numbers. They matched and turned to their puzzle sides. One box was blank, and the other showed a curved line at an odd angle. That was all. With hardly a moment's hesitation, the contestant shouted, "Brigitte Bardot!"

I couldn't believe my ears. Why would he have come up with a guess like that so early in the game? But when I tore the tape off the answer, I could hardly believe my eyes. In plain black and white, it read: BRIGITTE BARDOT.

My heart nearly stopped beating. I concentrated on not betraying to the audience that something might be amiss. Had we somehow fallen into the same fraudulent conspiracy that had destroyed the other game shows?

"Tha-a-a-t's right!" I shouted, trying to keep my tone as neutral as possible. I was sure something must have gone horribly wrong with the security backstage.

I decided to take a chance with my future. On the air, I asked him how he could possibly have made such a wild but accurate guess.

"I'm a structural engineer," he replied. "And I know what the catenary drag of the cable on a suspension bridge looks like. I took a wild guess that 'bridge' might be part of 'Brigitte Bardot.'"

I was relieved. Again, the show's leakproof structure had stood up. Unfortunately for this contestant he had made the correct guess so early that he hadn't racked up any worthwhile prizes.

When people called Concentration a quiz show, I would remind them that it was neither a quiz or a show. It was a game, more like a sports event than a memory test. It was real, just as an athletic contest was real.

When people asked me, "Is this show fixed?" I'd say, "No, it isn't even broken." In 1958 that seemed like a pretty clever riposte.

If they persisted in this line of questioning, I would ask them my own question: "How much do you think it would be worth for me to run a rigged program? A million dollars? Five million? Even if I was the worst mercenary in the world, it wouldn't be worth it."

I was obviously hoping to make more than that throughout a long career in broadcasting.

The rationale for fixing the quiz shows was that it was all show business anyway. People, so the saying went, want to be entertained. Van Doren had been told that by cheating, he would be furthering the cause of higher education. Besides, he had been assured, no one would ever know. And, of course, *everyone* on television does it.

Concentration stayed on the air with high ratings as proof that none of that had to be true. People were willing to be entertained and excited by the simple joy of playing the game or by the vicarious thrill of watching others play to win or lose. I enjoyed playing the game myself, when I got the chance. I played it twice against my announcer, Bob Clayton, for charities. Though I have a very good memory for some things, I wasn't very good at *Concentration:* Bob beat me both times. But there was no agony in defeat—I knew it had been fair and square.

Prime-time prize shows virtually vanished after the scandals. But with the success of *Concentration*, NBC began to ponder the profit potential of trying a nighttime version. In this business there is an old saying: stagehands hear everything first. One night a stagehand on *The Tonight Show* pulled me aside.

"There's going to be a nighttime *Concentration*," he said.

"No there isn't," I told him. Nobody had said anything to me about it.

The next morning I opened up *Variety*. Sure enough, NBC was contemplating a prime-time *Concentration*. And the article said they were planning to ask either Hal March or Milton Berle to be the emcee.

I fired a letter off to Robert Kintner, president of NBC.

"From a legal, profit, and ownership standpoint," I wrote,

"*Concentration* belongs to NBC. But from a moral, audience, and entertainment standpoint, *Concentration* belongs to me."

I concluded by noting that if they went ahead with the show as planned, I would not only quit daytime *Concentration*, but I would also leave *The Tonight Show*. With that petulant gesture of bravado, I was in a position to storm off into a mop closet. But a few days later they offered me the nighttime job. I accepted.

Several weeks later I was sorry I had made such a fuss. I had begun to feel a proprietary interest in *Concentration*, and the nighttime version was not shaping up as I had hoped. The problem was that NBC wouldn't leave well enough alone. To help us make the break into prime time, they imported a whole collection of show doctors from the West Coast to give the program some pizzaz.

Unfortunately for all of us, their concept of pizzaz did not exactly mesh with mine. Their suggestions for "improvements" were so ludicrous I was embarrassed even to hear them. For one grand prize, they wanted to offer a six-month supply of hamburger meat. The visual punchline to this strained gag was to be a live cow. The heifer would be brought right out on stage; chopped steak on the hoof. Apart from the problems with the ASPCA or Cleveland Amory, I didn't find the idea cute.

"Why don't we just haul out a hammer and some boning knives and butcher the cow right up there on the stage?" I asked. They didn't look horrified. I was never entirely sure that they didn't take me seriously.

Of course the opening title on our show was too dull for prime time, they said. One show doctor wanted to bring out a line of chorus girls with letters stuck to their fannies. When they all bowed away from the audience, in a line, it would spell out CONCENTRATION. Fortunately that idea was butchered early.

As a matter of personal policy, I tried to discourage the entire proscenium arch approach. *Concentration*, I explained, was a straightforward event, played out on a plain stage between the two chosen contestants. As far as I was concerned, nothing more was needed. I even tried to get them to dispense with the electric organ music and vibraharps, the indispensable trappings that spelled "game show."

I marveled that Norm Blumenthal, the original deviser of the rebuses and the producer at the time, didn't have a nervous breakdown. He knew what made the show work. The problem was that the new "conceptualizers" wouldn't listen. At first, the Los Angeles whiz kids wanted to throw out the puzzle format altogether. On that crucial point we succeeded in hanging firm.

They did win one major victory. They managed to "enhance" the Big Board. NBC spent a fortune on a new display that did everything but send out fireworks. It absolutely screamed "Prime time! Nighttime! Hollywood! Show Biz!" The new board came suitably outfitted with acres of flashing bright lights, loud colors, and all sorts of gimmicky accessories. Most of their wilder ideas died on the drawing board or were killed by me or the producer, but the new nighttime *Concentration* did end up with louder music, a faster format, and a generally higher volume.

Our nocturnal version ran only once in prime time, and was pulled by NBC. One thing was sure: nobody liked it. We didn't like it. It was too big and glitzy. The L.A. programming whizzes didn't like it. They were sure it was dull. Los Angeles blamed us for blocking their new plans. New York blamed L.A. for screwing things up.

One thing we would never have allowed was any change in our method of selecting contestants. Contestants are crucial to any game show. Since so much rides on their reactions to winning or losing, there is always a temptation to select people for their dramatic possibilities. I hear many game shows do that now, as a matter of course. But we did not.

The only applicants we screened out were those who flunked an extremely simple rebus test, on grounds that such a person would be an embarrassment to himself or herself, as well as the show. We also refused to allow anyone on who had been a participant on another prize show within the previous three months. After a while we stepped up that limit to three years. As game shows became more popular, a group of professional contestants started taking advantage of the easy pickings. After all, game shows offered far better odds than any other form of legalized gambling.

One woman, if not quite a professional player, lied about being on another show in the last ninety days. It turned out she had played, and won, on another show within the past few weeks. I didn't want to give her the car she had won, I felt, under false pretenses. But she threatened to sue, and NBC let her keep the car.

I was upset about that decision, seeing it as moral weakness on their part. I argued that to give her the car was as wrong as withholding a prize from someone who had rightfully won. She knew the rules when she lied about her past. But NBC buckled under on the pragmatic grounds that fighting a lawsuit would cost more than the car. I didn't threaten to quit or go public with my complaint, but it seemed vitally important to me that we stick by our rules at all costs. After all, it was a deviation from publicly accepted standards of conduct that nearly wrecked the whole field in the first place. I never felt right about that decision.

Unlike other game shows, we tried to be relatively modest about our prizes. At most, our grand prize would occasionally be worth $50,000. We also had a couple of inexpensive gag prizes in each game. On our premiere show, the first game was won by a contestant who had racked up only a wet noodle and a cup of coffee. One critic wrote, "It's a cinch *this* show isn't rigged. Who'd want to rig it?"

Our biggest prizes were typically cars, boats, furs, furniture, or jewelry. But the most exciting prize, for some reason, was always the car. In those days a compact car cost about $2000 or $3000. We gave away first-class around-the-world vacations, diamond necklaces, or sometimes rare furs worth many times the price of a car. But the wildest audience response, the buildup of tension, always took place whenever anyone won a car, even a compact. The automobile was still the standard fixture of the American Dream.

We didn't buy our prizes directly from the manufacturer. A number of independent companies act as brokers for prizes on game shows. They calculate the worth of the commercial exposure of having a particular item as a prize on the show. Then they approach potential suppliers and work out a deal between the supplier and the show. The price is discounted to account for the promotional value. Smaller prizes are often acquired for nothing. Larger prizes, in the boat or car category, might have cost us wholesale price, if that.

But let the player beware. Contestants were taxed by the IRS for the full retail value of the prize. Some of them resented this. They felt that if they won, they shouldn't have to pay tax on the proceeds. A few contestants even boldly suggested that we should be paying it for them. But we couldn't have done this, even if we had wanted to. The IRS takes a very strict position on that. If we had offered to pay the tax bite, the IRS would simply have counted that additional amount as extra income for the contestant, and the contestant would have paid tax on *that*. We settled the question as every other prize show did. We simply handed out the prizes and let the winner handle the IRS payments. After all, it wasn't as if they were losing out in the end.

There was one particular grand prize I'll never forget. That day, the big booty was a boat called an Aqua-Patio. It came with two large steel tank floats, a large deck, and a little awning on posts. Powered by a small outboard motor, it was suitable for cruising inland waterways and other calm surfaces.

Before the grand prize was revealed, my announcer, Bob Clayton, would give a glowing description of whatever object the contestant had just won. For the Aqua-Patio, we had a line of copy which read, "For hours of pleasure cruising." Bob hardly ever fluffed a line, but when he did, it was an extraordinary blooper. When it came time for his description of the Aqua-Patio, Bob intoned the copy and ended it with, "For hours of pleasure screwing." I still have a tape of that at home.

I had my own share of bloopers. We had been on the air only

a couple of months when the doors flew open and a stunning contestant stood there before us. She was a housewife, not an actress, but she was real movie star material. Her card indicated that she had been married eight years and had a nine-year-old child.

Innocently, I twitted her about what I thought was a typo. But she just shrugged matter-of-factly and said, "Yes, well, I had to get married." The audience tittered, but I decided I'd better not kick that ball around anymore. So I fell back, without thinking, on my legal obligation to establish that all the contestants understood the basic rules of the game.

"Well," I said, "I guess you know how the game is played."

At that point the audience absolutely caught fire. This was all live, and broadcast at a time when remarks like that were rare on the air. But she stayed extremely poised through it all and laughed along with everyone else.

Dick Auerbach, our floor director, was the only man I've ever met who knew how to hum dirty. If he spotted a particularly good-looking contestant, he would invariably drift behind me and start humming to himself, eyebrows raised, in a lyrical leer. It's hard to describe, but if you ever heard it, you instantly knew what it was. It was a lecherous hum, intended to proclaim not his own lechery, but some imagined lechery of mine.

One morning the sliding doors opened and another absolute knockout walked out onstage. The camera focused directly on her. I was standing off to one side. From there, I could clearly see Auerbach, standing behind her but out of camera range. He was holding up a cue card on which musical notes had been written, with the letters *h-m-m* written beneath. I stared at the card, wondering what it could possibly mean, when suddenly it struck me like a gong. It was Auerbach's visual version of his dirtiest hum! I couldn't help but burst out laughing. After the show, Norm Blumenthal, our producer, asked me what had been so funny. I found the joke a little hard to explain.

Though it was not easy to get rich as a *Concentration* contestant, our prize bank was nearly broken by a baseball player, Ralph Branca. He was probably the best Concentration player in world history. He won twenty-one games in a row, and took home multiple cars, furs, jewelry. As his victories mounted, the studio audience became curiously split between those rooting for him and those who didn't like the idea of someone winning so much.

Under the rules, Branca could stay on as long as he remained undefeated. After Branca, we fell under a certain amount of pressure to set a limit on the number of games a single contestant could win. But we never changed our rules. I strongly opposed the idea of a limit, on the grounds that if that was how the game was always played, maintaining consistency was the best way to establish trust. After all, how often did a Ralph Branca come along? The answer: just once in nine years.

I wanted to host *Concentration* for ten years, which would bring me to the end of 1968. After I left, I wanted Bob Clayton, my long-time announcer, to succeed me. He had done the show frequently in my absence, and he was the only person who ever did it the way I wanted the show to be done. (And the only substitute who kept the ratings up.) Bob was an old friend, and he loved *Concentration.* NBC wanted Ed McMahon instead.

When it finally came time for me to say goodbye, NBC asked me to stay on for another few months. I agreed to extend my contract for eight more weeks. In return for that favor, I asked that Bob get the job as host. They agreed.

I did what they asked, and they seemed to be doing what I asked. When I left in January 1969, Bob immediately got the job as host. But four weeks later they simply fired him, without explanation, and brought in McMahon. I felt betrayed. The show was holding up under the transition. It hadn't sagged in the ratings. But it was clear that NBC had intended to use McMahon all along, and had apparently abused my good faith to squeeze another couple of months out of me.

I tried to raise some hell at the network, but at that point I had no more leverage. I did have the satisfaction, several weeks later, of getting a call from NBC in the Virgin Islands, where I had gone on vacation. They wanted to know if I knew how to get hold of Bob Clayton. When I told them, I hoped there was no hint of smugness in my voice.

Ed McMahon is an excellent broadcaster, and he does many things well, but hosting *Concentration* required a style the audience had become accustomed to. Bob and I were the only ones they seemed to accept. The ratings had slumped drastically and the company was ready to make a change.

Bob stayed on as host of *Concentration* for four years, until the show was finally canceled. The fourteen-year-run was close to a record for a game show, beaten only by *Hollywood Squares.* Today, I constantly run into people who stop me in the street, in stores, on planes, on boats, in hallways.

"You probably don't remember me," they'll say. More often than not, they are right. "I was a contestant on *Concentration.*"

Then I take a closer look. Even after all the years, I do occasionally remember a face. And I always ask the same question: "Did you win?"

If they did, they tell me about the boat, the car, the fur coat, the jewelry, and what it meant to them. If they lost, they remember the consolation Polaroid camera and say, "Well, I had a good time anyway."

I can say the same thing. As host of the most-trusted game show on television, I can honestly say it didn't matter so much whether anyone won or lost. It was, as they say, how we played the game.

7

THE HIATUS

For nearly fifteen years I had experienced maximum pressure on camera. By the time Sid Caesar finally dropped off the air in 1957, I was already busy with *The Tonight Show*. By the time Jack Paar retired from television five years later, I was hosting *Concentration* and about ready to start work on *Today*. Then, after nine intense years of hosting *Today* early every morning, I was prepared to let it all go.

On October 11, 1971, I formally handed over my post to my successor, Frank McGee. They gave me a portrait of myself in oils, in lieu, I suppose, of a gold watch. I was, after all, severing not only a nine-year relationship with *Today*, but a relationship with NBC stretching back over three decades.

This was to be my farewell show, but I managed to keep outpourings of nostalgia to a minimum. Somehow, effusive sentiment seemed inappropriate. I was leaving entirely of my own accord, and making no bones about my desire to escape the pressures of regular broadcasting.

By then I had racked up more hours on camera than anyone else in the medium. As I've said, it's all formally recorded in *The Guinness Book of World Records*. My closest competitor is Johnny Carson, with some 7000 hours, but it would take him another fifteen to twenty years on *The Tonight Show* to catch up. I'm not worried. Part of this longevity can be ascribed, I am convinced, to my propensity for changing paths—not getting stuck in one slot.

I never enjoyed running on only one track. I kept doing *Caesar's Hour* when I started *The Tonight Show*. I stayed with *Tonight* when I started *Concentration*. I kept doing *Concentration* when I started *Today*. And after leaving *Concentration*, I did seven NBC specials while hosting *Today*.

My decision to leave *Today* after nine years seemed just one more in a string of difficult choices. Hard to make in the short run, but beneficial over the long term. As much as I had enjoyed hosting *Today*, the hours sometimes made it feel like a debilitating disease from which it might take years to recover.

Now I had to see if there was life after *Today*. Whatever happened, I would be deprived of the amplified voice I had grown so used to over the years. There is a subtle but immense power that visibility in the world's most powerful medium gives to you. I had enjoyed its benefits for so long I could hardly imagine life without it. But I had taken a comparable leap two decades before, when I left the security of an NBC staff position for the free-for-all of New York television. I had survived that transition, and eventually prospered. Heading into my new life, I could only hope I would make as good an adjustment.

As soon as I finished that last *Today* broadcast, Ruth and I hopped in a car and drove to Arizona. It took us three and a half days. This was what we had been waiting for all those years. After three decades of life in big cities, we were finally heading for home.

For years, Ruth and I had been searching the globe for a place to put down roots. Both of us had been born in the Midwest, but had lost any connections with the area long ago. Neither of us are urban animals by nature, but we had lived most of our adult lives in big cities, first in Chicago, then in New York. Whether one admits it or not, that is an experience which leaves an indelible impression. Fulfilling Thomas Wolfe's famous title, "You Can't Go Home Again," neither of us was willing to try the Midwest. We ended up wandering the world when we could, enjoying the carefree traveler's life, but always with an eye out for a place to settle down.

We looked everywhere, from Tahiti to Portugal. We were strongly drawn to both these places, but never found the right spot. We knew we would know it when we came to it, but we were occasionally fooled by initial impressions.

We fell in love with Portugal at first sight. It is a beautiful country, utterly unspoiled but still thoroughly European. You can still live well there on very little money, something to be considered when contemplating an early retirement. But in 1971 Portugal was still a military dictatorship, even if a relatively benign one. It was also a very poor country just beginning the painful process of modernization. Portugal turned out to be a fine place to visit, but we really didn't want to live there.

We also fell in love with Tahiti. Having spent a few idyllic weeks there at the conclusion of my Pacific sailing voyage, we seriously thought about establishing a more permanent base on the island. But we finally decided that the island mentality, that sense of confinement peculiar to all isolated landmasses, would eventually drive us to drink. After such restless roaming, we found ourselves no closer to our destination. We felt a bit like lovers who, after a string of infatuations, long for the fullness of a more permanent relationship.

We finally came to the not-very-original conclusion that there is no place like home. We decided on America, but wanted a place we didn't know well. In 1967 a business organization based in Phoenix asked me to speak at their annual gathering. Ruth and I flew down to Arizona and drove around the surrounding countryside. We both were struck by the same thought. This might be the place.

We had no desire to live right in Phoenix. As cities go, Phoenix is perfectly pleasant, but we weren't about to abandon one city just to live in another. We wanted to be relatively isolated, but with proximity to the resources and services of a large metropolitan area.

Out from Phoenix in a radius as far as Wickenburg is some of the finest land either of us had ever seen. Around Cave Creek we found a generous section of rugged, utterly unspoiled territory, adjacent to the Tonto National Forest, which includes the Mazatzal Mountains, an enormous Designated Wilderness. The area can be entered only on foot or on horseback. Next to Cave Creek is a place called Carefree. It was here we bought a piece of land, drew up some plans, and before long started to build.

The main house sits nestled in the brow of a mild hill. A separate guesthouse lies down by the road. From the main house, you can see sixty miles clear across the Phoenix Valley. As night falls, beads of light string across the sprawling northern suburbs of the city. Our view of the valley from fifteen hundred feet up is equaled, in my opinion, only by the panorama of Port Royal, Jamaica, from the heights of Kingston, and the grand sweep of the French Riviera from Mougins. What makes the view so unique is not only what you see, but what you see it *through*. The clarity and quality of the light and air in Arizona is absolutely breathtaking.

As climates go, I've never found anything quite like Zone 12 Desert. That is the technical term describing the ecology of the area. The landscape is not like the Gobi or the Sahara. Still, it is a dramatic desert, punctuated by giant Saguaro cacti, strawberry hedgehog and prickly pear, octillo, and other exotic vegetation of that arid terrain. The plant life tends toward the thorny, the most effective survival mechanism in such an environment. At the same time, the vegetation is sparse and uncrowded. You can walk through all that bramble and not get scratched once. The plants seem polite, giving you plenty of space to navigate a safe course.

For us, adapting to life in Arizona was no problem. Geographically, we were conveniently located. We had a grandchild in New Mexico, a brother in Texas, another in California. When my father came out and happily lived out his last decade in Arizona, I felt as if I'd finally come home. To symbolize this sense of connection, for several years I kept a cactus in my apartment in New York. I watered it only when the weatherman said it was raining in Arizona. Which meant of course that I hardly watered the poor plant at all. Like the desert plants we grew to love and admire so much for their tenacity, we quickly sank roots in Arizona that were, if not remarkably deep, unusually wide.

As a social environment, Carefree is not easily categorized. Unlike some comparably attractive areas back East, it does not represent any narrow slice of society. Expensive and humble homes can be found on the same road, with no particular sense of social or economic hierarchy. There are some political dinosaurs still in the area who think Barry Goldwater is pinko, but also a good number of people who could only be described as progressive. There are many retired people, but it is far from a geriatric ghetto. (Retirement communities of exclusively older people might be fine for some folks, but I never liked the idea of living in one.) In any case, I hardly felt ready to retire at fifty. I felt more like I was starting to live.

I was not planning a permanent vacation, just a more leisurely life. I didn't want to quit working, I just wanted to work when I wanted, where I wanted, on what I wanted. I was, in short, not forcing myself into early retirement so much as achieving an occupational change of rhythm. I expected to keep working on television, doing special projects, commercials, occasional shows, but I was also looking forward to pursuing other interests including writing, teaching, lecturing, and private consulting in communications.

I had already committed some of my time to a number of nonprofit organizations, including the National Space Institute, UNICEF, and the Center for the Study of Democratic Institutions, founded by Robert Hutchins, former president of the University of Chicago. As a consultant to that organization, I conducted two symposia at their headquarters in Santa Barbara, one on the subject of aging, the other based on an article I wrote for the center's magazine on the resources of space.

My commitment to space exploration had taken off gradually over the years, like a very slow rocket. In 1955, two years before Sputnik, I narrated and reported NBC's first documentary on space exploration, *The First Step Into Space*. Produced by Reuven Frank, later head of NBC News, it featured Dr. Heinz

Haber and some of the early rocket men, discussing and debating the future of the embryonic U.S. space program.

Dr. Nathan Kaplan, head of the National Academy of Sciences, was working on coordinating space projects for our government. In that pre-NASA era, the Air Force was working on the Titan rocket, the Navy on the Vanguard program, and the Army on its Redstone project, all at cross-purposes. Each was being run in total secrecy from the others, and with duplicative budgets. The formation of NASA under Dr. Wernher von Braun was initiated largely in response to this problem of waste of resources—out of a desire to put our space program under a civilian umbrella.

Wernher von Braun was a brilliant scientist. During the war he was effectively trapped at Peenemünde and ordered by Hitler to improve on the V-1 rocket, at that time blitzing London. He developed the V-2, which was markedly inferior as a weapon, but a very good rocket. For his pains, he was arrested by Himmler and held for ten days under sentence of death for sabotaging the German rocket program. The Nazis had ordered him to destroy London, but Wernher was trying to fly to the moon.

As the Allies advanced on his position, he and all but one of his colleagues sought American protection, for fear of Russian capture. Von Braun entered the United States by streetcar from Mexico to apply for United States citizenship. At the Redstone Arsenal at Huntsville, Alabama, his devotion to space research contributed enormously to our catching up with and surpassing Soviet space activity.

Prior to the Soviets' launching of Sputnik, President Eisenhower had declared 1957–1958 the International Geophysical Year. Then Sputnik took our country by surprise, at a time when most Americans were convinced the Russians didn't know how to drive a tractor. The IGY program stimulated enormous interest in Arctic and Antarctic research. It also gave our fledgling space program an additional push toward mapping and studying the earth from the vantage point of space. The idea, of course, was for the effort to be truly international, but the Eisenhower administration clearly hoped that it might give the U.S. the leading edge in this strategic area.

That year I became NBC's supervisor of science programming, which, unfortunately, wasn't much more than a title. But it gave me access to important centers of space exploration in this country. During that time I attended graduate courses at Columbia University, studying astrophysics under Lloyd Motz. When the IGY ended, my post was abolished and science programming went back under the News Division of the network. But I never lost my interest in space travel and science in general.

Toward the end of his life, von Braun founded the National Space Institute to foster a wider public interest in the scientific benefits of space exploration. He invited me onto the board. When I left *Today*, Wernher was already ill with the cancer which would eventually kill him. Somehow I had wound up becoming vice president, and when Wernher finally became too sick to work, he asked me to take over as president. At first I protested on the grounds that they needed a space expert for the job. But Wernher said Dr. Jim Fletcher, former (and present) administrator of NASA, would be willing to become vice president. He felt that the president should be a communications person, not a space person. So I accepted the post and traveled the country delivering lectures designed to stimulate interest in scientific investigation of the world beyond our world.

In the meantime I taught a course in communications at Arizona State University. And I worked on a couple of books, a collection of science fiction and science articles entitled *Rings Around Tomorrow*, and a work on emotional maturity called *Potential*. With all these interests and activities, I had little time to miss being on television, or being a media personality. If it was recognition I needed, I had enough. If it was money, I had enough. And if it was fame, I didn't need more of that than I already had. I was doing what I wanted to be doing, and was content with my lot.

Occasionally I was reminded that the broadcast industry was

not beating a path to my door. I did a number of educational projects, special reports, guest shots, and commercials, but it wasn't as if my phone were ringing off the hook. There was no flood of offers to fly out to New York or Los Angeles to host the latest prime-time network special. The mass-media work was obviously going to those who were still in the swing of things.

When a lecture agent suggested that I should lower my speaking fee, since I was no longer a big network star, that rankled. I felt I was doing as good a job at public speaking as I ever had, perhaps better, but this agent made it clear that on his circuit, fame is the only hot commodity, not what you say from the podium.

I knew he was right but for my injured pride, I decided to let my fee stand. And during those years I was out of the spotlight, I never detected any drop in opportunities to speak. Apparently the public had not yet forgotten me.

In 1972 I was asked to become the national spokesman for the Ford Motor Company. I had no problem doing it. The money was good, and Ford went to considerable lengths to demonstrate to me that the product was good, and that they were putting pride of craftsmanship back into the assembly line. I've always believed that in a free society there is nothing wrong with telling people—on a commercial basis—about a product, as long as they have the freedom to go back to Brand X, or ignore the message, or buy the product. And as long as the message itself is not misleading.

After I accepted the Ford job, an executive at J. Walter Thompson, Ford's advertising agency, told me a story I found disturbing. I had not been Ford's first choice. They had originally hired Frank McGee, my replacement on *Today*. Frank had thought he could do free-lance commercials, but when NBC advised him of the exclusivity of his contract, Ford was left without a spokesman. I learned later on that when the advertising people were agonizing, on deadline, about a replacement for a new Ford campaign, one of them suddenly said, "How about Hugh Downs?" Another said, "Why we didn't think of him in the first place?"

172

That was my problem. They were no longer thinking of me in the first place. When you're out on the sidelines—in my case, the desert—minding your own business, people are going to leave you alone. Unless, of course, you get lucky.

In late 1975 I got a call from an old friend. Producer Jules Power and I had known each other since the Chicago days. Back in 1952, we started work on an NBC geriatric-medical special called *How Long Can You Live?* It turned out to be one of the most rewarding projects either of us had ever worked on. We were only thirty-one at the time, but the program sparked an interest in aging which grew stronger as we ourselves grew older.

Now, over twenty years later, Jules wanted to know if I might be interested in hosting a series about aging in America for the Public Broadcasting System. KQED, the PBS affiliate in San Francisco, had originally conceived the idea and sold it to the Department of Health, Education, and Welfare. HEW had agreed to provide a grant of $4,000,000 to underwrite thirty-nine weeks of half-hour shows, five days a week.

KQED had hired Jules to produce the series. Jules wanted me to host it. I knew it would be a massive undertaking, but it struck me immediately as something I ought to do. The subject intrigued me, it was for PBS, and though the pay would be a fraction of my old network income, I was more than happy to oblige if the project was right. I believed in noncommercial broadcasting, but I had never gotten a chance to try it. And I felt that a series on the subject of aging could be successful on a noncommercial basis.

I must admit I was somewhat dismayed at their commitment to the five-show-per-week format. But I figured that there might be some way to avoid spending all my time in San Francisco. I hated to leave Arizona.

It would have been more convenient, for me at least, to shoot the show out in Phoenix. A network could have done it just as easily there, or in Miami or Salt Lake City, as in San Francisco. But PBS is not a centralized network. It is a consortium of affiliated independent stations. Nearly all the stations in the system create their own original programming, which is then offered to the other stations. PBS has a number of wonderful stations: WNET in New York, WGBH in Boston, KCET in Los Angeles, and KAET in Phoenix. The series was conceived and created by the people at KQED; thus it belonged in San Francisco.

I knew if I accepted Jules's offer I would be effectively shattering my dream of staying in the desert and returning to television for an occasional special or documentary. In fact, without really understanding the implications of this move, I was paving the way for a gradual return to full-time broadcasting. *Over Easy* was not on the scale of a commercial network production, but it was regularly scheduled.

I accepted the job under the assumption that I could fly up to San Francisco once a week for a day or two and spend the rest of my time at home in Carefree. From my experience on network daytime shows, I knew it was possible to do two and three shows in one day, sometimes as many as five. I thought the same would hold true with *Over Easy*. I was wrong.

I was assuming a level of network professionalism that just wasn't there. Jules Power, with years of network experience, demanded production values corresponding to that level. But despite the enthusiasm of the KQED staff, bringing *Over Easy* up to network standards took time and effort. We took three full days, in fact, just to tape our first show.

"At this rate," I told Jules glumly, "It'll take ten years just to wrap up one season."

Jules assured me things would improve. Gradually, they did. The show finally pulled together enough to allow us to shoot more than one show in a day. But we never laid down a routine that would have permitted squeezing a week of shows into one day. Ruth and I had to move to San Francisco. The house in Carefree, rather than remaining our permanent residence, became a vacation retreat once again. The show put a crimp in our life-style, but the satisfactions it brought were worth the trouble.

Over Easy quickly grew from a show that critics derided as a one-month concept into a highly respected program. We could have gone on for a hundred years without scratching the surface of the subject of aging. At the close of our first season, we had 273 stations in our lineup, including one or two commercial outlets. If a PBS station didn't have room for us, the program could be offered to a commercial station. Before long, *The MacNeil/Lehrer Report* was the number-one PBS program, we were number two, and Dick Cavett was number three. Given the specialized service-oriented material we were providing, the high ratings were enormously gratifying.

The original grant of $4,000,000 funded our first forty weeks. But KQED had to refurbish studios, expand space to produce the show, and incur considerable start-up expenses. Our actual production budget was far from lavish. Still, the government sent out a crew of watchdogs to make sure, among other things, that none of our expense accounts included alcohol or tips. In principle, I had no problem with the rule. I didn't think that we should be tipping or tippling on taxpayers' money. But it was a little irksome knowing that the costs of sending those agents out to check up on us far exceeded any petty drink tab. We tried to figure out how much tipping we could have done using *their* expense accounts.

Over Easy ran for four successful seasons, in spite of losing our HEW funding after the second season. Our forty-week season was cut back to twenty-six. This had nothing to do with the quality of the product or the size of our audience. It had everything to do with the vagaries of the federal funding process.

The June 1978 Nielsen ratings estimated our national viewership at over 2,300,000 households, watching at least once a week. In our second season, our HEW grant was cut back to $2,300,000, or one dollar per household reached. We thought that was a tight budget on which to keep the public informed about issues affecting a fast-growing segment of the population. Finally, we lost all HEW money and got our funding from the stations, foundations, and large corporations.

Robert Benedict, the young commissioner on aging, didn't approve of our inspirational material depicting those who had been successful at aging. He wanted us to focus more on the problems of the elderly. But the whole subject is infinitely more complex than a simple portrait of disease and impairment. Focusing on these problems perpetuates the agist attitudes that make things unfair for our older population.

HEW displayed a self-serving attitude. Since they had put up the money, they demanded that we focus on what they wanted us to show. They didn't mind upbeat material as long as it featured specific services such as the kneeling buses they were trying to provide. Anything else of a positive nature was considered irrelevant. This raised an irksome question: was HEW putting up grant money so its services could be advertised and promoted on television?

Our conflict with Benedict came to a head when we scheduled a segment on teenage pregnancy and HEW protested. What had teenagers' sex problems to do with the elderly? they wanted to know.

Everything, we responded. Old people have grandchildren, and issues like that are close and real for them. But this reasoning proved to be too much for the federal government and we lost our funding.

The government wanted us to focus on stereotyped, and often false, images of the aged. In fact, less than 5 percent of the aged ever become senile. Out of the 27,000,000 Americans over sixty-five, only 5 percent will live in nursing homes. Only about 12 percent live below the poverty line. The vast majority of older people live fulfilling lives and are interested in people around them—including their grandchildren.

Neither did we want the show to be aimed solely at an older audience. We wanted to help shape a new ethic concerning aging. You can't create a new ethic by preaching to the choir. We wanted people of all ages to understand the issues of aging in this country. Much to our satisfaction, we found ourselves reaching a significant number of viewers in the eighteen-to-thirty age group, those who will eventually change fundamental attitudes toward older citizens if anyone will.

There is nothing wrong with being old or growing old. But there is always something wrong with being lonely, broke, sick, and discriminated against. It can happen at any age, but it is more common among the aged, and probably more distressing. When you are young and faced with those conditions, you at least have time to change that situation. When you're eighty, to be ill and neglected and gouged can be a real tragedy.

I came to the reluctant conclusion that my generation has caused many problems for my parents' generation. We were the ones who tried to deny the problem, shunting our older citizens off into nursing homes and forgetting about them. There was once a greater tendency to keep the older generation in the home. With the advent of the automobile that ethic changed. The technological revolution that was supposed to bring people together actually forced us apart.

We faced these problems on the air with the help of medical experts, social scientists, gerontologists, and dieticians, but to demonstrate that aging has a positive side, we also had many successful elderly persons as guests. We did features involving older people with second occupations, or artists, writers, and others who had something unique to say. And there were quite a few younger guests as well. Chevy Chase and Tom Smothers, for instance, talked about their grandparents, about their views of the world, and about their own inevitable growth. That always means growing older, even in our youth-oriented society, where this reality is often ignored.

We spoke with many vital older people. The Dalai Lama, spiritual leader of millions of Tibetan Buddhists, came on during our 1979 season. A man of enormous conviction, he spoke eloquently of his dream of revisiting his ancient kingdom of Tibet, from which the Chinese Communists had exiled him. He was one of the most powerful older men I have ever met.

Lowell Thomas, one of the most successful broadcasters in history, was another distinguished guest. A man who started broadcasting when the now-retired Eric Sevareid was only thirteen, Thomas had been with Allenby and Lawrence in Arabia. His career spanned decades of tumultuous history, most of which he covered himself. Still hale and hardy at eighty-six, he was a living model of how everyone would like to age.

On one memorable show, we had four generations of my family come on together. My father, myself, my son, and my grandson.

I asked each of them a simple question: what is the most important thing in life? I got thoughtful, even scholarly answers from my father and my son. But my grandson had a more straightforward response: "Eating," he said. His answer was probably as profound as the others.

In the end, *Over Easy* gave me a new perspective on an area I had never known: noncommercial broadcasting. Public television has had a hard time in this country. In Japan the NHK does beautiful programming on generous budgets. And they needn't beg the government for money, or solicit corporate underwriting, or endlessly plead for funding on the air. In Japan, every new television set carries a $15.00 value-added tax which goes to support public programming. England has a similar system. But one can imagine the forces that would rally against any such measure in this country. The networks, the set manufacturers, even the advertisers, would be up in arms.

Meanwhile, PBS has seen its government funding steadily cut back ever since the Nixon administration. For all its evident shortcomings, the ability of PBS to produce shows like *Over Easy* is a sign of its considerable dedication to the common good.

In May 1981 I had the honor of accepting an Emmy Award on behalf of myself and the program. The show also provided valuable material for a book, *30 Dirty Lies About the Old*, debunking a number of myths about aging, and *The Best Years Book*, a manual on late-years planning, which I wrote with Richard Roll.

I had been hosting *Over Easy* for only eighteen months when Roone Arledge asked me to join *20/20*. It was a conflict. I wanted to host *20/20*, but I told ABC I couldn't go back on my commitment to *Over Easy*. So for many months I commuted between coasts, spending half the week in San Francisco and the other half in New York.

Eventually, I brought my old friend Frank Blair from *The Today Show* onto *Over Easy* as host, maintaining a daily presence of my own with commentary and public service material, occasionally by remote from New York, while Frank handled the show from San Francisco. That made my obligation to both shows somewhat easier, but it eventually became an insane situation.

For what seemed like an interminable period, I spent eleven hours a week flying between New York and San Francisco—passing over my house in Arizona. Every Thursday night I would do *20/20* in New York. The studio stays "hot" until eleven that night in anticipation of any late-breaking news, which keeps us there until the show is over.

Then early Friday morning, I'd hop a plane and arrive in San Francisco by noon. We would do one segment of *Over Easy* on Friday, two on Saturday, and two more on Sunday. It would take all day Monday for me to get back to New York. I would spend Tuesday and Wednesday preparing for *20/20*, before starting this manic round-robin all over again. Only on rare occasions would we get to Arizona for a few days.

At one point we were maintaining so many different residences, I'd get up in the middle of the night for a drink of water and walk right into a wall. Fortunately, it didn't last too long. After a year of working *Over Easy* with Frank, I bowed out and Mary Martin and Jim Hartz took over the show for the next few seasons. I had loved the show, but I couldn't help but feel some sense of relief. I knew I had to concentrate my full efforts on *20/20*. ABC News's answer to *60 Minutes* was hoping to come into its own.

8
20/20

It has been eight years now since I started out as host on *20/20*. The show has carved a fine niche for itself in prime-time television. But on Monday, June 12, 1978, when I reported for work at ABC for the first time, I felt like the first mate on the *Lusitania*.

I didn't know quite what to expect. The premiere show had received such bad notices that there was no time for the usual shakedown process. Drastic changes had to be made before the second show went out on the network feed the next night. That was less than forty-eight hours away. I found myself suddenly drawn into a flurry of activity, working with a staff desperately trying to put together a new show along lines being laid down by news chief Roone Arledge.

Arledge had been keeping his hands off the production. Reacting to earlier criticism that he was wearing too many hats as head of both ABC News and Sports, and that his capacity for detail had kept him from delegating authority, he had refrained from any production work in building the premiere of *20/20*. But that all changed when he was handed a cassette of the first installment only hours before it was scheduled to air. After seeing the material, he caromed off the ceiling. He slashed and scrambled the premiere so severely that some staffers found the end product unrecognizable. He took the show off in directions he didn't have time to carry all the way through. He had brought himself in too late to change the downhill course of its disastrous opening.

But in the wake of the fiasco, Arledge conducted himself with statesmanlike cool. He told his secretary to clip out and throw away all reviews from the next day's newspapers. He didn't need a lot of sniping critics to tell him what was wrong.

At the same time he made no bones about his negative response. To one reporter he bluntly admitted, "The show was terrible. I hated it." There was something almost Churchillian about his resolve to take his lumps. He was determined to straighten out the mess and was willing to take sweeping steps to shorten the disaster period.

After the second show, he and I met at the bar of the Regency Hotel. We talked about what might be needed to help the program get off the ground. I had the impression he was hoping for something sensational, searching for some story that would immediately put the show in a high-wattage national spotlight. He seemed eager to do something that would cause people across the country to say to each other, "You've *got* to see 20/20."

We would have loved to accommodate him, but it was unlikely we could build a program by that route, at least a program that would last. Instead, we have done it by a slow, steady accumulation of core loyalty and an improved programming process. If we ended up taking the more plodding course, I think we gained something more substantial in the end. A rule of media physics might be that most objects of public attention that go up fast have a tendency to come down at about the same rate.

Roone had a strong influence on our early development. He was so traumatized by the opening that he couldn't help hovering over the proceedings. As one producer later remarked, "After promising to stay clear, he swung down out of the trees like King Kong, smashing bananas in people's faces." Arledge insisted on reviewing a tape of every segment before it went out on the air.

For a time we were, in effect, taping two programs, one on Wednesday—which Roone often didn't like—and one on Thursday. (We had moved time slots from Tuesday to Thursday.) I felt compelled to point out that I had been hired to do one program, not two. When Arledge brought in Av Westin as executive producer straight from *The Nightly News,* the show started to pull together, and the strain gradually eased. Thanks to Westin, the program began to inspire enough confidence that we went to a single studio day, eliminating wasteful expense while building a backlog of features.

Westin knew that *20/20* needed more focus and direction. That's not easy to do with a magazine program. A magazine lives off an endlessly recycled sense of variety. You bring a focus to a varied menu like ours by establishing a magical mix of subjects.

We were going up against the other networks' biggest guns, not the pallid competition *60 Minutes* faced on Sunday evenings. We needed something dignified but not stuffy, entertaining but not "entertainment," informative but not "educational." We had a tough balance to strike. If we did it, we would hit our intended jackpot: a fair share of the night's viewers on prime-time television, something a broadcast news magazine had never done.

After six years of struggle, trial, and error, our competitor, *60 Minutes,* achieved its own magic mix. That success was earned only after a timely move out of its initial overcompetitive time slot into the relative solitude of Sunday night. That transfer had been CBS's way of discarding a floundering show to the Sunday "ghetto" without killing it off altogether. But *60 Minutes* outlived the insult. It slowly gained a locomotive momentum in that low-pressure environment.

Av Westin ascribes much of *60 Minutes'* appeal to what he calls a "Sunday-go-to-meeting mood of absolution." People who feel guilty about not going to church, or not absorbing any culture, or concerning themselves with important thoughts, can redeem themselves at the end of the Sabbath by watching *60 Minutes.*

But we didn't have the advantage of that Sunday mood. Our first hurdle was to adapt the news-magazine format to the demands and values of prime time. We were up against the highly rated lust-and-blood entertainment programs on the air in our time slot—*Knot's Landing* and *Hill Street Blues.* *20/20* was airing in a time when most viewers preferred fantasy and escape rather than the reality we had to offer.

There are opinion surveys that supposedly help producers deal with such challenges. There is much nonsense in these surveys, but they can sometimes show a general outline of viewer preferences. ABC commissioned a few of them. They told us the obvious: rock stars, as a class, are about the most popular people on earth. For a while we profiled just about every teen idol able to fill Madison Square Garden on a Saturday night. Earlier, because Roone Arledge's programming background had been in sports, we had looked like a video *Sports Illustrated.*

During our heavy rock-star phase, we did an obligatory segment on Kiss, a musically thin group popular with nine-year-olds. The producers created a vivid picture of what the group was all about. The masks and the makeup, the spouting blood, the smashing guitars, the gleeful theatrical arson.

When Roone got around to screening the piece, he thought it was all right. He had only one question: "Why don't you go with one of their actual numbers instead of dubbing in that long tonic chord just sort of banging around in there?" To his amazement the producers explained that that *was* the actual number.

This didn't put a stop to our frequent forays into popular music. It was valuable at the time. We picked up a special audience segment, and still do an occasional feature on worthwhile personalities and groups.

I had been brought in to help set a certain tone, deliberately different from the disjointed banter of the first *20/20.* "Hugh Downs knows how to lead into a news story" was how Arledge put it to the press. Though I found the report complimentary, it alarmed me for some reason. I didn't want him to think that was all I could do.

Our current executive producer, Av Westin, defines my basic function as "bringing an audience with zero knowledge and zero interest up to a plateau where the story can begin to be told." This is a good description of news anchoring. Being an anchor, as *60 Minutes* producer Don Hewitt once said, has nothing to do with boats—even if a roving local reporter who acts as an anchor is absurdly dubbed a floating anchor. The term anchor really referred to a relay race in which the anchor leg is the strongest runner.

The borrowed term provides only a loose analogy. On *20/20*, I have people around me who are superior to me in various skills, such as investigative reporting, biography, and consumer issues. Even though I function as a correspondent on features dealing with health, science, the emotions, and adventure, my main job is to provide the mortar between the bricks of material, to give a varied feature program some element of continuity. I like to think of myself as a representative of the viewer, on the other side of the tube.

I've been described as cool in a hot medium. From the days with Jack Paar on *The Tonight Show* to my decade-long stint as host of *Today*, my job has always been to supply a stable center around which fiery segments can spin. Hot stories, hot correspondents, can benefit from being presented through the cool device of an interchange between reporter and host. The British term for the task is linkman. On the first *20/20*, not only did many of the individual segments miss, but the glue that might have held them in place was missing. I was going to have to supply that missing link.

After erring too far in one direction, we didn't want *20/20* to go off half-cocked in another, if we didn't want to slavishly imitate *60 Minutes*. Nor did we want to give up our own claim to investigative reporting. In the first few weeks of the show, our own Sylvia Chase scored impressively on that front with a hard-hitting investigation of the flaming gas tanks on Ford's subcompact Pinto.

I was pleased that *20/20* was looking at a subject that desperately needed probing. At the same time I was feeling some heat. The target of our first major investigation happened to be Ford, a former employer of mine, although I had never been involved in Pinto advertising. I handled this potential conflict in the only way I knew how: I brought the whole business out into the open, on camera, and left it up to the viewer.

It was our third show. I led off with the story. I pointed out that *Mother Jones,* a small California magazine, had first reported the dangers of the Pinto gas tank. ABC News editor Jules Bergman had broken the subject on television with the first government crash-test film. Sylvia Chase had gone on to reveal that Ford had tested a safer Pinto gas tank but had never put it into production.

The risks were caused by the so-called drop-in fuel tank. In this design, the top of the tank is also the floor of the trunk. This places the tank itself only inches from the rear of the car. The driver was exposed to a high risk of explosion and fire in the event of a rear-end collision.

At the close of Sylvia's superb report, I felt compelled to point out my prior involvement with Ford.

"You know, I advertised Ford products a few years back," I said. "At the time, of course, I didn't know, and I didn't think anyone else did, that this kind of ruckus was going to unfold."

I certainly didn't. The Ford people first approached me in 1972. They made it clear that my job would be to emphasize a "return to quality" on their part. I had no problem with that. If they could convince me the quality theme wasn't just bunk, I would be happy to say so. And the Ford folk took some pretty persuasive steps to prove to me that they weren't just talking through their hats. I met personally with Henry Ford, II. I toured assembly plants. I came away impressed by the visible efforts the Ford production people seemed to be making to "return pride of craftsmanship to the assembly line." That was Henry Ford's personal phrase.

My advertising spots were all oriented around the quality theme. I invited customers to test for themselves whether a Ford was indeed a quality product. At first, dealers were worried that thousands of customers might come in to take their showroom models apart. But in time they came to believe, as I did, that the quality concept was not only a sound idea but a genuine corporate policy extending right down through the assembly line.

After a year of this, the company and their ad agency decided they wanted a punchier delivery, louder music, flashier visuals, with emphasis on style, speed, and glitz. In other words, the old Detroit fantasy sell.

They asked me to do one of those now-trendy car ads. The kind stressing speed, with loud, stylized delivery of copy and a lot of gratuitous glitter. I told the Ford people that if that was what they wanted, there were plenty of people out there who could do it better than I.

"But we want you," they said.

It turned out they didn't want me all that much. They wanted their shiny new campaign more. It was all part of a long marketing process that culminated in the basically meaningless slogan: "Have you driven a Ford lately?" Out went the spokesman, the emphasis on gas mileage and solid construction. In went a lot of pretty shots featuring fast Fords rounding hairpin curves.

Now, just two years later, Sylvia's report had turned up the fact that as far back as 1967, crash tests performed at UCLA had shown that the drop-in tank of the Pinto was a time bomb. A safer design, with the tank mounted over the rear axle, would have cost Ford $8.29 more per car. On our show, a Ford engineer said that the decision not to go with the safer version had been part of a "corporate policy." Apparently, the policy was to cut assembly-line costs, not promote quality.

When Ford and I parted company, there had been no hard feelings. But after our 20/20 broadcast, a Ford public relations man wrote me an extremely wounded letter. He accused me of using Sylvia's report as a vehicle to somehow "get back" at them. There was nothing I could write, do, or say, to persuade this man that this was not the case. There was nothing to "get back" for. It was simply a piece of legitimate journalism.

Lee Iacocca, who was then head of Ford, seemed to understand my position. When I approached him for a corporate contribution to the National Space Institute, of which I was then president, he made a generous contribution to our cause through Ford Aerospace, with no mention of our Pinto story. It is possible that *20/20*'s investigation of the problems at Ford may well have done more to bring about a "return to quality" at the company than any pronouncements Henry Ford, II, himself had made.

Throughout that first year on *20/20*, we tried to achieve a balance between such hard-news stories and softer feature material. Occasionally we found ourselves veering somewhat unsteadily between Mick Jagger and Agent Orange, from discos in Manhattan to dissidents in Moscow. By spreading ourselves out across the globe and across as wide a range of subjects as possible, we were trying to present the world as we saw it. At the same time we were establishing our family of correspondents as a global news-gathering team to be reckoned with.

While our "family" in the field was like a football team running a complex formation, I played my part by making the necessary introductions, forming conceptual bridges, adding conversation and context as events spun around me. I also did ten or twelve pieces a year, and still do, as correspondent. I interviewed the nonagenerian champion of human rights, Roger Baldwin, founder and chairman of the American Civil Liberties Union. A few weeks later I touched the lighter side with a whimsical piece on automobile art.

I have always been intrigued by people who push themselves beyond the supposed limits of human endurance. I profiled Diana Nyad, the remarkable young long-distance swimmer, and Lauren Bacall, who revealed a different sort of person on camera. Her fabled toughness and savvy were made all the more endearing by her sensitivity and vulnerability. We rarely witnessed those qualities on the cinema screen, but they blossomed on the more intimate small screen.

Occasionally, in our compulsion to do a good job, we made mistakes. In an August 1978 piece on gas-price control, we aroused the ire of Herb Schmertz, Mobil's strong-willed public relations man. He ran newspaper ads across the country quoting a Cleveland newspaper which had denounced "Hughie Downs and His Band of Subjective Journalists." His basic gripe was that we failed to distinguish between so-called new gas and old gas in our report. Herb is a smart man. When we checked out the story, it turned out he was right. I duly admitted the factual error the following week: "We should have distinguished between old gas and new gas," I began. "The controls would continue on old gas under this compromise [legislation]. . . . Only the price of so-called new gas would be deregulated, until new gas controls are entirely lifted by 1985."

At the same time, I stood by the basic thrust of our report. It was that gas-price decontrol would have a marked and adverse effect on the wallets of the average consumer.

Programs like *20/20* often have to defend themselves from hailstorms of criticism. Over the years we have been sued and berated for lack of depth and quality, base intentions, poor methods, shoddy ethics, and inept or even malicious procedures, and attacked by opposing sides when presenting both cases. But nothing much ever comes of these storms.

One frequent allegation, which in the case of network news organizations has been largely unfounded, has been that we resort to "checkbook journalism." The term refers to buying news from the source, that is, from the newsmakers themselves. In one story, we found out more about the practice than we might have wished.

ABC policy, which is similar to standards at the other two networks, specifically states that the purchase of news is not the sort of business we want to engage in. A memorandum from our News Division puts it this way: "News requires a free flow of information uninhibited by monetary considerations. . . . The principle of not paying for news is clear. We recognize there will be difficult or borderline cases, but if we err, we should err on the side of not paying."

It was September of 1978, and our first season. The story we were pursuing was one of the hottest international scandals of its time. Jeremy Thorpe, a British Member of Parliament and head of the Liberal Party, had been accused of having someone try to murder a former homosexual lover. Thorpe was acquitted in court and cleared of the charge, but the case showed the power of "checkbook journalism."

Dave Marash managed to secure a dramatic on-camera interview with Andrew Newton, who claimed he had been hired to do the killing. Discussing a complex flow of payments in this bizarre bump-off scheme, Marash put his subject on the spot by disclosing certain key facts.

> *MARASH:* We at ABC are paying you for this interview, are we not?
> *NEWTON:* No, are you?
> *MARASH:* Yes, we are. We're not lying, Newton.
> *NEWTON:* How much more?
> *MARASH:* Want the truth?
> *NEWTON:* Please stop. I really don't want you to mention this. . . .

But Marash went on, gleefully overriding Newton's evident distress.

> ABC News does not, as a rule, pay news sources. But in Britain, checkbook journalism has become a way of life. . . . We quickly reached the point of either paying or packing up. . . . We chose to pay. . . . It would have been neater and cleaner to do without the aid of a checkbook, but we could not.

Which does not precisely prove that rules are made to be broken. But as long as the show decided to suspend one, it felt more comfortable telling the audience why.

In television journalism the investigative method has given birth to a new breed of on-camera performer. This hard-hitting type adopts what some people call a prosecutorial style to achieve dramatic results in the field.

If Mike Wallace is seen as a black belt in this most modern of martial arts, our own Geraldo Rivera certainly developed a more freewheeling version, leavened by a countervailing layer of genuine compassion. Geraldo's first training for this role came as a lawyer. He is readily outraged by injustice. Wallace developed his own style on *Nightbeat*, a 1950s local New York talk show that featured all the bright interrogative lights, lit cigarettes, and the tough confrontations of a sitdown version of *Dragnet*.

I am not an aggressive broadcaster by nature. I could never even play the unctuous game-show host, which demands a hundred front teeth and the ability to tell people they are having fun. I find it virtually impossible to do a piece involving ambush journalism, a controversial technique involving an on-camera confrontation with an unsuspecting subject.

The ambush is only one weapon in the arsenal of investigative journalists pursuing an undercover story. Television reporters often use hidden cameras and play assumed roles. I don't use such techniques because I was never very good at investigative work of this kind. However, I find it completely defensible. It fits my belief that there is no such thing as an embarrassing question. There are only embarrassing answers. As long as you don't lay hands on someone, bar his or her way, or infringe on his or her civil rights, you have a right to ask anyone anything. The subject has a right to answer or not, as he or she so chooses.

When unorthodox techniques such as ambush journalism are used to report, and not distort, the news, they are perfectly legitimate tools. Geraldo produced some astonishing reports for us, several of which could never have gotten on the air without using such methods.

I don't do undercover work myself, but I have had to ask some hard questions on the show. One particular case was a story I did in 1980 on nuclear power plants. Out of the 65,000 letters that had come into our offices from viewers across the country, one caught the eye of a staffer, who saw its story potential.

Robert Gray, the mayor of Mexico, New York, a tiny town in

the sparsely settled Upstate county of Oswego, wrote to us asking why the utilities were trying to turn his politically powerless community into an "overbuilt nuclear park." I went up to Mexico to see what happens when a rural town gets caught in the power grip of an energy crisis.

On the shores of Lake Ontario, not far from the Canadian border, Oswego County is mostly wetland, woodland, and farmland. A lone nuclear power plant built in the sixties was rapidly joined by three more in the seventies. By 1980 local utilities had applied to build two more reactors, all in the same region. The power wasn't for the local people: much of it would be sold to affluent customers on densely populated Long Island, where the power was welcome but the nuclear plants were not.

In such a report, it's often more important to ask the right question than it is to get any conclusive reply. I asked an executive at Niagara Mohawk, the utility responsible for much of this buildup, a simple question: "How do you answer the charge that in the main, nuclear power plants tend to be located in areas where the least effective opposition exists?"

His answer was not at all surprising: "I don't know whether there is any cause and effect."

In his flat denial of the problem, I had gotten what I wanted. In my closing I pointed out: "Ironically, as construction of these plants was increasing, power consumption had gone down over the past six years. Nuclear overbuilding will add to the surplus of energy. . . . We are now producing thirty-three percent more electricity than we consume." That was in 1980.

Then came Three Mile Island. On the air, I delivered a commentary on our long-term survival options.

Two books selling out in Harrisburg, Pennsylvania, during Three Mile Island were *The China Syndrome* and *The Rand McNally Road Atlas*. It sounds all too human. In a crisis we try to keep on top of what's happening. But get ready to get out, if you can't. . . .
That's how most of us are responding, psychologically, to this threat of nuclear disaster. . . . But we ought to be looking around for something besides road maps to get us to safety.

Try this on for size—the sun safely pours 150 trillion continuous horsepower on the dayside of the earth. This power is free, cannot be stolen, and will not burn out for five billion years. This shift to solar power is clearly indicated, and we would be insane not to move seriously on this starting now.

Whether offering opinion, ad-libbing, or reading from a prepared script, everything we do is communicating with the broadcast public, who either will—or will not—accept you. I don't think it's a matter of skill. There's never been an actor good enough to invent a *person* whom people will accept if the real person isn't acceptable. I suppose it's a way of saying, Be yourself.

My early experiences in radio taught me another thing. If you concentrate on the meaning of what you are saying, and not on the sound of your own voice, your effectiveness as a communicator will improve notably. On television, if you're concerned with your personal appearance and the sound of your voice, what you're trying to say will tend to get lost.

What I have tried to do is maintain what media people call a cool approach.

In acting it means letting the character show through, not the performance. In classical music it means letting people hear the music and forget about the musicians. One New York critic attacked Zubin Mehta, the music director and conductor of the New York Philharmonic, on the ground that he lacks charisma. Good orchestral conducting should be transparent. Mehta's a very forceful personality if you meet him, but when he conducts Mahler, you don't hear Mehta—you hear Mahler.

In television anchor work, which is a visual medium, you will exude an identifiable personality, no matter how cool you try to be. The viewers will then decide if it's something they can relate to. But the idea of constantly shaping a charismatic façade, or forcefully imposing your personality on the material, goes directly against the purpose of the job, which is to put the message across—not to become the message yourself.

The role of the linkman, anchor, or host, is to provide perspective, distance, even a touch of detachment to the far-flung events reported on by field correspondents. A "hot" approach sits better with the viewers if used by a correspondent than if imposed from the top by the anchor. The anchor position enhances the credibility of the reporting itself, by supplying a sense of context, by building trust, by keeping the intrusion of personality to a minimum. It tries to deal effectively in an essentially visual medium without resorting to a flashy bag of actor's tricks.

I rarely have ethical problems with stories I help present on the air. Fortunately, my own values usually coincide with network policy and the innate taste of our producers. But occasionally a segment comes up with which I have a problem.

In July of 1979 Pierre Salinger profiled a famous Spanish bullfighter, El Cordoba. At forty-three, "the Man From Cordoba" was taking a chance with his life by staging a fast plunge back into the bullring. Bullfighting is a young man's game. As comebacks go, this was almost like Mickey Mantle deciding to return to the Yankees next year.

The story was aired, and despite all the usual disclaimers, it still left a bad taste in my mouth. It looked like a powerful promotion for the cruel sport of bullfighting.

"Bullfighting is a sport abhorrent to many Americans," Pierre began. "But we should realize the Anglo-Saxon ethic is not universal. For the people of Spain, bullfighting is not a sport but a ritual, whose origins are deeply rooted in man's age-old struggle with nature."

All well and good. My problem was that the breathtaking visual presentation, combined with our correspondent's evident admiration for this daring matador, didn't balance the unpleasant truth. No matter what aficionados say, the bull is not just a hunk of hamburger who dies happy at the hands of the matador.

"I know the rationale here," I prodded Pierre on camera at the close of his piece. "The bullring might well be less inhumane than the slaughterhouse. But the bull is outnumbered any way you cut it, and it is very hard to justify."

"I understand how you feel, Hugh," Salinger replied. "But I

think the point of this piece is that we're dealing with another culture, and other cultures have different ways of expressing deeply held feelings."

My on-air objection to the bullfighting story came from my concern for animal rights. But I also know there is excessive posing and posturing on both sides of this controversial issue. I no longer hunt game. At the same time, I refuse to categorically condemn all hunters. Many hunters, I believe, genuinely want to put meat on the table. I will respect a staunch antihunting stance only if it is taken by a strict vegetarian. If someone denounces hunting while munching a Big Mac, I can't buy it.

In another segment, Sylvia Chase was investigating an arthritis clinic in Mexico run by a certain Dr. Corillo. The American Arthritis Foundation and other medical groups had denounced this man for coaxing Americans across the border by the thousands to be treated with drugs not allowed by the FDA.

Sylvia went down there and took back a sample of Dr. Corillo's arthritis preparation, which Corillo claimed contained no dangerous hormones. But laboratory tests in this country showed the medicine did contain certain powerful steroids.

I happened to know of three separate cases in which responsible people have taken the medicine for a decade, and swear by it. They are convinced, and I have no reason to doubt them, that they would not be alive today except for the benefits of that drug. Non-FDA-approved preparations might indeed have adverse side effects, they argue, but what side effect can be worse than death?

I have considerable respect for the FDA and the immense task it faces in testing all drugs sold in this country. But certain useful, even lifesaving, drugs have been needlessly denied entry into the U.S. because of the prolonged, overbureaucratized testing process. As in all bureaucracies, the FDA people want to keep their jobs. For example, no one will be fired if he or she *keeps out* a controversial drug that might prevent ten thousand asthma deaths per year. But heads will roll if someone lets *in* such a drug, and it turns out to have negative side effects.

When viewing both sides of the argument, we should remember that if aspirin were tested today, it might not be allowed on the market by the FDA because of its main side
effect—stomach bleeding.

In the case of the bullfighting story, I felt I had to voice my
objections on the air. But in the case of the Mexican arthritis
clinic, I ended up holding my tongue. Two obvious facts uncovered by our investigative team prompted me to take that
course. First, the piece covered the testimony of those who had
been helped by the drug. And, second, Dr. Corillo had lied on
camera about the presence of steroids in his compound. I was
satisfied that it was a sound piece of journalism, but I winced
when it was aired, knowing the feelings of the patients who
believe they owe their lives to Dr. Corillo.

Over the years, I have felt it important for me to say my
piece, in most cases, with the full support of the network. In
1985 I took a definite on-air stand on a drug issue. We did a
piece about the Mafia and its longstanding involvement with
the smuggling of illegal drugs into this country, particularly
heroin. I thought it was the right time to reiterate a position I've
taken before on the air. Fifteen years before, I made a plea for
the legalization of marijuana on *The Today Show*. At the time,
the roof fell in on me. The suggestion was not very popular. In
1984 I spent about ten minutes laying out the rationale for
legalization on an ABC Radio show called *Perspective*, to which I
sometimes contribute. This time the mail ran three to two in my
favor.

After the *20/20* story on the Mafia and heroin smuggling, I
made my case once again. I emphasized that I believe in the
law. But as soon as you put certain activities and substances
outside the law, you automatically lose control of them. Criminal elements go into these prohibited areas to make money,
which ends any reasonable hope for control. I came out for
legalization and strict regulation. The mail which came in ran
about two to one in favor of legalization of drugs. Shortly after
the broadcast, columnists Mike Royko and William F. Buckley
separately supported the idea in their columns.

In my eight years on *20/20*, my strongest conflict with the network came quite recently. In October of 1985 a *20/20* segment based on Anthony Summers's book *Goddess: The Secret Lives of Marilyn Monroe* was canceled by ABC News. The book presented a number of shocking charges involving a dead President and his brother, then the attorney general of the United States.

For years, rumors had been darting around that there were romantic links between both Kennedy brothers and Marilyn Monroe. But the Camelot aura was so strong, and the Kennedy mystique so difficult to challenge, that a veil of secrecy surrounded them.

That all began to change when Summers, a former BBC correspondent and author of *Conspiracy*, a book about the assassination of President Kennedy, decided to try to solve a long-term mystery: the death of Marilyn Monroe.

20/20 had entered into an exclusive arrangement with the publisher, Macmillan, to draw on the book for a segment produced by our own people. By the time *Goddess* was published in September of 1985, we were prepared to air a visual version of the author's investigation. Av Westin had handed the assignment to Stanhope Gould and Ene Riisna, two of our top producers. The correspondent was Sylvia Chase. The result was a twenty-six minute, in-depth report that surprised everyone. It went even further than the Summers book in digging up the Marilyn Monroe–Kennedy connection.

The piece was given a tentative air date of September 26, 1985, our season premiere. At the last minute, the segment was postponed until the following week, October third. The reason given by Roone Arledge was that the piece needed more work. All of us at *20/20* believed we were going to air the segment after certain requested "clarifications" were inserted into the narrative. But after being heavily edited—at the request of management—from its original length of twenty-six minutes down to seventeen minutes and finally to only thirteen minutes, the signal from ABC News was that there was still no green light to go on the air. Something was holding the piece up.

At six o'clock Thursday night, October 3, 1985, Sylvia Chase was in the studio, just going into makeup, when I first learned that the piece had been killed. We were astounded. A standby feature was substituted. Angered by the reasons given, Geraldo Rivera impulsively suggested that Barbara Walters and I should join him in a vow to "not let the company get away with this." All of us felt jolted by this preemptive strike against what we considered a balanced and revealing piece of television journalism.

Geraldo, who is more easily outraged by an injustice aimed at a friend than at himself, did not let the matter sit there. He expanded his views to Liz Smith of the New York *Daily News*. The following morning they were splashed all across her gossip column.

"We were appalled that Roone would override a respected, honorable, great newsman like Av [Westin]," Geraldo said. "We were appalled that the head of this network would suddenly show such an interest in this particular story when he hasn't shown interest in so many others we've done."

Meanwhile, Roone was giving his own, and ABC management's, explanation to the New York *Times*.

ABC had decided to kill the piece, he said, because "it was gossip-column stuff" that did "not live up to its billing. . . . It set out to be a piece which would demonstrate that because of alleged relations between Bobby Kennedy and John Kennedy and Marilyn Monroe, the presidency was compromised because organized crime was involved. . . . Based on what has been uncovered so far, there was no evidence."

At *20/20* we disagreed. The unaired segment was backed by enough evidence to warrant raising the questions it presented—including eyewitness accounts of the wiretapping of Marilyn Monroe's home by teamster leader Jimmy Hoffa, along with eyewitness accounts of repeated meetings between her and both Kennedy brothers. Fred Otash, a detective who claimed to be the chief wiretapper, was interviewed on camera. His account of the wiretapping procedure was corroborated by three other wiretappers, all allegedly hired by Hoffa.

This confirmation of old rumors was startling enough. But

the research finally pointed to a visit by Bobby Kennedy to Marilyn Monroe's house on the day of her death. This visit apparently prefigured a mysterious ambulance ride during which Marilyn may have died on her way to the hospital. According to these accounts, the ambulance was turned around after her death and driven back to her house, where her body was later found by the police.

The actor Peter Lawford, a Kennedy relative and a neighbor of Marilyn's, is thought by some to have helped "sanitize" her home after her death, possibly removing a suicide note, papers, and diaries that could have linked her to the Kennedys. Bobby Kennedy's secret affair with Marilyn may have begun, according to some accounts, when his brother Jack sent him to tell her they would have to break off their relationship.

The *20/20* research, along with the Summers book, compiled all this evidence in exhaustive detail, including on-camera interviews with Deborah Gould, Peter Lawford's third wife, and Eunice Murray, Marilyn's housekeeper. Some of Ms. Murray's recall was cloudy, but journalistic accounts are not bound to levels of proof demanded by a court of law. And, on the unshown segment, we made it clear whenever the facts remained murky.

To the press, Roone Arledge maintained that his decision to kill the piece was based solely on the grounds that "so far nobody has found the tapes of the wiretappings" made—allegedly at the request of Jimmy Hoffa—of Marilyn's phone. But the actual tapes (and Marilyn's diary), as I told Roone at a meeting at ABC the next day, were probably about as accessible to us as Hoffa's body, and for perhaps the same reasons. As far as we were concerned, taped interviews with those who claimed to have done the wiretapping were reasonable presentations on the air.

Arledge disagreed. "Television's impact is so great, so much greater than print," he told Liz Smith, "that if we devote two-thirds of *20/20* to a premise, we'd better be able to prove it. . . . My objection to the piece as it stands is that it's a piece of sleazy journalism. Just not good enough for us."

When that quote hit the stands, I was concerned enough about damage to want to talk to the press. We had been advised by ABC Public Relations that if the press were to contact any of us about this controversy, the best comment we could make would be "no comment."

I had made no public comment until the "sleazy" quote came out. But now I took the calls of reporters and columnists.

The New York *Times* asked me what I thought, and I told them: "I lament the fact that this decision reflects badly on people I respect, and it reflects badly on me, and the broadcast," I said. To the Washington *Post*, I added, "I don't work with sleazy programs or sleazy people."

There were other, larger, issues involved. I felt we had to make our views on this subject clear, or concede to ABC News, with all its might, the power to rewrite history. I could not agree that the Marilyn Monroe affair did not affect the presidency and did not touch on national security. I could not agree that the story merely pandered to morbid curiosity and was not the sort of journalism we should be engaged in. A dead President belongs to real history, not to some continual rewriting of history simply to protect an image.

Liz Smith's column the following morning carried a retraction by Arledge of his use of the unfortunate word. "Roone says now he never used that 'sleazy.' But I believe he did," Liz said. "Maybe he didn't mean to do so. I'm sure he didn't intend it to reflect against his own staffers . . . it just came out in a way he had not meant."

The same column carried a general statement by me: "I live comfortably with network news policy, and a network has the right to control what goes on the air. What disturbs me about this incident is the implication that people I respect more than any others in this business—Av Westin, Stanhope Gould, and Ene Riisna—were all overruled. And it now looks as if their accuracy and integrity are under fire."

By now I had begun to see that Arledge had not really intended any harm to our people. The decision to kill the piece fanned the fire of publicity rather than squelched it. After knocking locally around the New York press, the national media couldn't resist such a juicy controversy.

For a moment it seemed to be getting out of hand. The October 21 *People* magazine presented an account of the Thursday-night cancellation of October 3 which overdramatized Geraldo's suggestion that we unite in our dissent: "When the decision came down, Barbara Walters, Geraldo Rivera, and Hugh Downs stood together on the set of ABC's *20/20*," *People* said. "Linking arms to symbolize their unanimity, the trio of TV news personalities vowed to protest the network's last-minute decision to kill an investigative segment on the mysterious circumstances surrounding the 1962 death of Marilyn Monroe."

People quickly got down to specifics: "The suggestion is that the network's many connections to the Kennedy family influenced the decision to snuff the controversial segment. Arledge, for instance, is a long-time friend of Ethel Kennedy, Bobby's widow. Jeff Ruhe, 33, an Arledge assistant, is married to Courtney Kennedy, 29, the fifth of Bobby Kennedy's 11 children. David Burke, vice-president of ABC News, is a former aide to Ted Kennedy."

For my part, I was not interested in such speculations as to why ABC did what it did. I was more concerned about protecting the people and the reputation of a program I had been involved with for nearly eight years.

For his part, Roone flatly denied allegations of cronyism: "Ethel Kennedy is a friend of mine like hundreds of people we do stories on," he told the *Times*. "That has never affected our judgment." As for the reported role of David Burke in the decision, Burke told me that because of his relationship with the Kennedy family, he had expressly excused himself from a review of the program.

The affair soon died down in the press, but it left a permanent mark on our staff at *20/20*. The following week, Geraldo Rivera resigned his correspondent's position at ABC after ten distinguished years at the network. Whether, as Liz Smith so vividly speculated, Geraldo "stepped off or was pushed off" was never publicly revealed.

My belief is that he left because he wanted to. Conditions at the network, with the imminent merger of ABC with Capital Cities, made contract negotiations complicated. The climate may have been unfavorable for renewal under circumstances Geraldo felt he deserved. He hadn't had a real vacation since *20/20* first went on the air, and he and I had talked more than once about my 1965 voyage across the Pacific in a small boat. It will not surprise me if he does this. Whether he takes an extended voyage or not, as he said on his last *20/20* broadcast, he will undoubtedly return to broadcasting.

Today's *20/20* would not be the same without Barbara Walters. Barbara is an American superstar and an enormous boost to the show. I like to think I gave her a leg up by showcasing her talents on *The Today Show* twenty years ago. In the fall of 1981 we came together again. In the early days I had hoped to get her on the show as a frequent correspondent, but she was still co-anchoring the ABC *Nightly News* with Harry Reasoner and wasn't really available. Reasoner had been with *60 Minutes* for two years before going over to ABC to anchor the news. With the help of Howard K. Smith, he pulled ABC's news ratings sharply up. Today ABC News, under Roone Arledge, is a nationally respected news-gathering organization, but up until recently, NBC and CBS have always shared the leading edge in news among the three networks, with ABC a distant third. Under Reasoner, ABC started running a respectable race.

Then Fred Pierce took over as president of ABC. He decided to offer Barbara Walters, who had by now become a co-anchor of *The Today Show* with Jim Hartz, the job of doing the nightly news with Harry Reasoner. It was a bold, headline-making move, and added to ABC's image as the up-and-coming news network, prepared to innovate to stay in the race. As the first female nightly network news anchor, Barbara jumped immediately from stardom to superstardom.

Her new image as the Million-Dollar Baby—a reference to her widely reported annual income—may have been good media hype, but it didn't enhance her position with her fellow journalists at ABC.

Harry Reasoner was not pleased with the new arrangement. He worked out an oral agreement with ABC which he publicly referred to as his "Barbara Walters escape clause." He agreed to co-anchor the newscast with Barbara if they cut two years off his contract. In effect, this gave him a trial period during which he could see how things worked out. As far as Reasoner was concerned, things never did work out. When his new contract ran out, Harry went back to CBS to rejoin *60 Minutes*.

After Reasoner's departure, ABC was forced to rethink the arrangement. They didn't want to risk keeping Barbara as the sole anchor. They were willing to be innovative but not revolutionary. That left Barbara without a regular berth at her own network. She was still signed exclusively, she still did her own popular specials, but ABC was not prepared to give her her own show based on the celebrity-interview format.

In the spring of 1981 the company came up with a proposal to have Barbara come on *20/20* every week, in some special, not yet defined capacity. I certainly had no objection to that. But the proposal, when finally formulated, turned into an offer for her to co-anchor the broadcast with me. This was not acceptable to me. I had no objection to Barbara's increased presence. I respect her work, and we're friends. This was more of a philosophical problem. Co-anchoring is inherently awkward. It really works only when the co-anchors are in different locations, like Huntley in New York and Brinkley in Washington. But some broadcast executives believe that if one experienced anchorperson is effective in the studio, two should be even better.

When I learned that ABC was offering Barbara a co-anchor position on *20/20*, the first thing I did was to go straight to Barbara herself. She knew I had wanted her on *20/20* more often, but I had been hired on a solo anchor basis and wanted to leave it that way.

I then made my position clear to Av Westin, and finally all of us ended up working out a compromise.

I stayed at the anchor position. This meant I was the only person squaring off to the camera, talking directly to the audience, supplying the bridges between different segments of the program, and between the program and the audience at home. I remained the linkman, as the British call it.

Barbara, meanwhile, worked at the anchor desk alongside me. But her function was to debrief the correspondents at the end of each story, plus add observations on the segments, then enter into conversation with me at the end of the program.

We thought that, given my reluctance to share the anchoring, this would be the best way to take advantage of her talents. It seemed like the best possible compromise at the time, but neither of us was quite happy with it.

I appeared to launch each story with great enthusiasm and then turn my back on it after my introduction, leaving Barbara to talk with the correspondents. At the close of the program, I occasionally gave a commentary alone or discussed the pieces with Barbara at the anchor desk. When Barbara did her own story, I interviewed her at the end. When I did my own story, she interviewed me. These worked, but the format of the program now seemed to limit Barbara to short interviews, and it left me out of the discussions I felt I should be part of.

Finally, I had to ask myself if sharing the anchor work might not be the lesser of two evils; and why was I holding out against an idea that seemed to have the approval of everyone else? Particularly since there was a danger of losing Barbara if we couldn't come up with something that worked.

So, in late 1985, with a new desk, an upgraded set, and a positive attitude, we launched a new format for *20/20*, with Barbara Walters as a full co-host. It seems to be working.

I had feared that the very qualities she has which make her valuable as an interviewer and field correspondent might work against her as a co-anchor, but that has not been the case. The anchor hat sits attractively on her head, both in working with me and by herself in my absence.

NBC should have listened to me when I told them they should give *The Today Show* to her when I left.

20/20 is evolving with the years. We continue to do hard stories about crime and malfeasance, but there has been far less undercover material in recent years. We have seen something of a climate change in the public mood. For years, the American viewer seemed endlessly fascinated by the relentless exposure of nefarious deeds, particularly in fairly high places.

Journalists won awards, politicians and other authority figures winced and suffered, businessmen walked in fear of being called before the carpet of Mike Wallace or Geraldo Rivera. Much that was exposed needed to be exposed. But after years of emphasizing hard-hitting exposés, people have developed an enormous thirst for more positive stories—the brighter side of American society.

While there will always be a role for investigative reporting on television, many of our features have gradually taken on a new dimension—an emphasis on what we call an involvement approach. These tend toward service stories which may point out a problem, but also point toward a solution. We did a story on impotence, demonstrating that this condition affects as many as one out of ten American males, but we also showed that in a majority of such cases positive steps can be taken for correction.

Our features on depression, anxiety, anorexia, and bulimia, on which I was the correspondent, all demonstrated the existence of effective remedies for these tragic conditions. We don't want to leave our viewers simply angry and depressed. We want to present grounds for hope, if it exists, and inspire a sense of participation and control in the viewer.

I've seen interesting ideas come up in story conferences. I've heard Av Westin ask, "Is there any hope for this situation? Is there any reason to be telling people about this other than just to depress them?" We can't do every story, so if there is no possible solution, we'll go for a story where we *can* offer people some way out, some positive direction. We don't mind sounding an alarm, but we want to offer the reasonable hope of a remedy as well.

In July of 1981 the nation was shocked by the collapse of walkways at the Hyatt Regency Hotel in Kansas City. On a Friday evening as a tea dance was being held in the lobby, 111 people died, 188 were injured, and many more were pinned under tons of concrete and steel. The night of the show, we asked the human question, "When a community is suddenly hit with an overwhelming disaster, how does it react?"

Within hours, the tragedy was being thoroughly documented by daily reports of body counts. The news media were focusing, almost obsessively, on a near-frantic search for people to blame for the disaster. They had their jobs to do. But we had begun looking for something else—a different perspective. Our correspondent, Tom Jarriel, went to Kansas City and found a magnificent story of selfless human action.

We told the story of "Country Bill" Alman, the jackhammer operator who had been breaking concrete on a nearby construction job when he rushed to the hotel. He began hammering holes through tons of concrete under which many of the still living lay trapped.

We outlined the heroism of Dr. Joe Waeckerle of nearby Baptist Hospital, who had just finished duty in the emergency room when he rushed to an even greater emergency. He worked through a long night to save hundreds of survivors. We located a number of heroes who risked their lives to rescue the trapped victims.

Though we dealt firmly with the origins of the tragedy, and the complex structural questions surrounding "long-span spaces" like the Hyatt Regency Atrium, we strove to leave our viewers with an indelible impression of natural heroism, of human capacity for altruism in the face of catastrophe.

A multisubject news hour is timeless and can rejuvenate itself after every program. Each week brings new events, personalities, and problems that need to be examined in a less rigid environment than the nightly news.

Dramatic programs tend to have a life-span of growth, peak, and decline. It isn't easy for writers to come up with new devices and new inventions to keep their characters consistently interesting. Shows like *Dallas* or *Dynasty* or *Knot's Landing*, like many real-life romantic relationships, often demonstrate that time erodes initial infatuation and replaces it with a deadly boredom.

If a show like *20/20* is going to grow and stay young, our three or four mini-documentaries presented each week must inform, educate, and, above all, *hold* the television viewer's restless attention. We have to reach the emotions of viewers as well as transmit facts. The success of *20/20* is no surprise to me. Having been involved in television news and entertainment for more than four decades, I understand why the visual news magazine has become the most powerful program our industry has yet produced. Its great strength lies in its variety—and in the power of reality itself.

9

ADVENTURE

On Friday, December 10, 1982, at 6:10 P.M. Eastern Standard Time, on assignment for *20/20*, I took a short walk to the South Pole. In my right hand I held a fifteen-foot bamboo pole with a small green flag on top. This nondescript object was meant to mark the precise point at which all longitude vanishes, where the sun is no higher in the sky at noon than at midnight, and where it rises and sets once a year. Where all time zones converge. The end of the earth.

My job was to move the South Pole to its true location.

Since it was first known that our earth is a ball, and that it turns once a day on an axis that can be located, this spot has possessed an unearthly significance. Lives have been lost in vain attempts to mark this spot and return safely to civilization. I had arrived not by traditional dogsled or snowshoes, but by Hercules C-130 Navy Transport and a sporty Sprite Sno-Cat made by John DeLorean. Then for the last few meters on foot, by Bunny Boots.

Bunny Boots. These marvelous thermal boots, designed for the U.S. Navy, put impressive layers between feet and ice. Tube socks connect to a nylon mesh layer, under which is a layer of rubber, a layer of felt, two thin layers of wood, a layer of air, a moisture barrier, more felt, and finally a sole of rubber so thick I felt as if I were wearing elevator shoes.

Now, perched warm and dry an inch and a half above the frozen snow, I followed twenty-three-year-old Dr. Laureen

Utz, a cartographer with the U.S. Geological Survey, to a surveyor's pin. It was stuck in the ice at the spot I had come to stab in the bottom of the earth.

Dr. Utz had used the latest satellite readings and a surveyor's transit to pinpoint the Pole's correct location at precisely 90 degrees South Latitude, a marking that was probably accurate to within twenty inches. The new location—created by polar icecap drift—lay just over ten meters from where the pole had been stuck almost a year before, in January.

I yanked the pole out of its old hole and walked some thirty-four feet to the surveyor's pin. There, with cameras rolling, I punched the long bamboo shoot straight down into the white crusty surface, to what was now the "true pole."

This trip to Antarctica was one of the high points of my lifelong interest in science. It all began when I was five, and I asked my father how far away the moon was. Rather than brush me off with "very far" or "too far to go," he answered: 238,000 miles. I was so flattered at being given an adult answer that I've been interested in science ever since.

I have shared a similar interest in what might be called adventure. Places remote and inaccessible have continued to exert a powerful influence on my often restless imagination, and in a general spirit of exploration, I've taken the trouble to learn diving, sailing, flying, ballooning, and high-performance driving for racing cars. I've never been in love with danger for its own sake, but I do often seek out certain relatively safe sorts of adventure. Since I've had the privilege of knowing some of the great divers like Cousteau, sailors like Irving Johnson and Bus Mossbacher, glider pilots like Joe Lincoln and Dieter Loeper, and drivers such as Mario Andretti and Mark Donahue, I've always felt like a chihuahua at a convention of Saint Bernards. And as a devout coward, I have always made sure to stack the deck in my favor whenever possible.

Early on, television programmers learned that if people were sitting safely at home watching the set, they enjoyed seeing on-camera people doing adventurous things. Almost as if the passivity of television-watching needed an antidote. Television was also best served if we could venture forth out of the tame confines of the studio environment. This is particularly true on talk shows. Producers are always trying to come up with ways to get us out into the open, doing something exciting.

Broadcasting has been kind to me. In addition to everything else, it has given me the chance to indulge some exotic interests—all under the guise of working—such as traveling to the South Pole or flying an airplane. Millions of television viewers share these interests and would be happy to sample these pursuits if they had the time or the money. In my case, the networks often handle the cost. I just supply the body and, I hope, the mind when needed.

I try not to do anything on air unless I feel it is safe. Part of my job in demonstrating these sports has been to show people that if they venture into the unknown correctly, they can be reasonably sure of their safety. In fact, some supposedly risky sports are really safer than routine activities like night driving. Although 1 out of every 1600 motor vehicles in the U.S. will be involved in a fatal accident in a calendar year, only 1 out of every 2000 gliders will suffer the same fate. Yet I am sure most people would consider gliding riskier than driving.

On *The Today Show*, and now on *20/20*, we have found that these adventure segments work better if we participate in them ourselves. If we showcase an expert doing these things, the audience can always say, "Well, that's a special person up there with special abilities." But if it is just me or another correspondent doing it, then people might think, "Maybe I could do that too."

I was always a timid kid. When other kids were playing rough, I'd hang back because I didn't want to get clobbered. I suffered from an unusually high level of physical fear. At around thirty, having successfully conquered a number of professional fears such as a bad case of mike fright and a related disorder, camera fright, I first started to develop a taste for things I should probably have already outgrown.

It may have been a case of delayed adolescence, but I began

to test myself physically—to conquer the fears of my childhood. It may have also been an antidote to some of the pressures of broadcasting. For whatever reasons, I acquired a strong desire to scuba dive, glide, explore, race cars, sail boats over long distances, fly airplanes and balloons. God knows what all. If I could pursue these outdoor interests as part of my on-camera career, so much the better.

It was this lust for challenge that led me to the South Pole at the end of 1982. It is a strange sensation to stand at the end of the earth. The spot is extremely desolate, quite high (about 9300 feet above sea level), and almost featureless. No matter what advances of technology and transportation have since intervened, the ghosts of the great explorers from the heroic age—Scott, Amundsen, Shackelton—crowd in on anyone who reaches here.

There is something positively overwhelming about the sheer emptiness of it all.

"God what an awful place," British Captain Robert Falcon Scott wrote. No one could have known better. Scott and his four companions froze to death on this ice on their way back to base camp from the Pole.

December is midsummer in Antarctica. The temperature was a relatively balmy −26 Fahrenheit, and there was almost no wind. Despite a prudent knowledge of the dangers at the Pole, I felt safe and comfortable. I was wearing heavy twill pants lined with a synthetic wool, over lined chinos and thermal underwear. Above my waist I wore a thermal undershirt, a heavy wool shirt, a vest of quilted insulation, and an enormous orange down parka with a lined hood. For extra protection, I had covered my head with an orange Balaclava hat, a perfect padded headpiece were I to decide to stand on my head.

Standing on your head at the South Pole makes some backward sort of sense. In fact, it has become something of a cliché for visitors to the Pole to perform this banal balancing act—even if the ghosts of the great Antarctic explorers would view it with icy disdain. I thought about it, but after stabbing the green flag into the ice, I decided to abandon the idea. Moving the marker was enough of a stunt. Besides, we looked ridiculous enough in those oversize Bunny Boots and bright red puffy parkas, like giant orange penguins rallying around some alien flag.

Once, much was made of going around the world in eighty days. More recently, astronauts have orbited the globe in about ninety minutes. Now I had conceived a magic plan to beat them all.

I calculated that if I walked around the true South Pole in a circle somewhat under eight feet in radius, each step would take me into a different time zone. I could go around the world in twenty-four steps, in about half a minute. I started out at Zero Meridian, the longitude shooting straight through Greenwich, England, in the center of the Prime Time Zone. At step five, I was on New York time, step eight in Los Angeles time, step ten, Hawaiian time. When I crossed the International Date Line, I was theoretically losing a day. But, as I said with a shrug to the camera, "At the South Pole, what's a day?"

I stepped smartly across the meridians marking Australia and Japan and India, then trudged, as gracefully as possible given my ungainly costume, finally around back to Zero Meridian, with hardly anyone knowing I had been gone.

The South Pole loves to get the best of you. When we reviewed the tape of my circumambulation of the globe, it turned out that the color had frozen out. It looked more like dense black-and-white footage taken years ago, perhaps of Scott's expedition. Fortunately, cameraman Jim Watt was using tape and not film to shoot all the Antarctic sequences. We were able to reshoot the sequence, then play it back immediately in the warmth of the dome of Pole Station. The second time around, the color was fine.

It was 6:10 P.M., Eastern Standard Time, when I moved the Pole, but time at the bottom of the world is purely conventional, even arbitrary. The U.S. Navy uses Greenwich Mean Time, but Americans at Pole Station fly in and out via Christchurch, New Zealand. There is obviously no point in realigning your biological clock to an entirely new frame. So

New Zealand time is used for the mundane purposes of eating breakfast or falling asleep, while Greenwich Mean Time is used for the gathering of scientific data.

The "Pole People" got so tired of wrangling with the Navy over the time issue that they finally said, "Okay, we'll set our clocks to Greenwich Time, but that means we'll be eating lunch at midnight and be sound asleep at noon."

I have been fascinated with the South Pole since I was a child. My interest stemmed, surprisingly, from an elementary-school physics question. How was it, I wondered, that people visiting the continent of Antarctica managed not to fall off the earth and into oblivion? That was before I understood that "down" is toward the earth's center.

Later on, my curiosity was further aroused by reading about the tragic drama of the race between Raoul Amundsen, the Norwegian, and Robert Scott, the Britisher, to be the first man to the South Pole. Amundsen reached his goal on December 14, 1911, while Scott failed to arrive for another month. On his way back, Scott and his four companions froze to death only eleven miles from safety.

Respect for the courage of these adventurers was uppermost in my mind when I contemplated my own journey to Antarctica. I was entranced by an image of endless white ice, with no permanent population, and—inland from the shore—no animals, no plants, no insects, no germs. In its sheer sterility, it is the closest environment we have to outer space. How the tiny international band of scientists who winter over manage is a fair model for colonizing other planets. Experiments now being conducted at the Pole, far beneath that icy landscape, are giving us clues to earlier atmospheric conditions, to the origins of life on this planet, and by extension, on other planets as well.

About a quarter mile from the actual pole marker stands a ceremonial pole. It is, not surprisingly, a barber pole, circled by flags of the countries that have signed the Antarctic Treaty. In 1959 only twelve nations were involved, but it now has thirty-two adherents, including India. Half are active on the continent and qualify for participation in periodic conferences on the treaty. Though the pole itself might be purely symbolic, the treaty is very real. It could well prove a model for peaceful cooperation, as opposed to competition, in any future extra-planetary venture. It sets aside all rival territorial claims, prohibits any military activity or weapons testing on this continent the size of the U.S. and Mexico combined. The treaty also provides for unimpeded inspection to ensure strict adherence to its provisions.

I had wanted to come to the South Pole for about as long as I could remember. Some years before, I had done a story on Admiral Byrd for a syndicated television series called *American Lifestyles.* I had hoped to get to Antarctica for firsthand research, but our budget wouldn't cover the fare to New Zealand. I found myself in the awkward position of doing a story on Admiral Byrd without going to Antarctica. The setback only strengthened my resolve to make it someday. I have since learned that I was not alone. There must be something about the Pole itself that induces a mystical, perhaps irrational, desire to reach its remoteness.

For some years I had been in touch with both the National Science Foundation and the U.S. Navy regarding the possibility, and it now looked as if it might be feasible. If you get permission to go, all transport and food from New Zealand are handled by the NSF and the Navy. No airlines land in Antarctica. But crew and equipment costs, and transport to and from Christchurch, New Zealand, are not paid by the U.S. This was a formidable budget item. Still, we locked the trip in at *20/20.* George Orick was the producer, and he started immediately on lists and logistics.

When I heard in August of 1982 that the South Pole was going to be moved in December, I had a talk with Dr. John Slaughter, then president of the National Science Foundation, the organization in charge of American scientific activity in Antarctica. I told Slaughter I'd like to be the one to move it. The next month they called me from Washington to say they had suggested this to the scientists down there, who thought it was a good idea.

In the television news business, trips across the world are

arranged on a twenty-four-hour basis. ABC News president Roone Arledge failed to appreciate the levels of time and planning it takes to set up an expedition to "the end of the earth." A few weeks before I was due to go, our producer, Av Westin, called me aside.

"Roone doesn't want you away for so long during December. He wants the trip put off awhile."

I was flabbergasted. All I could think of to say was, "Av, on December tenth I'm going to be at the South Pole. I sure hope it's going to be for ABC." Av's understanding and intercession saved both the trip and my contract.

Permission from the National Science Foundation, the United States Navy, and the head of ABC News were essential, but I had another problem. A physical exam by a private doctor turned up an incipient hernia. I was surprised. Not long before, I had helped my father, then in his eighties, lift some heavy object. "Hernia is one thing you don't have to worry about," he said. "The Downses have good planking."

The Navy did a reexam and found no hernia, but they insisted I sign a waiver before I could go beyond Christchurch. A year and a half later, I finally did develop a hernia, which was corrected by surgery. It must have been there all along. Fortunately, the South Pole marker was not heavy.

I had become somewhat obsessive about the trip, compelled by the eloquence of Scott, who kept a journal of his last, fatal days at the Pole. Though I was confident our expedition would end differently, one entry in the journal kept coming back to me: "After all, it is not what we see that inspires awe, but the knowledge of what lies beyond our view. And we, little human insects, have started to crawl over this awful desert, and are now bent on crawling back again."

The Pole is located on a continental plateau, where the ice is two miles thick.

After lugging more than two tons of camera equipment and gear to Christchurch, we took off two days later on a C-141 Navy Transport to McMurdo Station, Antarctica.

There are no alternate landing sites, and no land between

New Zealand and Antarctica. Unless radio communications informs a flight that McMurdo is open, a plane must turn back at the point where it still has enough fuel to reach New Zealand again. It is the point of no return.

The worst cliff-hanger of the expedition came when radio transmission with McMurdo blacked out on an intermittent basis. Not knowing if McMurdo was clear, we turned back for three minutes. I thought the whole mission was scrubbed. Fortunately, the point of no return is closer to McMurdo than to New Zealand. When we finally made radio contact, we were able to turn around again toward Antarctica, with just enough fuel reserve.

We landed on sea ice eight feet thick. Almost immediately, we boarded a Hercules C-130 for the Pole Station. There was a danger, due to the blackout, that we might not get there the next day. Or, if the blackout continued, at all.

Inside the geodesic dome at Pole Station are a number of buildings—mess hall, labs, dormitories. Unlike McMurdo, there are private rooms for those who live at the Pole. I found my room excessively warm, and couldn't locate a control to make it cooler. Ironically, the only way I could sleep at the South Pole was to take off all my clothes and lie on top of my blanket.

During December, Antarctic midsummer, the sun never sets. It hangs in the sky at the same 23 degrees off the horizon all day and night as it moves slowly around the sky. By March 21 it sits squarely on the horizon, neither rising or setting, but traveling the full 360-degree sweep around. Then, in the winter, which is our summer, the sun never rises, and it is perpetually dark. The long Antarctic night is not an experience for the average tourist. But sixteen to twenty Americans do "winter over" here every year, strictly for research purposes. Once committed, they are frozen in for the duration, as no airplane can land until after sunrise in the spring.

A few days later, we helicoptered from McMurdo Station across the Sound to Taylor Valley. McMurdo Station is the main United States installation in Antarctica. As we neared the magnificent Transantarctic Range, we could see thick tongues of glacial ice flowing, like cold white molasses, out from the valleys. We set the 'copter down on a glacier near immense ice-fall spills the size of Niagara. Their vast tonnage moves at a stately pace, taking weeks for the topmost ice to reach the level of the glacier.

Standing before one awesome cataract, I found myself unable to speak. A wave of emotion came over me in the presence of such a remote natural wonder of the world. Finally, I taped a short essay for *20/20*.

Here, among these magnificent "dry valleys," which truly resemble the moon, I staked out a claim to Ruth Downs Land, covering roughly 66,000 acres located across McMurdo Sound from McMurdo Station. I have walked on it, photographed it, and marked off its coordinates on a map.

Compared to some claims, Ruth Downs Land is a pretty small spread. Queen Maud Land and Marie Byrd Land each cover millions of square miles. But modest-sized Ruth Downs Land does follow true Antarctic tradition, in being named after a woman. Following the example of Admiral Byrd, I named the land after my wife.

After breakfast on Monday, December 13, we headed out in a track vehicle to the survival training area north of Scott Base, the New Zealand station. This is the Ross Ice Shelf, which extends for nearly a thousand miles down to the Ross Sea. The shelf is a solid sheet of freshwater ice hundreds of feet thick and almost as large as Alaska. Glaciers pour down off the Polar cap and flow majestically down to the Ross Sea, where they finally break off at the edge in huge chunks. The shelf has been known to calve icebergs bigger than Connecticut.

Near the edge of the mountains the ice starts to buckle under extreme pressure from the glacial flow. Treacherous ridges called *sastrugi* rise in giant ripples. Between them, crevasses open to various widths. This is an ideal site for survival training for scientists and support people scheduled to remain here for any length of time. We taped some New Zealand mountaineers teaching training parties how to build an ice shelter.

The fierce wind was blowing snow that severely cut our visibility. This snow, flying across an open crevasse, can first form a cornice, a lip of snow out over the abyss. Then, reaching the other side, it creates a bridge of snow that thickens in time. This is truly the cruelest natural menace I know. The snow-bridge completely conceals the crevasse and will support the weight of a human being just long enough for centering over the opening. Then it gives way, dropping the unsuspecting traveler into a crack that goes down dozens, even hundreds of feet, narrowing as it goes.

After videotaping Antarctic mountain teams roping themselves together for safety, we followed them to an area known to be pocked with ice crevasses. Producer George Orick and I hung back in the rear with Dr. Frank Williamson of the National Science Foundation. There were not enough ropes and slings for all of us. After a demonstration of how a member of a roped team who falls into an ice crevasse can be pulled out by his team members, I read, on camera, an appropriate passage from the Antarctic Survival Manual: "An unroped fall into a crevasse is inevitably fatal. Should you survive the tumble, your death from hypothermia is only hours away."

Not more than fifteen minutes later, Frank Williamson struck out a few yards from the rest of the party, trying to avoid a treacherous-looking area in the snow. He headed sideways and somewhat north to a firmer-looking area where he thought he saw footprints still left from one of the student training teams.

At first I thought he had fallen to his knees. Then I decided he had fallen into some sort of shallow hole or depression. Then with horror I realized, "Oh my God—he's fallen into a crevasse!"

He had plunged through the snow up to his waist. From where I was standing, only a few yards away, I could see him, now visible only from the chest up, desperately holding himself up by both arms, grabbing the crumbling ice edges with both hands.

George Orick was closest to him. Frank would surely have

fallen through to his death if George hadn't rushed over and dropped to one knee, pinning Frank's arm to the ice, finally grabbing hold of his hand. When I got there, Frank was still sliding down the narrow ice walls, making it almost impossible for me to get a grip on his right arm. I managed to reach a hand down to his shoulder, but he was slowly slipping out of his clothes.

All in a flash, I grasped two awful facts. First, as George and I tried to pull Frank up, all we seemed to be doing was making it impossible for him to breathe. And when we relaxed our grip slightly to let him get air, he slipped farther down in his clothing. At the same time, I was sure I felt the edges crumbling, threatening to throw all three of us down into the bottomless hole.

I threw myself flat down on the surface and tried to keep my feet back as far as possible to act as an anchor. Holding on to Frank's right arm, I could see past him down to a shelf of snow about fifteen feet below. Beyond that was open darkness, continuing on for what looked like miles.

George said, "Hold on, Frank—you're going to be all right. Everything's going to be okay."

Frank said, "No, it isn't." I could hear doom in his voice. He didn't think he was going to get out of that hole alive.

The members of the training team quickly went into action. Four minutes later they had a rope around Frank and were hauling him out of the crevasse.

Jim and Tom, our camera and sound men, were roped, and hung back as anchor for the rest of their team. But they had a clear shot of the proceedings and taped the whole thing from the point when George first fell onto Frank's hand.

As for Frank, he handled the situation with courage, and with the humor that so often masks the terror of a brush with death:

FRANK WILLIAMSON (to cameraman): "Did you get it all? How'd I look?"

What I might call my physical on-camera exploits began over

thirty years ago, when, in 1955, I learned to scuba dive for *The Home Show*. We were shooting a short diving segment from the pool of the Beverly Wilshire Hotel in Beverly Hills, hoping to show viewers how people would go about learning for themselves. In those days the sport was fairly new and basically unregulated. The theory was that if you didn't know what you were doing, the only person you could hurt was yourself.

I learned the basics, and when that tame swimming-pool segment proved popular, we searched out more authentic excitement. The art of underwater photography was developing rapidly, and we took advantage of the new technologies to bring our viewers an undersea world few had ever seen. We did a number of dramatic diving segments out of Silver Springs, Florida, with Rico Browning, a champion diver and underwater dolphin trainer who handled the undersea sequences for the popular show *Sea Hunt*, starring Lloyd Bridges.

Later I would dive, both on- and off-camera, in the Bahamas, the Virgin Islands, various coastal and Great Lakes locations, the Great Barrier Reef off Australia, and in Tahiti and Hawaii. I was even tempted to dive under the Antarctic ice with a rather daring scientist performing experiments in a lake of glacial melt in the Taylor Valley. But when I got a closer look at the diving conditions, I was glad they wouldn't let me.

I did do a night dive—without lights—off San Salvador with scientists from the Ocean Trust Foundation. On a cloudy, moonless night we rode out a mile to sea, to the edge of an undersea shelf dropping off into a trench hundreds of fathoms deep. We had been diving that afternoon in the same place. But after dark, using a little mooring buoy with a small light on it to mark the right spot, we dropped an anchor sixty feet down to the shelf. The running lights on the boat were then doused. With more than a little shock I realized that we were really going to dive without lights. I had dived at night once before, off the Great Barrier Reef, with lights, but never in total darkness.

The prospect of getting lost in that infinite blackness wasn't inviting. I thought to myself, "Well, I'll just lower myself down into this ink and climb down the anchor chain to the bottom. If

I don't like what I find, I'll climb back up the anchor chain and reboard."

My enthusiasm flagged even further when I recalled the hammerhead shark we had encountered in these waters only a few hours before. He was about eight feet long, but he hadn't crowded us, so we let him alone. One of the scientists, Dr. Sylvia Earle, an expert oceanographer and record-holding professional diver, encouraged me by her confidence. She had done this sort of dive before. Once I was underwater, I was surprised. When my eyes began to "iris out," the world around me came alive. A spooky, silvery light was emitted from anything that moved, created by the phosphorescence of plankton—tiny organisms in the water. Incredible scenarios of marine activity were visible at those depths, and at that hour, that could never be seen by artificial light. Any unnatural light source would have frozen the magnificent movement. Or, even worse, frightened it away.

Among the more fascinating spectacles were photo-blephar, fish with phosphorescent bacterial sacs beneath their eyes that give off a flickering glow, like fireflies. This species, up to then found only in the Mediterranean, is called *crypto pharonon*. They seemed like miniature Chevrolets as they swam, their tiny headlamps lighting a path along a deep undersea highway. Dr. John McClosker, curator of San Francisco's Steinhart Aquarium, had predicted the presence of these fish. He took specimens, and his discovery made the New York *Times*.

I was thrilled by this rare aquatic drama, but still uneasy. Amid this exotic tranquility, I kept imagining the warlike visage of that hammerhead shark. When we finally got back to the surface, I did my best to hide a powerful sense of relief.

Deep-sea diving is not just a sport; it has valuable commercial aspects. The most romantic, and sometimes the most rewarding, is treasure hunting. For 20/20, Geraldo Rivera and I were given a chance to help search for a lost Spanish galleon on the Anegada Reef, twenty miles north of Tortola in the British Virgin Islands. The reef lies in the Anegada Passage, a preferred entrance to the Caribbean for ships sailing to and from

Europe as far back as the sixteenth century. Twenty-five miles long and hidden just a few feet below the ocean surface, hundreds of ships have foundered there over the centuries. Only a few have ever been successfully salvaged.

The leader of our undersea adventure was the veteran treasure diver Bert Kilbride, the "Lord of the Shipwrecks." I had known Kilbride for years, ever since diving with him at Buck Island Park, an underwater trail off the island of St. Croix. Bert was nearly seventy when Geraldo and I paid him a visit. He and his family had been exploring the area's reefs for over thirty years, and had located 138 sunken ships along this single reef. Many were found to contain substantial treasure, enough to enable the Kilbrides to comfortably inhabit their own private island and to handle the considerable expense of searching for sunken treasure in such treacherous waters.

The site we searched was reported to contain the wreck of the *San Ignacio*, which was sunk in 1742 with $10,000,000 in treasure aboard, including a cargo of uncut diamonds. That cargo, if recovered intact, would be worth at least $100,000,000 at today's prices. Under an exclusive agreement with the British Government, the Kilbrides are entitled to keep half of whatever treasure they find.

Geraldo and I wore full-length wet suits, not only to keep warm but to protect us from the sharp coral and debris on the bottom. At a working depth of fifty feet, we'd have less than an hour to dive on a single tank. A divemaster kept track of our bottom time, because even at that mild depth, the accumulation of nitrogen dissolved in the blood could cause the bends.

In thirty years of diving, I've seen few underwater sights more dramatic than the carcass of a sunken ship. Swimming through those tight spaces, in a maze of decaying corridors, can cause claustrophobia. I have experienced this in exploring relatively modern undersea wrecks. But after two centuries, the wreck of a wooden ship is pretty much gone.

Ancient wrecks are often nearly undetectable. The wood has rotted; the metal sheathing, stone ballast, and metallic cargo has disappeared beneath the sand of the bottom. Marine life has since covered everything, making the wrecks indistinguishable from the natural growth.

Such was the wreck of the *San Ignacio*. After clearing away hundreds of pounds of sand with a giant vacuum pump, we found our first identifiable metal object. It was one of the ship's cannon, heavily encrusted with coral. Geraldo wielded a heavy iron crowbar to wrest it from the ocean floor. A line and winch were rigged on the dive ship, and once on its way up, the cannon lurched toward me. I got out of the way just in time before it fell back to the ocean bottom.

Even as I watched the cannon ascend, I felt sure the boat winch couldn't possibly lift it. After breaking the surface, it swung wildly and with deadly force in the air as the crew tried to land it on deck. But the ropes and the winch finally held.

Before long the Kilbrides were chipping away at the layers of oxidation and sea life to try to make an identification. The cannon couldn't immediately be verified as belonging to the *San Ignacio*, but its crude design and markings plainly identified it as Spanish, and of the proper period, the early 1700s. Part of the evidence was that the cannon was made of iron, alloyed with 40 percent platinum, which the Spaniards called "bastard silver." By weight, these cannon are more platinum than iron, and thus extremely valuable.

My love of diving eventually aroused a passionate love for creatures that also dive, like dolphins. A fellow named Milt Santini used to capture dolphins out of the wild and train them or sell them to other trainers. When I met him, he had just gotten hold of a four-month-old dolphin. When I learned that Santini was planning to sell the dolphin to Dr. John Lilly, a well-known researcher into dolphin intelligence, I decided to buy the animal myself and keep it with Milt. I hadn't met Lilly at the time, but I didn't approve of his implanting electrodes in the brains of these animals.

I insisted on calling the dolphin Didi, even after learning that this winsome creature was a male. Didi was also something of an actor, though his show-biz career was limited to a brief stint as the swimming partner for Mitzi, the first Flipper on television.

224

Finally I asked Milt to set Didi free.

The John Pennekamp Coral Reef State Park in southern Florida has an undersea program for returning animals to the wild. By setting up a feeding station in a wide underground pen, the animals come to know that they can always get food at the shore station. Then the fence is removed and they are on their own. Didi is now swimming free and happy, perhaps in the protected waters of this park.

In 1969 I was given another chance to test my devotion to sea creatures, including one of the world's most fearsomely named sea animals. With *The Today Show*, I flew out to San Diego, where we shot segments on the waterfront, at the Navy Yard, and at the famous zoo. But for me the main attraction turned out to be Sea World. There, a young Korean animal trainer, Tek Yun, had become the first person to ride a killer whale. I became the first nontrainer to try it.

Killer whales have been living in captivity for some time. The experts at Sea World had come to realize that these creatures are not really killers of human beings. They don't want to eat people—at least not in the ordinary course of things. In extremely rare cases they have been known to kill other mammals, but only when severely provoked. Still, I could tell that Tek was a little nervous about my getting into that tank—even as he assured me there had never been a documented case of a so-called killer whale killing a human.

"If I tell you to get out of the tank, get out fast."

"You won't have to tell me twice," I assured him.

I sat on the edge of the enormous pool, deep enough for the whale to dive in. He was sounding, then jumping twenty feet out of the water. Gingerly, I hung my feet over the edge. Tek was right. The killer whale made no move to bite them off. He was swimming placidly enough, only somewhat curious why this strange creature wanted to share his private pool.

Tek handed me a plastic kitchen sponge with a rough edge like a scouring pad. "Rub his skin, like this," he said, demonstrating. "They like having their skin rubbed because small sea creatures stick to it and it irritates them."

Somewhat tentatively, I reached out with that scouring pad

and rubbed the whale's skin. To my amazement, he actually slowed down. He swam, I swear, a little closer to me, like a cat sweeping by to brush up against your legs.

Finally, I took a handful of fish cut up into small pieces and dove to the bottom of the tank, with enough air for about half an hour. I lay there and waited. The whale's curiosity was now aroused. He came close and I rubbed him a little more while feeding him a bite of fish. His enormous mouth opened wide enough to put my whole head inside, but prudence dictated restraint. I figured such a move might frighten him as much as it would me. He had a double row of conical teeth, each the size of my thumb.

He opened that huge mouth and I fed him more fish. He seemed to be enjoying this little game. I thought to myself, "Well, if he likes having his skin rubbed, maybe he'd like having his tongue rubbed." I reached in to rub his tongue. He truly loved that. It was at that point, I think, that we became friends.

When it came time to ride him, I got out of my scuba gear but stayed in my rubber suit. I tried a few times, unsuccessfully, to mount this creature, whose skin was as slick and smooth as a bald car tire. Finally I got hold of his dorsal fin. I slung one leg around in front. Very carefully, I positioned myself. As soon as I thought I was set, he decided to take off like a rocket. I fell off the whale.

I got myself more firmly seated, with the dorsal fin planted squarely at the base of my spine. It felt like the cantle of a saddle. He took off again, this time more gently. Miraculously, I stayed on. It felt like riding a greased horse, bareback. Nothing but the grip of my knees kept me from sliding side to side as if in some aquatic rodeo.

After a few times around the pool, I retired. From then on I decided I'd stick to dolphins. Didi would never have given me such a hard time.

I later heard that my friendly whale killed a 400-pound dolphin with whom he was sharing a tank. I have always assumed that the dolphin must have done something to irritate him.

*   *   *

Having survived undersea sports, I went on to flying—again because of television. One day in 1962, Al Smith, a *Today Show* producer, came up with a brilliant idea.

"We'd like to do a serious segment on what is involved in getting a private pilot's license." He thought they would take a beginning student through all the stages of flight training.

I said, "That sounds wonderful. How about making me the student?"

I proposed this on the reasonable ground that if I could learn to fly, anybody could.

Under proper conditions, flying is not a dangerous activity. But I ran into trouble on my very first lesson—while still on the ground. At Westchester County Airport, we filmed my flight instructor showing me the walk-around check, to make sure all was right with the plane. We did this inside the hangar. Outside, the wind was quite high, with gusts up to forty knots. When the lesson was finished and the film crew had wrapped, I noticed that the wind wasn't howling anymore. I took a quick look out the hangar door.

"The wind's really dropped," I said. "Why don't we take her up?"

The instructor called the flight service station, which confirmed that the wind velocity was down to about zero. For the moment, conditions were safe for a light plane. But they said, in effect, "You're on your own."

We took the plane down to the end of the apron and taxied into position for a runup. It was still eerily calm. Just as we began our takeoff roll, the wind came up and hit us like a giant hand, picking up the light plane and driving it nose down onto the runway. The little Cessna 172 stayed in this position, tail up to the sky, the prop and nose smashed.

I had my feet on the instrument panel. I undid my seat belt, wrenched the door open, and crawled out onto the wing strut. Just as I was trying to climb down off the plane, the fuselage began to fall backward. I jumped as far as I could, imagining gas tanks rupturing behind me. I hit the ground rolling, with no idea which part of the plane might hit first. Fortunately, neither I nor the instructor was hurt.

The following week I took my second lesson, at a different airport, with a different instructor—and with a new airplane. I drove out to Linden, New Jersey, an airport completely surrounded by smokestacks, bridges, oil tanks and high-tension lines. If you can fly in and out of Linden, you can fly anywhere.

Out the airport window I could see a brand-new Cessna 172. I recognized the number. I wanted to get a jump on the situation and look good to the new instructor. I went out and started performing the walk-around check, a routine I had learned the lesson before.

I had just about completed the check when a man fell into step behind me. I didn't want to break my train of thought, so I didn't introduce myself. He seemed to be evaluating my performance. When I finished the check I asked the man, "Should we take her up?"

"Sure."

"Which seat should I sit in, the right or the left?"

"Which seat do you want to sit in?"

"Well, I'd like to sit on the left, the pilot's seat."

"Fine," he said.

I climbed into the pilot's seat and we had the engine started before we realized something was wrong. He wasn't my instructor. He was a new student who thought I was his instructor. We were just about to take up an airplane that neither of us knew how to land.

I was beginning to think that airplanes and I were jinxed until Dick Collins, my new flight instructor, came upon this unlikely scene. Once Collins took over my instruction, I made rapid progress.

The Today Show filmed all my lessons except my solo flight. That, according to tradition, is a surprise cast at the new pilot by his instructor.

It happened on Martha's Vineyard. I had sailed a boat out to the island, and my flight instructor flew out to meet me. I'd had about eight hours of flight instruction by then. We flew around the little Vineyard airfield twice on a particular flight pattern and landed smoothly each time. We were on the runway for a third takeoff. I assumed we were going to repeat the same routine when Collins opened the door to the Cessna and stepped out.

"I think you ought to take her up by yourself," he said. Then he was gone.

I was alone for the first time in an airplane cockpit. I taxied into position and carefully ran through all the procedures, made a clean takeoff, and climbed to my assigned altitude. After my first scheduled turn, I was in the pattern. All I had to do was come back downwind, make my base leg and line up final to land. I would have completed my solo.

But as soon as I flew downwind, there it was. A big DC-3 coming into land at the point at which I was preparing to enter my final approach. That is no situation for a neophyte pilot. But I simply expanded my flight pattern and came around behind him until the DC-3 touched down and turned off the runway. Then I landed safely, a solo pilot.

To qualify for my license, I needed to fly something like forty solo hours, a certain percentage of it cross-country. I flew to such fascinating places as Allentown, Pennsylvania, with *Today* filming some of those flights. After I passed my test flight with an FAA inspector, Dick Collins gave me a final piece of advice: "Now you are a licensed pilot. That means you can legally buy a surplus P-51 and put your grandmother in the back seat and fly to Alaska. But I wouldn't recommend it. Americans tend to think that anything that is legal is safe." He didn't need to add that some of them are now dead Americans.

From flying to gliding was an easy transition. An airplane, after all, is really a glider with an engine on board. Anyone who learns to fly can learn to glide. There are 20,000 licensed glider pilots in the United States, ranging in age from fourteen to over eighty. I am one of them.

Still, the fact that there is no engine and no propeller distresses some people. My father, for one, would fly with me in any airplane but not in a glider. Actually, I think gliding is a safer sport. The two glider ports I fly out of regularly have operated daily for dozens of years without a fatal accident. There is an occasional accident, but unlike regular plane crashes, the pilot and passenger almost always walk away from it unscathed, if shaken up.

My first gliding experience took place in Elmira, New York, the Glider Capital of America. Not coincidentally, it is also the headquarters of Schweizer Aircraft, the nation's foremost sailplane manufacturer. In 1962 I was in Elmira for *The Today Show* to do a segment on the New York State vineyards, and I decided to drive over to the glider port run by Schweizer.

I took a couple of glider rides with the instructor, Bernie Caras. We were sitting on the ground with the towplane all hooked up for a third time. I hadn't even undone my seat belt when Bernie hopped out the back door and reclosed the canopy. I was about to get out myself when he said, "You're a licensed pilot. I think you can take her up by yourself."

"No, thanks—I really don't think I'm ready," I said a second too late. The towline had snapped taut. I had the choice of either releasing the tow or heading on up. I went up. Once aloft, my main concern was losing the airport. Other than that I had no problems. The thrill of gliding silently through the open sky was unlike any other I've experienced. I later bought an acrobatic sailplane and now spend a good portion of what spare time I have gliding in it.

I have always been fascinated by speed, and there is nothing speedier than a jet aircraft except a rocket. I've flown two jet military aircraft, the Lockheed F-104 and the McDonnell Douglas F-101. Once I was over Chesapeake Bay in the F-104 with pilot Chuck Toffero. Since he could take over if I did anything stupid, he asked if there was anything special I'd like to do. We were at 28,000 feet.

"Sure," I said. "I'd like to do a loop."

He turned the controls over to me. I must say I didn't do a brilliant job. I lost 12,000 feet trying to close that loop. An F-104 is a Mach 2 aircraft, which means it can go twice the speed of sound. We were going about 1200 miles an hour, and at those speeds you need a lot of sky to move around in. When I pulled out of it, I hadn't made a tight enough loop, but—for-tunately—we were high enough to handle it. There was still 16,000 feet between us and the ground.

Speed on the ground is a different matter. As a small-town boy, I had been driving since the age of nine, and it was second nature to me. But until I was well over thirty I had never even thought of racing cars. It all started because of the persuasive skills of a high-powered press agent. Coupled, of course, with my willingness to explore what might prove to be an adventure.

It was 1970 and California's Ontario Speedway was ready to open. The promoters of the track had organized an inaugural Celebrity Pro-Am race in which various amateur celebrity drivers would be paired off with top-ranking professionals. I was asked to participate by Kirk Douglas, who had some interest in the track. Lou Cowan, of the public relations firm of Rogers & Cowan, like all great practitioners of his profession, has a tendency to exaggerate, if only in his clients' best interests. When the subject of the Pro-Am came up, my name somehow came up with it.

"But does he race cars?" someone asked.

"Sure," Lou said, confidently.

My name was entered along with six celebrity amateurs, almost all experienced drivers: Paul Newman, Dicky Smothers, Dean Martin's son Dino, astronaut Pete Conrad, and tennis champ Pancho Gonzales. There was one difference between these drivers and me. I had never been in an auto race.

I was picked up at the Ontario airport by one of the promoters of the speedway. Just making conversation, he asked me how many times I had raced.

"Oh, this is my first time," I said candidly. We drove the rest of the way in a rather uncomfortable silence. He later confessed that he had spent most of that drive figuring a polite way to drop me from the roster. His mind was conjuring up morbid headlines not conducive to promoting his new track: TODAY SHOW HOST KILLED AT NEW SPEEDWAY. But he grudgingly consigned me to my fate.

The Ontario Speedway is a replica of Indianapolis except for a few fine points. The Ontario track is an oval, but the area within the oval is laid out as a curving road-track for road racing. The Indy 500 is a straight speed race, running counterclockwise, and the cars turn in only one direction—to the left. A road race involves turns both right and left, and the direction at Ontario was clockwise. We were going to drive performance-model Porsche 914s, with five forward speeds and enough power to take you up over 150 mph on the straightaway.

Since we had only a few days to practice, I drove diligently under the tutelage of Bob Bondurant, who ran a high-performance driving school at the track. I learned, in time, how to turn the car using little more than the throttle and clutch, accelerating into the turns, hardly moving the wheel. Racing cars tend to "squirrel" somewhat on the turns, so I learned, slowly, how to hold the drift to a respectable limit. After a few days and a good many hours racked up on the road, I was able to push the car up into an acceptable competitive range, giving us a chance at the trophy.

My assigned partner was Mark Donohue, one of the great drivers of his generation. Paul Newman and Dicky Smothers, the leading celebrity drivers, were each assigned to one of the famous Unser brothers, also top-of-the line racers. Pete Conrad's partner was Mario Andretti. After every three laps the drivers were to switch off, so pros and amateur drivers were carefully matched according to size. Our harnesses were buckled so we could snap out of them and change places without extra time lost for size adjustments.

The celebrity drivers would begin the race with the strenuous Le Mans sprint, which requires the drivers to run for their cars at the start. The pro drivers were to be in the cars with engines running. As each sprinting partner touched the car, it would move out.

In practice runs, I would dash to the car, slap the rear fender, and stop just short of the low wall back of the pit. Before getting to my own car, I had to cross in front of a car driven by Parnelli Jones, a driver famous for letting nothing stand between him and winning. Before the race started, someone said to me, "Whatever you do, don't fall down in front of Parnelli's car. He'll run right over you."

When the actual starting gun went off, Mark was in our car, in gear and ready to slip the clutch. I made my dash as practiced, except that I ran faster than before. When my hand hit the top of the rear fender, I vaulted over the car *and* the pit wall. Fear can be a great motivator.

We ended up doing fairly well, all things considered. We finished fourth out of a pack of seven teams, which left us respectably in the middle, three ahead, three behind. If we hadn't been hit by one pit stop of excessive length, we would have made a better showing.

One minor consolation was that we finished one step ahead of Paul Newman's team. I can hardly consider that a serious victory, since Paul's car had mechanical trouble. Paul is such a gentleman that in an interview he told the story of how I finished ahead of him my first time out on a road track. He eliminated the key detail about his engine trouble.

The Ontario Pro-Am remains my only competitive car race. In retrospect the thrill doesn't compensate for the danger. I've seen too many drivers injured or killed in that sport. I had gotten to know Peter Revson, Mark Donohue, Graham Hill, Art Pollard. All are now dead.

I think it's simply too dangerous a sport for any but the youngest, best-coordinated, and most dedicated. Too much is dependent on muscle response and reflex time, which inevitably slow down as you get older, no matter what shape you're in. Paul Newman, still driving at sixty, is perhaps a brilliant exception.

Though I stopped competitive racing, I didn't entirely stop speed driving. In 1971, when I was still with *The Today Show,* I was given the chance to drive a Formula A racing car the day of the Indy 500. A Formula A car is so powerful that one touch of the throttle makes you feel as if a giant hand is pushing you from behind. Speedway rules permit practice on the Indy 500 only up to the day before the race. The day of the race, the track becomes off-limits to drivers.

By 7:00 A.M. I was out with the camera crew doing pre-race

coverage. I took a quick (very quick as it turned out) spin in the Scorpion, a Gilmore Race Team car built by Clint Brawner. The driver, Art Pollard, had been bumped in the time trials, and could race only by using their number-two car. This left the Scorpion free for me to drive before the race.

As I was belting in, one of the drivers told me that some of the mechanics and driver Cale Yarborough had a five-dollar bet that I would stall the engine just getting out of the pit. With that challenge in mind, I carefully let the clutch out after I had the engine well up and running. I barely, just barely, let my foot off that pedal until I was halfway down the first straight-away. I knew I was riding the clutch in a car costing upward of $80,000, but I was determined to come out on the right side of a five-dollar bet.

As it turned out, I was clocked at about 175 mph on the straightaway, a horrendous speed for me. The pavement on those turns flashed by at such velocity that I felt as if the world had dissolved into a blur. After surviving that quick run, I was wrapping up the segment of *Today* when one of the drivers called the track. He was furious because he thought one of the other drivers was breaking the rules by practicing on the day of the race.

There are people who go through life never feeling a need to test themselves physically. Then there are others who live for danger. The human spectrum of challenge runs all the way from fear and timidity about even mild risks to a thirst for danger that can be interpreted as self-destructive.

Either extreme is clearly abnormal. Perhaps the norm is someone who enjoys a moderate sense of danger, to add a certain spice to life. If that is true, I suppose I could classify in the range of normal.

I have always felt that our general concept of courage is cloudy, perhaps even false. If someone is truly fearless— so dumb as to not be afraid of anything—then bravery has no meaning. Courage requires that you feel fear and over-come it. Other valuable qualities require their opposites to have meaning. You can't enjoy a nice fire in a fireplace in a steam-heated room or enjoy a good meal unless you are hungry. Similarly, adventure is thrilling only when there is some fear that you are dealing with, perhaps even determined to conquer.

To develop a workable way to handle fear, you have to occasionally scare yourself. The process can be pleasant. It's the same sort of pleasure people get out of horror movies or roller coasters. A little danger provides seasoning, but too much is overwhelming. Even though I was not in much immediate danger in Antarctica when Dr. Williamson fell into the crevasse, it certainly wasn't fun. Close proximity to death is truly horrible. Once you've felt it, it's not an experience you would ever want to repeat.

Of course, many popular fears are utterly unfounded. People avoid swimming in the ocean for fear of sharks. That's as sensible as not walking across the street because there are cars in the road. Cars and sharks can both kill you, but the chances of sudden death from either are certainly not very high. Fear is compounded by ignorance. People who come out to Arizona are always asking about rattlesnakes. I point out that more people are killed by lightning in Arizona than by rattlesnakes. But houseguests have never asked me if I have a lightning rod on my house.

At the same time, ignorance often breeds carelessness about things that could reduce risk. If you don't know what you're doing, you're likely to be afraid of the wrong things and careless about the real dangers. In the case of active sports such as blue-water sailing, sky diving, scuba diving, gliding, ballooning, and general recreational aviation, the fears are often exaggerated. Statistically, more people die in automobiles and from accidents in the home, and from eating too much or smoking cigarettes, than while pursuing recreational activities they may consider dangerous.

I try to keep this in mind when pursuing all outdoor activities. It helps to check my fear.

Born in landlocked Ohio, I have always been fascinated by large bodies of water. When you are a child, you develop obsessive feelings, feelings almost like love, toward objects of magical fascination. I felt that way about water. I was driven toward water. At the same time, water frightened me half to death.

My uncle had a cottage on a lake a few dozen miles from our home in Lima. We would go down there in the summer and I'd go boating with an older cousin. I was always in the rowboat with my father or my older cousin, until once I decided to take the boat out by myself. I was shocked but thrilled to learn that the boat stayed afloat without anyone else being aboard. When it kept on floating for me, I felt like an admiral. I had an idea it took some special skill, like knowing how to ride a bicycle. From then on I fantasized about sailing an ocean, though I was still bound to small freshwater lakes.

In 1949 my wife and I and our four-year-old son took a short vacation at Bangs Lake in Illinois. With the little cottage we had rented came a rowboat equipped with a one-and-a-half-horse-power motor. One day I got out on that lake with my boy. Quite a way from shore a bad wind came up. The lake lay east to west, so there was a long fetch for the wind. I suddenly realized that the boat did not have flotation compartments and we didn't have life jackets. Though I could swim to shore if I had to, I wasn't sure I could make it with a four-year-old. And I was sure that I didn't want to make it without that four-year-old.

I really was in fear of death. I kept the bow into the waves. The boat seemed to be riding them, though we were shipping a great deal of water. I knew if I turned to make for shore, there was a real danger of broaching, and of capsizing. I found myself in the uncomfortable position of making promises to heaven that if I ever got out of this scrape, I'd start doing all sorts of things the right way.

The wind finally subsided a little, and we eventually made it back to dry land. But I so resented feeling afraid of the water that a seed was planted. Eventually it grew into the idea that I had to conquer the biggest body of water on this planet. That of course is the Pacific Ocean. In 1965 I sailed a boat from Panama to Tahiti, with my son aboard. By then he was nineteen. Simultaneously, I expunged that demon of fear first felt on Bang's Lake, and enjoyed one of the most rewarding experiences of my life.

I was still host of *The Today Show* when I made my Pacific voyage, and many of my friends thought I was crazy to go. The trip would take the better part of five months. It would be extremely expensive, and it would take me out of the public eye for an extended period. The public, they said, was fickle.

For me, the point was that I wanted to go, and that was enough. If the public (which is not so fickle) was going to forget about me, they would do it right while I was on the air. As for the expense, sailing across the Pacific was precisely the sort of project my money from broadcasting had been earned to fulfill.

Another common objection was that the trip would be dangerous. I couldn't disagree, but a certain degree of danger adds texture to life, and as someone who believes in life even more than adventure, I was determined to take all possible steps to ensure the safety of the expedition.

I studied ocean pilot charts for weather and wind averages over a five-year period. I read and reread the Sailing Directions and pored over approach and harbor charts of our stops. I read accounts of other trans-Pacific voyages. I boned up on celestial navigation, always an abiding interest. And I spent a lot of energy planning our trip down to every niggling detail, including the type of boat, the makeup of the crew, the provisions and supplies we would need. Even the watch system to adopt or modify.

We began our journey in Fort Lauderdale, stopped in the Bahamas and Jamaica, and made a languid passage through the Panama Canal. My wife met me, the crew, and our son, Hugh Raymond, better known as H.R., at each port and accompanied us through the Canal. Although Ruth's ancestors were Phoenicians who sailed out of the Mediterranean to the British Isles and possibly to the New World centuries before Columbus, she is not a sailor. She insists that her ancestors were practical people who traveled by the most modern means available at the time. If the old Phoenician sailors were voyaging today, she says, they would fly jets. Ruth said goodbye in Panama, planning to meet us in Tahiti when we made landfall there some eight weeks away.

It was in the Caribbean that we had our first serious mishap. A large steel barrel containing spare fuel broke loose from where it was tied to the mizzenmast and rolled around on deck like a blind metal elephant. It damaged materials stowed on deck and smashed the cockpit coaming until we finally secured it. In my captain's log I noted that a state of "normalcy" on a trip of this type is not at all normal. Only a few nights later, just east of the Galápagos, we were visited by a mysterious leviathan, possibly a shark, which followed us silently under the surface, glowing with phosphorescence for a few hours before vanishing.

We made a landing at the Galápagos, where Darwin voyaged in the *Beagle*. We visited there with a number of rather eccentric residents, including two German brothers who made their home in that remote spot. During World War II they had pledged to go as far away from Adolf Hitler as possible.

I was privileged to spy Tahiti before anyone else in the crew. We were anxiously crowded on deck, awaiting that last landfall. All eyes were focused on the horizon, hoping to be the first to glimpse land. I happened to sweep my eyes higher into the haze than the rest. Rising up out of the water was the volcanic mass of Tahiti itself. I felt like Cortés.

"Land ho!" I said quietly.

"Where?" everyone asked.

"You're looking too low," I said.

They then saw that faint discontinuity below which the sky seemed a tiny shade darker.

Within minutes, Tahiti's silhouette emerged in the hazy afternoon sky. We got to the break in the reef outside Papeete just as the sun was setting.

We stayed on Tahiti for a few weeks. My wife and my

daughter had been waiting there to join us. I threw a surprise Tahitian birthday banquet for Ruth, which actually remained a secret until the last moment. As our time ran out, we were saddened by the thought of flying back to "civilization." One of our company, Bob Dixon, was so taken with the island that he decided to stay for an indefinite period. It was a one-way trip for him. He still lives there.

One of the first things I did on landing at Los Angeles in October was to visit Johnny Carson on *The Tonight Show*. At the start of the voyage, I had shaved my head in order not to be bothered with haircuts. It had grown back in unevenly, at best. To make matters worse, I now had a beard.

In those days, Johnny Carson did a little bit called "The Mystery Guest." When I strode onto *The Tonight Show* stage, looking nothing like my former *Today Show* self, Johnny was dumbfounded. He had no idea who I was.

I sat there, grinning at my own transformation. Suddenly, a male voice in the audience shouted out, "It's Hugh Downs!" I had made a few radio broadcasts back to *The Today Show* during the trip, so it's possible this man knew where I had been.

I'll never forget the look on Johnny's face as he squinted at me and said, "Hugh, is that really you?"

I had to admit it was. I also had to admit, with satisfaction, that I felt like a changed man.

That trip across the Pacific has given me more personal satisfaction than any other travel experience I can think of, including Antarctica. I have considered embarking on this voyage once more, this time with my grandson, my daughter's boy. I have considered it, but I haven't decided. I hesitate only because of the worry it would cause my daughter, and, once again, my wife.

My one last adventurous dream, still intact and unfulfilled, is to fly into outer space. So far, I have been able to live out that dream only in the lifelike environment of flight simulators.

Flight simulation is quite an amazing technology. The Space

Shuttle simulator at the Johnson Space Center in Houston generates such realistic images and effects that when you're in the cockpit you can look out the windows and see open space, the earth, and the array of stars, focused to infinity, just as they would appear from the space shuttle.

On takeoff, you can actually see the launch tower falling away as you lift from the earth. As you move upward, the sky turns dark. You see stars in the night sky, the same ones you would see on the date and location entered into the computer systems.

Then, into that vast night sky comes a view of the earth's surface. You are moving around it just as you would through space. On re-entry you break through the heat barrier at about Mach 25. In the drag of the earth's atmosphere you finally slow down to less than Mach 1. Through this, you really have no power. You are in a high-speed, very long glide. You put the nose down in order to keep the speed at about 245 knots, more than twice the speed of landing for a commercial airliner. At that enormous, shrieking pace, you get the gear down and level off. Then you begin your flare, when you put the nose up and the plane lands on its hind legs. The flare acts not only to hold the plane up but also to bleed the speed off.

For 20/20, I made five simulated shuttle landings for a piece on the Space Shuttle.

My first two landings were pretty bad. I came down in excess of fifteen feet per second, which blew the tires. After those attempts I landed safely but ran off the runway. On the fourth and fifth tries, I finally made decent landings.

I have even made a few moon surface landings in the Lunar Module Simulator at Cape Canaveral. Landing the lunar module is unlike any form of flying. You have to put the ship down at precisely the right attitude, or angle. You can set it down wherever you want, provided it is level, but it's still very tricky. There's no atmosphere, so you don't glide in. You come, more or less, straight down. If you come down at too tilted an angle, you can fall over on your side. Then you would have permanent residence on the moon.

Fortunately, technology can sometimes make up for human

error. If you bring the lunar module in at too critical an angle, the computers will take the ship away from you. As I made my landing listing too far to one side, I felt the stick jump right out of my hand. Those computers are programmed to save the ship at all costs, even the pilot's self-esteem.

As president of the National Space Institute, I had made a formal request to NASA to be allowed onto the first orbital platform, the precursor to which was Skylab. This was before the Shuttle was even on the drawing boards. Unfortunately, the orbital platform was delayed. But work went ahead on the STS (the Space Transportation System), and the Shuttle was born.

After I left *The Today Show* and was no longer connected with a single network, Scott Carpenter thought I had a decent chance of becoming the first nonastronaut in space. It didn't happen, and now that I'm with ABC there would be a problem favoring one network over the other two. I know Walter Cronkite has applied. There are other journalists who have put in bids.

When the "first journalist in space" contest came up, I had considered myself a prime contender. NASA acknowledged that I was the first to apply, but the agency had never promised that I would be the first to go.

In late 1985 I withdrew from the competition. Not only did I know the people on the selection committee, but I was chairman of the National Space Institute. The very connection that I thought would be helpful now would give my selection the appearance of impropriety. In fact, it probably would *be* improper. I recommended Geraldo Rivera on the grounds that he would be able to recount the experience both from a reporter's standpoint and as an emotional, human experience.

After the shuttle disaster in January 1986, many journalists who had applied admitted to having second thoughts. But now that it appears to have been a freak accident, many are glad they left their names on the list.

I won't get into space as the first journalist, but perhaps when the shuttle flights become more routine, there might be room for me in space. That of course would be my greatest adventure.

10
FINAL CUT

I bought my first television set in 1951. One night I was watching an adult drama with my son, who was then six. The scene was set in a hospital room. A sick man was lying in bed. I sat there engrossed in the plot, wondering whether the man was going to make it or not, when my son nudged me, grinning.

"The wall moved," he said.

"The what?"

"The wall. When he moved his head back against it. Just then. It's not a wall. It's just *cloth*."

Forced to pay the wall some attention, I could see that the entire hospital room was nothing more than a backdrop, a stage set. My son had seen through an illusion I thought was real.

Magicians tell us that it is always more difficult to fool children than grown-ups. Adults possess a whole set of preconceptions that make it easier for them to be snookered. As more people grow up knowing the conventions of television, it becomes easier for us to be fooled by its capacity to generate a powerful, all-encompassing world of illusion. Television creates its own reality. As the most potent form of communication ever invented, it casts its own magic spell.

Of course, the illusion of television could be justified on the grounds that all reality is an illusion. The tabletop we see as solid is really just a mass of particles, all in constant motion. And the particles themselves are not even made up of solid matter, but of electrical charges. What we see as an unbroken surface is, to the physicist, mostly empty space.

But television is even more magical. It can change things we consider objective reality into a hall of mirrors. If a camera crew is assigned to cover a political rally in a stadium that is less than a third full, the director can easily alter that reality. The advance men can compress the crowd into the line of the cameras. This will make the stadium *appear* full.

The camera's eye can distort almost at will.

1. The shot could show the stadium full, by confining itself to a tight view of the massed crowd.

2. It could show the stadium deserted, by focusing on the empty seats.

3. It could pan around the stadium, revealing that the stadium is only a third full.

4. It could ignore the crowd and focus on the speakers.

The built-in bias of the camera's eye can never be entirely avoided, but it can be neutralized if objectivity is a goal. As David Brinkley once said, "You can't be objective, but you can try to be fair."

Trying for objectivity is one goal of television news, but if we listen to polls of listener attitudes, it is not always achieved. One reason—and I think this is mainly true of local TV news—is the supposed need to add the dramatic trappings of show business. When this happens we are looking for trouble.

There is nothing wrong with news being diverting. Reality, if properly presented, should engage as well as inform. But if producers, in a misplaced attempt to juice up their product, shape and contour the news to fit a preconception of what "sells," that is a disservice to the public. They are eroding the professional goals they are supposed to serve.

The electronic media so amplify everything that both distortion and a perception of distortion—even where none exists—pose a constant threat to their credibility. Striving for objectivity while at the same time seeking to hold attention is the challenge of any television news show, whether it be the nightly news, *60 Minutes,* or *20/20.*

244

Television is the only channel of communication called upon to deliver both entertainment and reality, fictional drama and real-life drama, fantasy and information. We don't expect reality from movies or from the stage. We are disappointed if we don't get entertainment. But in television we expect both.

It's a tall order, but the medium is trying. In the early years we were sometimes off the mark. But today I see signs all around that our medium is maturing rapidly. There is a growing realization that providing information is what we do best. Television is superb at covering late-breaking news and current events, imparting information, and presenting an accurate visual window on the world, from an inauguration to an election, from a hijacking to an earthquake.

One reason is that the traditions of good journalism are beginning to take hold. Another important reason is that the networks now recognize that reality sells. They can make money, a lot of it, by presenting the real world and the real truth.

Nobody endows commercial television. To survive, it must move merchandise by generating large national audiences for its advertisers. The fact is that magazine shows like *60 Minutes* and *20/20* are now some of the most successful programs in the business. News programs, even some full-length documentaries, consistently draw significant audiences. So if truth does sell, as I believe it does, there doesn't have to be a conflict between large audiences and good, accurate television.

Television is powerful. So powerful that it exerts an influence on "reality" itself. When events are choreographed by or for television, we are faced with a problem. For example, television now controls the timing of sports events. By creating a need for regular breaks in the action where commercials can be inserted, television has made the sports industry conform to the needs of broadcasters.

The projection of national election results, by using exit polling and other sophisticated opinion surveys, is another controversial example of the impact of the medium on the message. Some critics are convinced that broadcasting the results of a poll before all the election booths are closed has a damaging effect on our political choice and therefore on our freedom.

Personally, I think the danger that last-minute projections actually influence voters is exaggerated. For every voter who will vote only for the winning candidate, there are an equal number who will support the underdog. If elections are close, the knowledge that two candidates are running neck and neck might even draw more voters out at the last minute. There has been talk of legislation to curb TV projections before the polls close. I don't think that's a good idea. The precedent would not be healthy to the cause of a free press. However, I would favor voluntary restraint by the networks themselves. And this appears to be happening.

When we think about TV coverage, the case of political conventions comes to mind. There, the networks are beginning to agree with the critics. Most producers now think that such events should be the politicians' show, not a television show. Don Hewitt, producer of *60 Minutes*, has said that television should not be shaping a national political consensus. George Watson of ABC News has said that television should try to keep a spotlight on the process, but should avoid becoming a participant in it. Again, the answer is for broadcasters to act as their own watchdogs.

All these questions bear directly on a larger question. Are the networks slanting the news? Obviously, at various times, there are slight differences in political cast at the various networks. Some anchorpersons and correspondents are more liberal, or conservative, than others. But that political balance is constantly shifting. In the end, I am convinced all three networks are basically centrist. Any significant differences among the networks are balanced out simply by the existence of the triumvirate.

At ABC there has been a deliberate attempt to balance political commentary by drawing on opposing segments of the political spectrum. For example, the self-professed conservative George Will and the openly liberal Sam Donaldson balance each other every Sunday morning with David Brinkley.

I have been in television for forty years, and at dinner parties and even in casual conversation I have always heard the same fear expressed: that television would prove to be a sinister force. It would destroy young people's ability, or desire, to read, and it would corrupt their morals. It would drive newspapers, magazines, books, and radio out of the marketplace. But there are no signs of this happening. In fact, the opposite seems to be true. Book and magazine sales have grown since the advent of television. Newspapers, though fewer in number, are still strong. Many TV miniseries or documentaries based on books have promoted the publishing industry, and publishers have promoted their wares, without cost, on scores of TV talk shows.

Another bogeyman has been the networks' supposed control of the airwaves. This is becoming less true every day with the dynamic growth of "narrowcasting," including cable and pay television, the proliferation of ground station receivers or satellite dishes, and the amazing growth of VCRs.

The pie of television revenue is being sliced thinner all the time. In 1978 the networks commanded 95 percent of the national prime-time audience. By 1985 they were down to 78 percent. What was once regarded as a broadcasting structure dominated by three large companies is becoming a media free-for-all.

I think the advent of these new media is healthy for everyone. It might even get networks off the hook when it comes to federal regulation. In the days when only a limited amount of air space was available to get a message across, the rationale for federal regulation of the broadcast marketplace was strong. But today, when audio and visual images can be transmitted directly to the home and office over telephone lines, coaxial cable, and fiber optics, or hauled directly down from the sky by means of a satellite dish, the need for governmental regulations has gone the way of the Model T.

Why regulate network news, for example, when millions of Americans can watch cable news and other specialized news programs around the clock? C-Span, for example, offers us selected congressional debates and total coverage of political conventions—something that is becoming too expensive for the major networks.

Over the years I've heard a lot of criticism of television for tolerating various forms of pandering. This includes sponsor pressure, ratings pressure, and the pressure of having to sell time in a commercial medium. These forces obviously do exist, and at times have exerted considerable influence over what goes out on the air. But we need to put those premises into perspective.

First, other media have successfully operated under similar pressures. For example, newspapers and magazines were accused of downplaying the health aspects of the first surgeon general's report on smoking. They were afraid to jeopardize the enormous revenues generated by the tobacco companies. The television industry had never advertised distilled liquor. Now it would forgo all cigarette and liquor revenues rather than be involved in such a conflict—one between the news and sales departments. News departments had always been fiercely independent within the networks and they have fought hard to keep that independence.

There once was a direct, and unhealthy, interference in television programming by sponsors. That was in the day of the single-sponsored program, a system broken by Pat Weaver, who once headed NBC. When *Your Hit Parade* was sponsored by Lucky Strike, George Washington Hill, head of American Tobacco, would review songs before they were allowed on the air. Hill had an aunt who would tap her foot if she liked the music. If she didn't tap her foot, that particular song would simply not appear on *Hit Parade* again. If the selection method wasn't exactly scientific, there was no one to challenge Hill's judgment. As sponsor, American Tobacco called the shots and the medium listened. In 1947 Hollywood made a movie about Hill called *The Hucksters*, with Sidney Greenstreet. Clark Gable played the hero, who lost his job rather than put up with that sort of pressure.

Sponsor pressure has largely become a thing of the past,

disappearing with the evolution from single sponsorship to participating or partial sponsorship. But ratings pressure has taken its place. It has become a new form of tyranny.

In theory, at least, the ratings system is valid. It certainly supports the notion that in a free-enterprise market we have to supply people with what they want. Otherwise we can't, or shouldn't, exist. But critics have made a good case for the notion that the audience is settling for what it gets. Cloning successful shows certainly stifles innovation.

In the early days of radio, audience response was judged more by seat-of-the-pants methods. Letters and phone calls and a general feeling that the show was gaining popularity were the unscientific hallmarks of success. In the early days of television, many of these methods were still used. There was a good deal more hunch betting and less of a tendency to play it safe. It's even probable that the so-called Golden Age of Television in the 1950s came about because of a blissful freedom from ratings pressure that gave artists the freedom to innovate.

But as competition grew more intense, more scientific means of judging popularity came into being. As a result, the medium plainly lost considerable creative momentum. For advertisers the first reliable scale was cost-per-thousand. Then, in the hope of figuring the relative worth of different classes of viewers, age and disposable income became important. Then came psychographics, which judged the purchasing habits of potential viewers.

On *The Home Show*, we found that cost-per-thousand was relatively high, but results per viewer were also high. Our viewers were more likely to buy a home product than the general viewing audience. A prime-time show might give a lower cost-per-thousand but generate fewer sales because only a small portion of the prime-time audience would be potential buyers of a home appliance. The greater part of the ad dollar would just be wasted.

Ratings criteria also change. When I first started hosting *20/20* in 1978, a program share had to be in the forties to be considered successful. Today, with increased competition, a

249

share in the high twenties is considered perfectly respectable. A share is the percentage of all sets turned on at any one time, while a rating point represents 1 percent of the country's 86,500,000 households with television sets. The widening gap between ratings and shares indicates that there may be less televiewing in general.

Ratings dominate television programming today. And as the race for ratings heightens, we have to ask a harsh question: Are the ratings real? Do they project an accurate indication of what people are watching?

In physics, the smallest particle of matter we can see contains quadrillions of atoms. We can't predict behavior of individual atoms under observation, but the collective behavior can be inferred statistically. When we sample only 2500 television sets to try to calculate the viewing habits of a nation of 237 million, we might well question our premises. Is the statistical base wide enough to be sound? And human beings are not atoms. Their reactions are far more complex.

The A. C. Nielsen company admits their system is not entirely foolproof, but they do maintain that their methods are the best available. Recently, though, the company announced that it would begin experimenting with a new instrument designed to gather data instantaneously from a larger survey group than they have been using.

AGB Research, a British-based Nielsen competitor, developed this "people meter." The device accurately measures what a set is watching without having to rely on the faulty memory or biased response of the viewer, as in the present system. Nielsen currently monitors 1700 households with what are known as black boxes. But the ideal system, according to AGB, would be a "passive" system that requires that the viewer do nothing except watch his or her set. The people meter represents an attempt to improve on the black box. But will such an enhanced ratings system really improve television?

Earlier I mentioned the difference between network news, with its increasing search for truth and objectivity, and some of the local "show-biz" news programming. I think that gap is steadily widening. The local news team has been described as a "jolly gang of jokesters with a frenetic weatherman and a hysterically shouting sports announcer." The news itself sometimes seems to be selected for superficial characteristics.

If, under ratings pressure, the networks were ever to mimic this broadcasting technique, a standard of excellence would be lost to the world. But I don't believe it will happen. The news departments of all three networks have become too strong, too prestigious, and too independent.

The tendency toward "show-bizzing" has always been present in broadcasting, and, outside of network news, it could increase with ratings pressure. Take the talk shows for example. Obviously they have evolved toward a more Hollywood format, partly reflecting the growing influence of Los Angeles on network entertainment divisions.

After forty years of television, and nearly ten thousand hours on the air, I have witnessed our medium's impressive development from a technologically backward, naive, unsophisticated medium that was radio-with-pictures into a powerful, sometimes arrogant, socially dominant, hyper-sophisticated business.

Television is often perceived as a juggernaut, blasting and withering, chewing up and spitting out people who have chosen it for their careers. Its pace is exhausting and seems ever to accelerate. But it still offers the world's best opportunity to get some things across to the public that might be useful to us all.

Maturity takes time. Age brings rewards and failings. Television has lost much of its early breathless sense of aspiration, the idealism that so brilliantly lit up its so-called Golden Age, when serious drama and offbeat comedy riveted millions of Americans. But we must remember they were held fast not only by the quality of what they saw, but by its novelty.

We have grown used to the illusion of television, less impressed by its magic. So as a medium, it stands at a crossroads—one created by advancing technology and changing social patterns. It is tempting for instance to think that the breakup of network dominance and the advent of cable and pay TV could promise a second Golden Age.

Unfortunately, that vast opportunity has not, and may never, materialize. Today most pay channels mainly recycle Hollywood's stalest offerings. Only a few of their original productions are of high quality. The widely touted cultural channels are largely out of business. They never quite located enough of the highbrow audience they imagined would support them in their early stages.

In looking back over four decades in television, I have tried to put myself in perspective. In the work I do today, I am, I admit, something of an anachronism. I know how to communicate on camera, but I am not a newsman by training. Nor am I an entertainer or a show-biz personality. I have done news shows and talk shows, game shows and documentaries, morning shows and late-night shows, prime time and daytime, commercial and noncommercial broadcasting. I was an announcer who became a second banana, then a host, and finally an anchor.

When I first joined *The Home Show*, I realized that if I were ever going to survive on this new medium I would have to play myself on camera, nothing less and nothing more. In a medium full of flashy entertainers, brilliant comedians, superb actors, and honey-throated announcers, I was none of the above. I was a well-spoken kid from Ohio with an absolutely ordinary personality.

It took me a few years to realize that if the twentieth century is the era of the common man—as H. L. Mencken so acerbically put it—then television is the medium of the twentieth century.

I think an important part of what I do is to try to represent the viewer. In a free society the media will rise and fall according to the power granted them by the people. If the audience ever senses that we are trying to fool them, they will turn away. But if they believe that we are doing our best to provide information, to persuade them of reasonable things if that is

our sincere intention, and to entertain them as best we can—
then I think we will have their support.

After 10,000 hours on television, I have learned one important thing: It is that the *real* magic of the medium is that *reality*
works on the small screen. Unlike the great silver screen of
cinema, we do not need to be larger than life. If we are to
provide a window on the world that will last, we must keep
that window as clean as we can.

If we are to live up to our promise, we have to leave the
mirrors to the magicians and go on trying to enhance an understanding of reality.

That job has occupied most of my life, and, overall, I'm
proud to be part of it.